THE DIVINE AND
THE DEMONIC

Based on fieldwork in the north Indian state of Rajasthan, this book focuses on supernatural affliction: illness and misfortune ascribed to demonic spirits or ghosts, or to other mystical agents such as sorcerers and witches. The author addresses a range of issues, including: *inter alia* beliefs about spirit possession, sorcery, witchcraft and the evil eye; and ritual practice, especially exorcism and healing ceremonies.

At a theoretical level, *The Divine and the Demonic* contrasts with much of the literature on spirit possession and supernatural affliction. Moving away from psychological or psychiatric paradigms, as well as from other forms of Western rationalism, the author offers fresh insights – both in terms of understanding supernatural malaise and its treatment, and in terms of the application of his phenomenological approach.

This book is also a wider study of the anthropology of South Asia, particularly medical anthropology and Indian ethnomedicine. The religious themes of Hindu priests and curers, popular Hinduism and pilgrimage are also discussed.

Graham Dwyer is Lecturer in Social Sciences at Greenwich Community College, London. He gained his D Phil in Social Anthropology from the University of Oxford, based on fieldwork in Rajasthan and funded by the UK's Economic and Social Research Council.

THE DIVINE AND THE DEMONIC

Supernatural affliction and its treatment in North India

Graham Dwyer

RoutledgeCurzon
Taylor & Francis Group

LONDON AND NEW YORK

First published in 2003
by RoutledgeCurzon
2 Park Square, Milton Park, Abingdon, Oxon OX14 4RN

Simultaneously published in the USA and Canada
by RoutledgeCurzon
711 Third Avenue, New York, NY 10017

RoutledgeCurzon is an imprint of the Taylor & Francis Group

© 2003 Graham Dwyer

Typeset in Sabon by LaserScript Ltd, Mitcham, Surrey

British Library Cataloguing in Publication Data
A catalogue record of this book is available from the British Library

Library of Congress Cataloging in Publication Data
A catalog record for this book has been requested

ISBN 0–415–29749–4

CONTENTS

LIST OF PLATES

LIST OF FIGURES AND TABLES

Figures

Tables

ACKNOWLEDGEMENTS

I gratefully acknowledge a particular debt to my fieldwork assistant, Khem Singh Bhati, and wish to thank R. Purohit and S. Soni at the Jain Vishva Bharati Institute, Ladnun, Rajasthan for providing language instruction as well as for helping and assisting me in my research. I am also indebted to Nick Allen who supervised my doctoral work when I was a student at the Institute of Social and Cultural Anthropology, University of Oxford. Nick Allen's comments on the chapters of this book have been invaluable, and I wish to acknowledge him for this and for the help, guidance and support he has given. Moreover, for equally instructive comments on many of the ideas and much of the analysis I develop in the book, I am especially grateful to Bruce Kapferer, Peter Flugel, Desmond Mallikarachchi and Antti Pakaslahti. I would like to thank Bruce Kapferer in particular, not only for his detailed comments on an earlier version of Chapter 2, comments that caused me substantially to revise it as well as other aspects of my work, but also for other helpful and encouraging comments he has given. Helpful comments on parts of this book have equally been advanced by Ron Bastin and by Peter Connolly (the latter with whom I have worked at University College Chichester and with whom I have had fruitful discussions). I would like to thank both of them. Thanks are due too to Bill Walters and to Valerie Isham, Professor of Statistics at University College London, for advice and instructive comments on the statistical analysis of the quantitative data given in the book.

The research upon which this book is based would not have been possible without financial support from the Economic and Social Research Council. The grant provided by this awarding body is thus acknowledged with gratitude.

ACKNOWLEDGEMENTS

Portions of this book include partially revised versions of two articles of mine: (1) 'The Phenomenology of Supernatural Malaise: Attribution, Vulnerability and the Patterns of Affliction at a Hindu Pilgrimage Centre in Rajasthan', 1998 *Social Analysis* 42 (2): 3–23, and (2) 'Healing and the Transformation of Self in Exorcism at a Hindu Shrine in Rajasthan', 1999 *Social Analysis* 43 (2): 108–137. I am grateful to the editors and publishers of *Social Analysis* for their permission to draw from this work.

Finally, I wish to thank my wife Bridget and my daughter Margaret for their loving support and companionship.

NOTE ON TRANSLITERATION

Throughout the main body of this book I have chosen to anglicise Hindi and Sanskrit terms. This choice, which is in line with the practice adopted in many contemporary books on Hinduism or on Indian religions, is specifically to aid readers who are unfamiliar with the conventions of transliteration that Indian language experts use. However, while this practice is engaged in the main corpus of the work, the interests and concerns of language specialists have not been ignored: key Hindi or Sanskrit terms that appear in the book are presented in conventional transliterated form (using standard diacritical marks) in the book's appendices and glossary.

Map 1 Rajasthan and Districts* (India Inset)

*From *Census of India*. Final Population Totals. Series 1, Paper 2. Delhi: Government of India.

Map 2 Mehndipur Village*

*From *Survey of India*. Delhi: Government of India.

INTRODUCTION

This book is based upon fieldwork carried out in Rajasthan, India, between September 1992 and September 1993. Its specific ethnographic focus is the small village of Mehndipur, which is situated in the district of Sawai Madhopur (see Maps 1 and 2 on the previous pages). Mehndipur is a famous Hindu pilgrimage centre, attracting visitors from the whole region of Rajasthan as well as from other north Indian states. The village of Mehndipur was selected for purposes of research, not only because many people journey to it in search of cure from affliction by malevolent spirits or ghosts (*bhut*s and *pret*s[1]), but also because of the daily rituals performed there on behalf of those held to be suffering from spirit malaise. Because I wanted to investigate spirit possession and its treatment in north India, and since little in-depth fieldwork at the time had been undertaken in Mehndipur itself, I decided to conduct research in the village.

Now, although I went to the village of Mehndipur specifically to carry out research on spirit possession, often the sick people whom I interviewed there said that they had become ill because they had been harmed by sorcerers (*jadu-tona karne vale*) or by other supernatural agents and forces. This, in fact, was not only given as the reason why many pilgrims had actually suffered adversity, but in a large number of cases it was also said to be the reason they had become possessed by spirits (*bhut-pret*). From the outset, then, it became clear that I would not be able to focus solely upon spirit possession, that it would be necessary to explore and examine other kinds of supernatural affliction as well. Moreover, because I found that Brahman priests and curers, such as *bhagat*s or *tantrik*s, are sometimes consulted in Mehndipur for the same or for similar reasons, particularly for purposes of diagnosing supernatural ailments or distress, it further became clear that it was necessary, not only to investigate the work of healers or magico-religious specialists operating in the village, but also to examine the practices of Brahman temple functionaries.

The book's structure, aims and objectives

This book is principally concerned with the different types of supernatural affliction, the healing ceremonies commonly performed for banishing spirits or for treating supernatural malaise, as well as the religious specialists consulted to diagnose and/or to cure it.

This Introduction briefly outlines the book's main theoretical and thematic concerns, concerns which are oriented by its phenomenological focus. Details of how research was carried out and a note on languages and transcription are also given here. Chapter 1 discusses the location or setting in which fieldwork was undertaken. It also gives relevant historical information about Mehndipur village and offers some introductory ethnographic data. Chapters 2 and 3 describe and analyse the different kinds of affliction thought to be caused by spirits and other supernatural beings and forces, varieties of affliction from which pilgrims often claim to suffer. Matters of causation, attribution and vulnerability, as well as the way in which persons come to be suspected or accused of harming others by means of magical or mystical agency are the major themes here. However, although these themes are presented and explored in each of these chapters, chapter 2 is based chiefly on the large body of quantitative data gathered at the pilgrimage centre. Chapter 4 focuses on exorcism and provides a detailed account of the main ritual performed in Mehndipur for expelling spirits and for curing those believed to be afflicted by various supernaturals, a ritual which I attended on over a hundred different occasions. Chapter 5 examines the practices of priests and healers and also compares these two types of religious specialist. Finally, the Conclusion provides a brief comment on the orientation of this book in terms of its theoretical and methodological goals – goals that involve and insist upon a movement away from the analytical focus of much of the anthropological literature on supernatural affliction and its treatment.

This book, in fact, has a number of aims or objectives. Besides contributing to the ethnography of north India generally and, in particular, to the ethnography of Rajasthan, the region where other researchers (e.g. Carstairs 1955, 1961, 1983; Carstairs and Kapur

1976; Gold 1988a, b; Kakar 1982; Lambert 1988, 1992, 1996; Mayaram 1999; Pakaslahti 1996, 1998; Satija *et al.* 1981; and Seeberg 1992) who have addressed some of the same or similar issues to those which I address have worked, one of the primary aims of the book is to provide a contribution to the understanding of supernatural malaise, particularly in terms of vulnerability. The attempt to ascertain why certain categories of person are specifically prone to spirit possession or to attack from other supernaturals and mystical agents, such as sorcerers and witches, is a central concern in the anthropology of religion generally. With the exception of anthropologists such as Boddy (1989), Kapferer (1991), Lambek (1981) and Skultans (1987a, b), however, many researchers have utilised the 'deprivation hypothesis', whose most notable proponent is Ioan Lewis (1966, 1978, 1986). This approach, which links affliction to subordination or marginality, has also been used extensively in the South Asian context. Many writers focusing on spirit possession in India, or in neighbouring countries, have tended to view this as being inseparably connected with oppression, especially the oppression of women by men, socio-economic inferiority, and the inability of subordinates to express their grievances openly (e.g. Freed and Freed 1964; Gellner 1992, 1994; Harper 1963; Jones 1976; and Opler 1958). But at a theoretical level there are major problems with the deprivation hypothesis, as I will show. Moreover, because it is particularly problematic as a general explanation of affliction, it is not adopted here. In this book, supernatural malaise is explored from a phenomenological perspective, as is its treatment, a perspective that in recent years has increasingly been engaged in the anthropology of religion (and in the anthropology of medicine, as well as at the religious anthropology/medical anthropology interface – see, for example, the work of Csordas 1997; Desjarlais 1992; Good 1996; and Kapferer 1991, 1997). The main argument I put forward about affliction is that certain categories of individuals become the prey of capricious spirits and often become victims of sorcery or some other mystical force because they see themselves and are seen by others to be exceptionally at risk from them. In other words, the attribution of illness and misfortune to particular supernatural agents or occult forces is largely connected with perceptions rooted in common sense, taken for granted assumptions and beliefs about susceptibility. Thus, following Bruce Kapferer, the Australian anthropologist who is well known for his work on spirit possession in Sri Lanka, it is contended that vulnerability is essentially a function of cultural typification (cf. Kapferer 1991: 128 and *passim*).

Another key purpose of the book is to show that, while sorcery suspicions frequently emerge in circumstances of perceived risk, in some cases diagnosticians or diviners may actually initiate them. Contrary to what anthropologists often assume, I demonstrate that sorcery suspicions are not always immediately present in the thoughts of those who seek guidance and help from occult practitioners. In fact, clients may be quite genuinely shocked or surprised when sorcery is identified by a diagnostician as the cause of adversity, having assumed that some other malevolent being, such as an unknown angry deity (*devata* or *devi*), has harmed them. And because the revelation itself may later lead to public denunciations, I argue that diviners or diagnosticians are sometimes instrumental in producing, not only sorcery suspicions, but also accusations. Indeed, because sorcery practice in north India is considered to be prevalent or widespread, I argue that this itself is an important reason why diagnosticians are able to initiate sorcery suspicions and/or accusations with apparent or relative ease.

A further aim of the book is to provide a contribution to the understanding of certain aspects of north Indian ethnomedicine. Now, the literature dealing with matters of illness and health in South Asia is voluminous and considerably diverse. Some studies of Indian medicine have been concerned only with the theory and practice of ayurveda (e.g. Tabor 1981 and Zimmerman 1978, 1980) or with the influence of Western and classical Islamic medical traditions on it (e.g. Leslie 1976). In addition, there are studies of indigenous conceptions of disease and healing other than those of the ayurvedic variety that have equally been concerned with the impact of Western or cosmopolitan medicine, as well as with issues of development and health care management, etc., such as Banerji 1981, Kakar, D. 1977 and Marriott 1955a. There are also studies that have not taken as a central focus the issue of Western influence on South Asian medical traditions, studies which have, nonetheless, explicitly utilised Western psychological or psychiatric paradigms, as in much of the literature on spirit possession and its treatment (e.g. Carstairs and Kapur 1976; Kakar, S. 1982; Nuckolls 1991; Obeyesekere 1970, 1977, 1984; Pakaslahti 1996, 1998; and Satija *et al.* 1981). Furthermore, a few studies of a wide range of popular or lay medical concepts and practices have been carried out too (e.g. Lambert 1988, 1992, 1996 and Nichter 1980). In this book, no attempt is made to describe or analyse the full range of Indian medical concepts and therapies. As indicated above, I am primarily concerned with indigenous notions of affliction in terms of the supernatural; and with regard to the treatment of supernatural malaise itself, I focus essentially upon exorcism.

In the book, a great deal of emphasis is placed upon the role of emotion in exorcist rituals. This is not merely because emotion is frequently displayed in the rituals, but, importantly, because it is seen by my informants as being critical to the curing project. Moreover, the book draws upon the literature on modern Western psychotherapies and argues that much of what takes place in them is similar to what occurs in exorcism. Thus, by understanding the first, it may be possible to illuminate the second and vice versa. Indeed, in both I contend that the patient de-identifies with pathological states of being and learns to re-identify the self (his or her physical and psychological condition) in accordance with positive feelings and conceptions. In psychotherapy and exorcism, the process by which the self is thought to be transformed, enabling the patient to get well, is clearly shaped by shared concepts and beliefs into which the sick person is socialised, a process that is held to be effected by means of emotion, the activation of an emotional charge. However, although participants in each of these healing milieus are expected to experience emotion and often claim to do so, this does not, of course, mean that it is present or that it is generated. Nonetheless, because a great deal of stress is placed upon it by participants, I suggest that it may often actually be produced and that this itself may help to facilitate the patient's recovery.

Yet, while fruitful comparison between psychotherapy and exorcism can be made, criticism is offered of the 'hysteria thesis' put forward by Sudhir Kakar (1982). His psychoanalytic explanation of spirit possession and exorcist rituals in Mehndipur is rejected, one important reason for this being that he does not take adequate account of the cultural construction of illness and cure.

Besides exorcism, the book, as I have also indicated, examines the practices of priests (*pujaris*) and healers (e.g. *bhagat*s and *tantrik*s) and the role that each plays in the treatment of supernatural affliction. It is argued that in Mehndipur they are complementary figures, not only in a hierarchical sense (cf. Dumont and Pocock 1957, 1959 and Dumont 1980 [1970]), but also in the sense that they do not compete with each other (cf. Babb 1975: 179). I show that priests and healers do not compete because they perform largely different functions – functions which might overlap at times but which tend to be seen by the practitioners themselves as well as by their clients to benefit pilgrims or patients in essentially different ways. Indeed, the book does not merely make a contribution to the understanding of the practices of Hindu priests and healers (while also providing an understanding of the relationship between these two types of religious specialist); it contributes to, builds upon or extends, the work of other anthropologists who have focused on the priest/healer relationship in South Asia too (cf. Babb 1975; Dumont and Pocock 1957, 1959 and Dumont 1980 [1970]; Marriott 1955b; Parry 1994; Srinivas 1965; Tambiah 1970; and Vitebsky 1993).

Research methods

Having outlined the major aims and objectives of the book – aims and objectives that are critically dependent throughout this volume upon the engagement of an approach originating in Edmund Husserl's philosophical work (see Husserl 1964) and closely associated with the sociology of Alfred Schutz (1967, 1970), an approach I present in detail shortly (see Chapter 2) – I turn now briefly to discuss how data were collected in the field. In Mehndipur, interviews and participant observation were the two methods used for gathering data. Informal interviews with pilgrims, with temple functionaries and with healers were mostly carried out at the healing shrines or in *dharmshalas*, the large halls erected from money donated by pious pilgrims. And at Balaji *mandir* itself, the main healing temple in the village, 734 patients and/or their accompanying carers were interviewed at some length, though these interviews, which were semi-structured, varied in terms of duration, as some of the respondents gave or volunteered more information than others. All these pilgrims were approached at the main entrance to the temple, and the interviews with them were conducted on different days throughout the course of my stay in Mehndipur, though most were done on Tuesdays and Saturdays, the days which, not only are believed to be sacred to Balaji, but also are the ones on which large numbers of pilgrims gather at the shrine dedicated to him. The mornings (from nine o'clock until twelve noon) were the period in the day when the interviews were held, when the new arrivals at the pilgrimage centre usually go to the temple for the first time.

It was on the basis of opportunity and willingness or agreement of pilgrims to be interviewed that the 734 patients and/or their carers were selected. Many other pilgrims who were asked to take part in an interview would not agree to it. In fact, of all those who were approached for this purpose, approximately one person in every three or four refused. Those who were unwilling to be interviewed declined the request for various reasons. Some pilgrims said that they were too busy or too upset and traumatised to talk about their affliction or their loved one's problems; and some of them stated simply that they had no wish to be interviewed.

On each occasion that my research assistant, Khem Singh Bhati, and I went to Balaji temple in order to conduct the interviews, the procedure outlined below was adopted.

The first pilgrim who came into the entrance to the temple was approached and was told that I was engaged in a study of the temple and of the pilgrims to it. He was then asked if he would be willing to be interviewed.[2] If he agreed to this, a number of questions were put to him. Firstly, he was asked: 'Why have you come to the temple in Mehndipur?' – *Ap Mehndipur ke mandir me kyo ae hai?* Typically, the interviewee would then respond as follows: he would say (1) that he had come to take *darshan* (i.e. both to view and to be viewed by the deity through the medium of the deity's image [*murti*]), and/or (2) to offer worship (*puja*), and/or (3) to make an oblation or to give a donation (*dan*) for some blessing or boon (*varadan*) received from Balaji, or (4) because he or a person he was accompanying was sick (*bimar*) or had *sankat*.[3] When either or both of the first two kinds of response were elicited, the informant was asked to comment on why he had chosen to come to Balaji temple in particular for such purpose(s); and when the interviewee said that he had come to make an offering for a blessing or boon received, he was asked to comment on this as well. But whether a pilgrim responded in any of the four ways mentioned, the interviewee was asked to give an opinion as to why persons are harmed by various supernatural forces or agents, such as spirits (*bhut-pret*). If a pilgrim said that he had come to the temple because he or a loved one was sick or had *sankat*, however, a number of other questions were put to him and/or to the patient whom he had brought to the shrine, though as often as possible an attempt was made to question the ailing person directly. (Approximately one half of these informants, most of whom were men, were the patients themselves; and in the majority of all cases, it was the sufferers who were asked to give details about the malaise or affliction from which they were held to be suffering.)

Now, in most of the 734 cases that I documented, it was not necessary to ask whether the patient was male or female; for the respondent himself was the sufferer or the patient was present and identified by him. But on the few occasions when the patient was not with the carer – because he or she was taking rest in one of the *dharmshalas*, for example – this information was obtained from the latter, as was information about the identity of all those who had come to the pilgrimage centre with the sick person. In those cases where the sufferer was questioned directly (questions otherwise, as I have indicated, were largely put to carers) the patient was asked the following:

1 'How old are you?' – *Apki umar kitni sal hai?*
2 'Are you married or unmarried?' – *Ap shadi-shuda hai ya shadi-shuda nahi hai?*
3 'Where is your place of residence?' – *Apka nivas sthan kaha hai?*
4 (a) 'Did you ever go to school or college?' – *Kya ap kabhi skul ya kolej gae hai?*
  (If this question was answered simply in the affirmative, or if no details were given, an additional question was asked.)
  (b) 'Up until what age were you educated?' – *Ap kitni ayu tak pare hai?*
5 'What is your caste?' – *Apki jati kya hai?*
6 'What is your occupation?' – *Apka vyavsay kya hai?* (When addressing a female patient, this question was rephrased to elicit information about her husband's occupational status [if married] or father's [if unmarried]).
7 'How many times have you been to Mehndipur; and how long did you stay each time?' – *Ap kitni bar Mehndipur gae hai; aur ap har bar kitni der thahare the?*
8 (a) 'What are the symptoms of your complaint?' – *Apki shikayat ke lakshan kya hai?*
  (b) 'What kind of illness (affliction/problem) is it?' – *Yah bimari (sankat/pareshani) kis tarah ki hai?*

(When questions 8 (a) and (b) were asked, the patient not only described or gave a name to his or her complaint (e.g. lethargy [*bharipan/susti*]), but also typically attributed it to a supernatural agent (e.g. a *bhut* or a *pret*) or to the work of a black magician (a *jadu-tona karne vala*). Other kinds of questions were then put to the respondent. Depending on the supernatural or mystical agent mentioned by the patient, questions such as the following were asked: (i) 'What kind of spirit (*bhut/pret*) is troubling you?' – *Apko kis tarah ka bhut/pret pareshan kar raha hai?* (ii) 'Why did the spirit afflict you?' – *Apko bhut/pret kyo lage?* (iii) 'Who is using sorcery?' – *Jadu-tona kaun kar raha hai?* (iv) 'Who has harmed you?' – *Apko kisne nuksan pahuncaya?* – and so on.) Moreover, the patient was asked:

9 'When did this illness (affliction/problem) begin; and for how long have you been suffering?' – *Yah bimari (sankat/pareshani) kab shuru hua; aur ap kitni der se bhugat rahe hai?*
10 'Have you seen a doctor?' – *Kya apne daktar ko dikhaya?*
11 'Have you seen a *bhagat, pir, mantrik, tantrik, vaidya?*' – *Kya apne bhagat, pir, mantrik, tantrik, vaidya ko dikhaya?*

The semi-structured interviews carried out at Balaji temple not only enabled me to collect biographical data on 734 different patients who had been brought to Mehndipur to receive supernatural healing or treatment, but they also enabled me to test for correlations between different categories of individuals in the sample who were said to be suffering from malaise and the types of supernatural or mystical being held to be afflicting them. In addition, the interviews that were conducted equally provided the opportunity to test for correlations between ideas about the kinds of person who are believed to be susceptible to supernatural attack – ideas rooted in the common-sense thought of Hindus and frequently expressed by them – and a large number of actual cases.

However, it must be pointed out that, while the semi-structured interviews yielded much valuable information, particularly about patterns of affliction by spirits and other mystical agents, uses to which the data can be put have some limitations. It has not been possible in this book to use the data I collected to offer generalised pronouncements about all pilgrims who travel to Mehndipur to receive cure from supernatural malaise; neither has it been possible to use the data to determine the incidence of supernatural affliction in the entire north Indian region, where the vast majority of the interviewed informants were domiciled. Because the informants were approached on the basis of opportunity, and because a population-based epidemiological survey would be required to make any claims about the incidence of supernatural affliction in north India as a whole, these types of generalisation cannot be made. More precisely, the statistical tests that were actually carried out on my findings (see chapter 2) are only applicable to, or make it possible for one to generalise about, those pilgrims to Mehndipur who would be willing to be interviewed if approached opportunistically for the purpose – that is to say, only those types of pilgrim who in principle would be willing to take part in the kind of interviews that were undertaken.

Besides the 734 semi-structured interviews at Balaji temple, as well as numerous informal interviews or discussions with other pilgrims, priests and healers that were conducted in Mehndipur, I also observed many healing ceremonies, ceremonies that are performed both in temples and in *dharmshala*s. As indicated above, this was a central component of my research too; and by attending these rituals, I was able to learn a great deal about the different ritual styles of curing that one encounters at the pilgrimage centre and about the practices of priests and traditional healers or diagnosticians operating in the village.

Note on languages and transcription

I began learning Hindi in the summer of 1990 after completing the degree of Master of Studies at the Institute of Social and Cultural Anthropology, University of Oxford. During the winter of the same year I also attended conversation classes in Hindi and Urdu at a tertiary college in my home town in the north of England. My ability to communicate in Hindi was further developed over a period of four months in northern India in early 1991 before I returned to Oxford to begin doctoral studies. And after returning from the sub-continent, I continued to devote attention to the study of the language, though at that time the focus was particularly upon Devanagari, the Hindi script. Prior to commencing fieldwork, then, I had gained a degree of skill in speaking the native language of northern India as well as a degree of competence with regard to reading and writing it. Moreover, in August 1992, four weeks before beginning the research, I received comprehensive tuition from a Sanskrit scholar at Jain Vishva Bharati Institute in Ladnun, Rajasthan.

However, despite the fact that I had acquired a more than elementary knowledge of, and skill in, speaking Hindi, it was still necessary to engage an assistant in the field. The research assistant was recruited on my behalf by members of the Jain community in Ladnun, the village in which he and his family were dwelling. He was educated (with a B. Comm. degree from the University of Rajasthan in Jaipur) and was a Sisodiya Rajput by caste. Without his help the research project would not have been possible. Perhaps the most important reason for his indispensability was the fact that many pilgrims interviewed in Mehndipur came from different areas of northern India, some of whom spoke complicated dialects, which to a non-native speaker of Hindi are often difficult to discern or understand.

Nonetheless, for the most part, interviews and discussions were conducted in Hindi, the lingua franca at the pilgrimage centre, used by pilgrims, priests and healers, though since a large number of the respondents in Mehndipur were well-educated and often fluent in English, they would sometimes insist on using the latter. This, of course, was also helpful but there were still occasions on which linguistic problems arose. In general terms, though, with the aid of my assistant, they were largely manageable. Furthermore, many conversations and informal interviews with pilgrims, priests and healers, as well as dialogues between religious specialists and their clients, were recorded on a small dictaphone, which my research assistant helped to transcribe and translate. This was also useful and enabled me to overcome a considerable number of language difficulties. Indeed, the key Hindi terms used by my respondents, and given in the book, were always written down and checked by my research assistant. This enabled me not only to ensure that their rendering or transcription was correct, but also that both the contextualisation and the way in which they were used, as well as their meanings and associations, were retained. Finally, it was also very helpful that the local priests and healers in Mehndipur communicate with pilgrims in Hindi rather than in Rajasthani. Some of the dialogues between these practitioners and their clients, in fact, are presented in the book, though only transcriptions and translations of key or unusual terms are given.

1

MEHNDIPUR

The fieldwork setting

Mehndipur village

The village of Mehndipur was initially brought to my attention through the work of Sudhir Kakar (1982), the Indian psychoanalyst whose writings on spirit possession and exorcism are well known in the West. He was one of the first researchers to go to Mehndipur. Together with Ashok Nagpal, a lecturer in the department of psychology at Delhi University, Kakar conducted a study in the village for a period of two months in the late 1970s (at a time when Satija and the team of psychiatrists who worked with him [see Satija *et al.* 1981] also did a short study there). Kakar's study, however, was not extensive; on the contrary, it was small-scale, not only in terms of the brief period of time he spent in Mehndipur, but also from the point of view of the subjects who agreed to take part in it: only twenty-eight pilgrims were interviewed (cf. Kakar 1982: 281 n. 6). More recently, Jens Seeberg (1992), an anthropologist from Aarhus University in Moesgard, Denmark, did fieldwork in Mehndipur. This was a more comprehensive investigation. Seeberg spent five months in the village, beginning in December 1989. His work provides important ethnographic and anthropological data on Mehndipur itself and on the pilgrims who journey to it. More recently still, another key study was carried out in Mehndipur by Antti Pakaslahti (1998). This particular study has an explicit psychiatric focus (as in the work of Satija *et al.* 1981) and is primarily concerned with family-centred therapy on offer in the village; nonetheless, it has major ethnographic and anthropological value too, as does the film Pakaslahti made in Mehndipur in 1996. Indeed, Pakaslahti's work is particularly noteworthy because it is based on extensive research in Mehndipur, research which the Finnish psychiatrist began in 1992 and which is still on-going.

12

Now, Mehndipur itself is approximately 100 kilometres from Jaipur, the state capital of Rajasthan. The three kilometre dust track that leads to the village from the main Jaipur–Agra road is traversed by *tanga* (a horse-drawn vehicle) or by jeep, for which each pilgrim (*yatri*) must pay the standard charge of two rupees.[1] On arrival the visitor who intends to spend the night or a longer period of time has the choice of staying either in a guest house or in one of the village's numerous *dharmshala*s. Indeed, my research assistant, Bhati, and myself were accommodated in one of these. The majority of *dharmshala*s are relatively inexpensive. In fact some are free, though boarding charges vary dramatically in some of them from seventy-one rupees a night to as little as five. The standard price, however, is around ten rupees.

History of the pilgrimage centre

According to the local inhabitants, Calcutta and Radhakishan Chamriya *dharmshala*s are the oldest in the village. They were built less than seventy years ago. Formerly, it is said that pilgrims travelled to the shrines during the day, returning home again a little after sunset. This, I believe, provides an important clue to the actual age of the village as a pilgrimage centre. Its popularity seems to have developed particularly since the 1930s. There were no lodging houses before 1930, and the local inhabitants claim that there were only one or two *prasad vala*s (sellers of offerings made to deities) operating in Mehndipur before this date, whereas today there are more than fifty. Furthermore, Balaji temple itself is less than a hundred years old. I was told by the shrine functionaries that it was constructed when Ganesh Puri was alive, a charismatic healer who was probably the first *mahant* (priest) at the shrine. He lived for eighty years. (According to his nephew, Ramjilal, Ganesh was born in 1899 and expired in 1979.) The second healing temple, known as Tin Pahar Vale Baba dedicated to Bhairava – so named because it is located on the triple peak of the largest hill overshadowing Mehndipur village – was originally built a little later, though the present, more recent construction was erected only forty-four years ago. A small plaque on one of the inner walls of the temple bears the names Punam Chand Jain and Hanuman Das Jain, the two men who donated money for this in 1959 (2016 Vikrama Era). Previously, as I was informed by the priests at the temple, there was only a small building on the site in which the principal *murti* (image of the deity) stood, the other important idols being left unsheltered outside. This temple was said to have been built during the period when Ganga-Nath (1877–1978), a senior contemporary of Ganesh Puri, was the incumbent.[2] Before this *mahant* took charge of it, the priests at the shrine told me that a few devotees from Udaipur, a small village three kilometres west of Mehndipur, used to perform *arati puja* there (worship with a lighted lamp [*dipak*]). But at this time and for many years after Ganga-Nath became priest, they commented that few pilgrims from beyond the local villages in the area journeyed to the temple. The temple on the hill adjacent to this, however, is evidently the most recent of the three original healing shrines in the village. It is dedicated to Sheshanaga, the thousand-headed serpent god upon whose hood, according to myth, Vishnu reclines during *pralaya* (the dissolution of the universe – cf. Brockington 1991: 195). It was founded only fifty or sixty years ago during the time of Kajor Nath, a priest who was ninety years old and who was still the incumbent when I carried out fieldwork in Mehndipur.

In addition to the relatively young age of these temples, and *dharmshalas*, it is clear that the pilgrimage centre only recently became popular from the dates marked on many of the *pitristhan* (literally, 'place or site of an ancestor'), which are erected at the rear of Balaji *mandir* and on the two hills rising out of the valley in which the village lies. I was informed both by priests and pilgrims, as well as by healers (*bhagats*), in Mehndipur that a *pitristhan* is made here when a deceased member of a particular family communicates his or her wish to reside in this sacred place. But it is also said that one may be set up after an ancestor spirit (*pitri devata*) takes rebirth (*punarjanm*) in memory and honour of it. None of these simple stone monuments seems to have been built before 1940, with the vast majority of them appearing since the late 1960s.

Nonetheless, according to every priest operating in Mehndipur, the village has been an important place of pilgrimage for millennia. The *Bara Hanuman Upasana* ('The Great Worship of Hanuman'), a book sold in the local bazaar, which contains information about the principal healing shrine as well as over 700 different *bhajans* (hymns) or mantras (magical formulae),[3] states that Balaji temple was founded 5, 000 years ago (Anon. 1990: 19). While this is, of course, unrealistic, one of the local myths recorded in the text is worth citing. Below is a summary of the story of the origin of the temple and of how Ganesh Puri became the *mahant*:

In the beginning there was a deep forest. Lions, tigers and numerous wild animals roamed about in it. Moreover, the people who lived there were continually full of fear because of thieves and bandits. Now, long before Kishor Puriji[4] became the *mahant*, his forefathers, whose names are unknown, had a dream, and in that dream-state they began to walk. They did not know where they were going. Then they experienced an amazing event. From one side flames appeared and there was suddenly a tremendous sound of animals. The animals encircled a place in the forest where the idol of Balaji appeared. They circumambulated that spot three times and prostrated themselves before the idol of Balaji. After worshipping the god, the great army of animals returned to the place from which it came.

There was a man called Gosaiji Maharaj[5] who travelled to this place and had a vision of this, an event that occurred long before his birth. He was slightly afraid and returned to his village but could not sleep. He was thinking about the happening, and as soon as he slept he had a dream that there were three temples in which there were three idols. At that moment he heard a voice saying, 'Get up. Take charge of my service, and my power will be increased.' But Gosaiji ignored the command. Finally, Hanuman revealed himself and told Gosaiji to worship him.

The next day Gosaiji Maharaj approached the idol of Balaji in the place where he had received the vision. He heard the sound of drums and trumpets, but no one could be seen. He gathered the people of the area and informed them about what had taken place. They decided to build a small house for Gosaiji and prepared food for him. Gosaiji performed many miracles. This was at a time when the ability to perform wondrous deeds had almost disappeared.

Later a king helped him to dig the idol of Balaji from out of the earth. They dug hundreds of feet into the soil. However, although they continued to dig, they failed to reach the feet of the idol. At last the king decided to leave.

Now, the image of the deity was not carved by any craftsman. It was a single piece of stone on the hill. In fact, it seemed to Gosaiji that the entire hill had become Balaji himself. At the feet of the god there was a small bottomless lake. From Balaji's left breast water flowed continuously into it. And even after the idol was dressed with clothes, water unceasingly flowed as a river into the lake. In this manner, Balaji established himself in that place, with two other helpful gods in accompaniment.

The village pantheon

The other two deities alluded to in the myth cited above are Bhairava and Pretraj. Balaji, Bhairava and Pretraj are the three main deities in Mehndipur. The second of these is a Sanskritic god and an *avatar* (incarnation) of Shiva, as is sometimes said to be true of the first (cf. *Siva Purana*: 3.8.2 and 3.17.70; Tulsidas' *Sri Hanuman Calisa*, Shloka: 6). The third, by contrast, is a local deity. In Sanskrit texts, there are numerous descriptions of Balaji and Bhairava. One of the best known sources for references to Balaji, the infant form of the god Hanuman, is the *Ramayana*. In this great epic, the core of which is thought to have been composed in the fifth or fourth century BCE (cf. Brockington 1991: 54) by the sage Valmiki, Balaji or Hanuman is portrayed as having immense power and strength (*bal*), which no demon foe can rival. But not only is Hanuman, son of Anjani and Vayu, the wind god, 'a fire to consume the forest of the demon race', as Tulsidas poetically describes him (1991: 596), he is also depicted as being full of compassion (*karuna*), as one who removes suffering, pain and distress. In the *Sri Hanuman Calisa*, written by Tulsidas (probable dates 1543–1623 CE – cf. Brockington 1991: 186), the author writes:

> With (Hanuman's) grace all the impediments
> And difficulties in the world can be overcome easily ...
> Evil spirits cannot come near your devotees,
> Lord Mahavira,[6] who chant your name.
> Chanting your name constantly, O Hanuman,
> One can be cured of all disease and pains ...
> Whoever comes to you for fulfilment of desire,
> Achieves great fruition in his life ...
> Shri Rama has great affection for you, O Mahavira,
> The decapitator of evil spirits and protector of saints ...
> One can reach Rama chanting your name
> And become free from suffering of many lives ...
> Other gods may not take care to take heed,
> But one who serves you, O Hanuman, enjoys all pleasures.
> (Shlokas: 20–35)

The deity's dual qualities of power or immense strength and compassion, which are emphasised by every pilgrim who travels to Mehndipur, are features of Bhairava's nature too, though it is essentially his fierceness (*pracandta*) that tends to be stressed. In Sanskrit literature, he is often depicted as brandishing various weapons, including a sword, goad, axe and arrow on one side, and a bow, trident, club, noose, and a skull mounted on a staff on the other side (*Agni Purana* 1.52.10). He has long protruding teeth and matted hair (cf. Dange 1986: 120). His appearance is terrifying, and in Mehndipur he is often referred to as the wrathful form of Shiva (*Shiva ka kruddh rup*). According to the *Siva Purana*, he came into existence when conflict arose between Brahma and Vishnu (*Siva Purana*: 3.8.1–66). Brahma, engulfed by *maya* (illusion), haughtily proclaimed himself to be reality itself, the sole unchanging entiy. Vishnu thus became enraged. But the rivalry between the creator and maintainer of the universe ended suddenly with the intervention of Shiva, the great destroyer. The latter manifested himself as Bhairava, the god with 'terrifying features' (ibid.: 3.8.47): 'By the time Brahma could reflect properly, the great being (Bhairava) was seen immediately as the third-eyed Nilalohita (Shiva) with the trident in his hand and an eye in the forehead. Serpents and crested moon constituted his ornaments. ... Bhairava ... cut off Brahma's head with the tips of the nails of the fingers of his left hand' (ibid.: 3.8.40–1, 52).

The severing of Brahma's head is alluded to in the *Kurma Purana* as well (also see Hiltebeitel *et al.* 1989: 8–9 and *passim*). But in this version, Shiva appears in a blackened form: 'After fighting a great battle with Brahma, Kala Bhairava cut the face of ... Brahma. The god died, his face being cut by god Shambhu (Shiva)' (2.31.30). Bhairava, in fact, is known to have eight different forms,[7] the Kala or black Bhairava being just one of these. In Mehndipur the term Kala (black) Bhairava is often used, as is the term Lal (red) Bhairava, and at Tin Pahar Vale Baba, at the feet of one of the five images of the deity, there is a small effigy of a black dog (*kutta*), the god's vehicle (*vahana*). But the term that is most commonly used at the pilgrimage centre is Kotval, meaning chief officer or chief of police. This term is a fitting one, since it is said that one of the god's major functions is to capture the malevolent spirits responsible for causing illness (*rog*) or calamity (*vipatti*) and to bring them into the court (*darbar*) of Balaji, the deity who, according to pilgrims, priests and healers, possesses supreme power (*sab se jyada shakti*). Because Bhairava's position in the local divine hierarchy is inferior to Balaji's (he is held to operate under Balaji's authority), he is viewed as being a little less powerful (*thori kam shakti*).

Pretraj, the third principal deity, however, is thought to be the least powerful (*sab se kam shakti*) and is sometimes referred to as Bhairava's messenger (*dut*) or servant (*sevak*). According to the local myth, which has a number of versions, the deity was originally an evil spirit whose tyranny knew no bounds. The valley between the two hills where the temple of Balaji now stands was his dwelling place, and he refused to allow anyone to pass by. Any person who attempted this was instantly killed or developed an incurable and painful disease. The people of the area out of fear thus decided to build a shrine and dedicate it to the ferocious spirit. This was an attempt to placate the ghost. But as soon as it was completed, it was destroyed by Balaji. This happened a number of times. On each occasion a shrine was constructed, the following morning the frustrated builders found that their work had been in vain; for the monkey god had reduced the monument to rubble. This vexed Pretraj who entered into a fierce struggle with Balaji. The former, however, was quickly subdued. He recognised that he was no match for Rama's help-mate. During the conflict, he also became aware that his actions were sinful (*papi*) and that they would have negative karmic effects. So he not only capitulated; he pleaded for forgiveness (*kshama*) and beseeched Balaji to include him amongst those who fight for the cause of righteousness (*dharmparayanta*). This is how Pretraj came to serve Balaji and why he now tortures (*yatna dete hai*) malevolent spirits rather than the innocent villagers upon whom he had previously preyed.

Despite the fact that Pretraj is considered to be a subordinate deity and the least powerful of the three major gods, two other minor deities are said to operate under his control or command: Divan Sarkar, his chief minister, and Kundivale Baba, Lord of the tank in which many spirit-afflicted pilgrims are instructed to bathe. Furthermore, according to some temple functionaries, there is also a third *devata* who acts as a messenger and servant of Pretraj. This deity is known as Bhangivara. I was told that his duties are to prepare reports (*rapat*) on spirits for his master and to purify (*shuddh karna*) them with fire (*ag*). Indeed, during the curing rituals in Mehndipur, kerosene fires are sometimes made by pilgrims to burn the spirits afflicting them, and this is viewed, not only as a form of purification (*shuddhikaran*), but as a type of punishment (*dand*) also. Some temple priests assert that Bhangivara was formerly an evil spirit, as were Divan Sarkar and Kundivale Baba. However, because they had received stern punishment from Pretraj, as well as from Balaji, for performing wicked acts, it is claimed that they decided to cease being malevolent and to do good works. Other temple functionaries, on the other hand, maintain that Bhangivara is not a deity at all. They comment that the word simply refers to a place, the site of an elongated *cabutra* (platform) that is located immediately outside, though connected to, the temple of Balaji where impure (*ashuddh*) spirits are not only made pure (*nirmal*) but beaten (*pita hua*) as well. Some of them also regard Kundivale Baba, not as a converted malevolent ghost (a *bhut* or *pret* that has become a *dut* of Pretraj), but as a kind of deified saint who in his life time was a *siddha purusha*, a man possessing magical or supernatural powers, and whose divine energy or *shakti* is considered to reside in the *kund* or tank. But, despite the different views that are expressed, all the respondents agree on one fundamental point, namely, that each of the above deities and the place known as Bhangivara emanate power from which every pilgrim gains benefit, whether their affliction (*sankat*) is thought to be caused by malevolent forces or not.

In addition, there are also two other minor deities known as Samadhivale Baba (or Samadhi Ganesh Puri) and Samadhi Ganga-Nath. Concerning the divinity of these saints, there is a complete consensus. All the *pujari* at the pilgrimage centre claim that these holy men both achieved *moksha* (liberation) and became *devata*s during their lifetime. A number of stories that are told about them testify to the conviction that they not only performed great miracles when they were alive but continue to do so today, their power emanating from the tombs into which their ashes were placed. Traditionally, a holy man or ascetic either decides to 'take' *samadhi* when he is alive or, alternatively, is 'given' it after death (cf. Parry 1982: 96). In the former case he enters into a state of deep trance or, as Parry points out, 'a perpetual cataleptic condition of suspended animation of deep meditation' (ibid.). But whether *samadhi* takes place before or after death, the body is arranged in a meditational posture called *padmasana*, a position where the spine is straight and the legs crossed, the hands or up-turned palms resting on the knees. The body is then placed onto a flat wooden board and lowered with poles into a hole in the earth. Immediately afterwards, this is covered with soil, and a stone construction (also known as a *samadhi* or *chatri* [cf. Carstairs

1957: 101]) is erected over the site of the grave. Ganesh Puri and Ganga-Nath, however, did not undergo the ritual process in the usual manner. For, in each case, it is claimed that the body spontaneously burst into flames due to the heat (*tapas*) in it.[8] It is said that these holy men were *brahmacarya*s (celibate), though Ganga-Nath became one only towards the end of his life. It is also said that they practised extreme austerities and were great adepts in the art of meditation, both of which enabled them to gain extraordinary suprahuman powers (*siddhi*s). Thus, even though they are now 'dead', from the point of view of the sick, or those who come to Mehndipur seeking relief from adversity, Ganesh Puri and Ganga-Nath still play an important role. Viewed as minor deities, they have been incorporated into the village pantheon, which, it should be noted, also includes all the major Sanskritic gods (*devata*s) and goddesses (*devi*s).[9] They are equally the object of worship (*puja*).

Having provided both essential information on the history of the pilgrimage centre and on the chief deities there, I now give details of two particular curing rituals – rituals to which reference will often be made throughout this book – and I provide a preliminary account of the practices of temple functionaries and healers in Mehndipur as well.

Curing ceremonies

Besides *arati*, the major ritual at Balaji temple which I describe and analyse in depth later (see chapter 4), a ritual that is performed for treating those suffering from *sankat*, as well as for purposes of worship, two other important curing ceremonies are also conducted in Mehndipur, namely, Arji and Darkhast.[10] These two names are Urdu legal terms, meaning 'request'. The rituals are held at the principal temple; but at Tin Pahar Vale Baba and at the Sheshanaga *mandir* only the latter is performed. During each of these, the supplicant must make food offerings (*bhog*) to the three main deities – first of all to Balaji, second, to Bhairava, and, third, to Pretraj. In the Arji ceremony, a large oblation is made, while in the Darkhast ritual a considerably smaller one is given. When fieldwork was conducted, the cost of the first of these was 41.25 rupees, the second was 2.25 rupees. For Arji, four items are required, namely, one and three-quarter kilos of *laddu* (a sweet food prepared from gram flour, sugar and ghee or clarified butter), one and three-quarter kilos of *urad* (a black pulse), the same quantity of *caval* (rice), and a small pot of pure ghee. The first three items, all of which have previously been cooked, are known, respectively, as Balaji *ka bhog* (Balaji's food offering), Bhairava *ka bhog*, and Pretraj *ka bhog*. During Darkhast, by contrast, five or six *laddu* balls, a few pieces of *potasa* (a sugar preparation) and a little ghee are offered.

Every pilgrim who wishes to undergo ceremonial healing must first give the Darkhast offering through the intermediary of a temple functionary. The latter takes a little of the oblation and puts it into the *havan* (sacred fire), which burns in small brass pots before each of the deities. When the patient is brought before Balaji, however, the priest also takes two pieces of the *laddu*, touches the feet of the idol with them, and returns them to the donor. The patient is then instructed to eat these. The part of the oblation that is consumed by the donor is known as *peshi ka laddu*. *Peshi*, meaning 'hearing', a legal term that usually denotes 'the hearing of a law suit', is another word of Urdu origin. Pilgrims claim that, as soon as the two pieces of *laddu* are eaten by the patient, the details of his or her request are examined by the god. Later, the remainder of the offering is taken to the rear of the temple. This is circled over the supplicant's head seven times and thrown over his or her left or right shoulder for the dogs and goats that wander freely there to feast upon. The action is viewed symbolically as freeing the patient from his or her affliction (*sankat*), of casting it off.

The whole sequence of events takes between five and ten minutes to complete, as does the Arji ritual, which in terms of procedure parallels the former in every detail. A patient who has taken part in the Darkhast ceremony, in fact, may choose to donate the large Arji offering a little later on the same day. Indeed, if after participating in the Darkhast ritual it is confirmed that a patient is afflicted by a spirit, this is considered necessary, and a patient may even continue to donate the large Arji offering on each successive day that he or she stays in Mehndipur. The precise pattern of daily offerings made in many cases, however, is determined in accordance with a particular senior temple functionary's (or healer's) instructions. Nonetheless, even if a priest or a healer (*bhagat*) directs a patient to offer Arji and/or Darkhast on a daily basis, it is said that before finally leaving the pilgrimage centre every patient must take part once again in the Darkhast ceremony. This, it is believed, is vital for the patient's welfare.

21

Plate 1. Mehndipur Balaji Temple

Plate 2. A Mehndipur pilgrim purchasing the Arji food offering from a
prasad vala

Plate 3. Pitristhan – ancestral shrines on a hill top in Mehndipur

Temple functionaries and healers

Regarding the duties of some of the senior temple functionaries, providing time for patient consultation is thought to be crucial, though in some respects most of them tend to give relatively mundane advice. For example, they may suggest that a particular patient should take part in the Arji ceremony every morning for a period of seven, eleven or even forty-one days. They equally exhort the sick to consume *prasad* (other sanctified food offerings), *bhabhut* (ash from the burnt oblation) and *jal* (holy water), which are available from all the temples in the village. Patients may also be advised to take special *prasad*, consisting of rice and *curma* (prepared from wheat flour, sugar and coconut). This is distributed at twelve noon every day from the Sita-Ram temple after first being brought before the idol of Balaji at the main healing shrine. No charge is made for this. In addition, patients are almost invariably told to avoid eating certain foods, especially chilli (*mirc*), onion (*pyaz*), garlic (*lahsun*) and meat (*mas*) as well as hot spice (*garam masala*). Consumption of these things is prohibited because they are held to be *tamsik*;[11] that is to say, they are considered to have an adverse effect on those who are sick due to their association with dark or malevolent forces (demons and ghosts) and with negative emotion, such as anger (*gussa*).

Furthermore, a patient or a patient's family, may be given a mantra and receive elementary instruction about how to recite it correctly, particularly if it is in Sanskrit.[12] For, according to some temple functionaries, if a Sanskrit mantra is not uttered correctly, it may prove ineffectual or, worse, exacerbate the afflicted person's malaise (cf. O'Malley 1935: 189–90). Alternatively, a patient may be given a particular *path* (a portion of scripture) to read and contemplate. The *path*s that are most frequently used for this purpose are the *Sri Hanuman Calisa*, the *Sri Balaji Path*, and the *Sundara Kanda*, the fifth book of the *Ramayana*, which narrates Hanuman's flight across the ocean to Lanka and how he subdues the demons there. If a pilgrim is illiterate, he or she may perhaps be advised to recite a *kirtan* (sacred utterance usually consisting of divine names) or a simple *japa* (a sacred phrase or sentence, or just a single word, such as *Om*) for a specified number of times every morning and/or evening for a certain number of days. A *kirtan* that pilgrims are often told to recite is one containing the names of two deities, Sita and her male consort Rama. However, it should be pointed out that, although distinctions are made between different kinds of sacred utterance – a *path* as compared with a *kirtan*, for example – they are not considered to be *absolutely* distinguishable from mantras; that is to say, all types of sacred speech, in a sense, are thought to be mantras and to have a similar magical effect or to produce the desired result for which they are employed.[13]

In contrast to temple functionaries generally, most of the healers operating in Mehndipur are extremely charismatic. Many of them become possessed by benevolent spirits (*dut*s), which are frequently said to be messengers and servants of Balaji. Indeed, some healers claim that the monkey god himself also possesses them. Those who do not become possessed usually work with a medium, a person through whom a curer communicates with helpful spirits as well as with malevolent ghosts. All practitioners, whether they become possessed or not, are known as *bhagat*s. This term is synonymous with the word *bhakta*, and in Mehndipur curers typically claim to be a *bhakta* or devotee of Balaji (Balaji *ka bhakta*). The ability to diagnose the nature and cause of illness, to identify the malevolent agents or forces responsible for this, to heal the sick and to expel evil spirits from the body is held to be a divine gift. In fact, the power healers believe and are believed by many others to possess is thought to come directly from Hanuman.

With respect to gender, most practitioners are male, and all of them belong to the twice-born castes (*dvija jati*). The majority of the healers are Vaishyas; a few, however, are Brahmans and Kshatriyas. In terms of occupational status, most curers are business men, though some are school teachers or have government service jobs. Generally speaking, all of them are relatively affluent and well educated. They are domiciled in towns and cities and usually come to the pilgrimage centre for a fixed period of time every month or for a number of days or weeks every year. Some of them informed me that they also visit other healing shrines in northern India in order to conduct séances (*darbars*) there and/or perform these rituals in their homes or in buildings close by, which they rent specifically for the purpose. None of the practitioners operating in Mehndipur demand cash payment for the service that they provide. To do so, they maintain, would be tantamount to committing a sin (*pap*) and an abuse of the healing gift bestowed upon them by Balaji. Moreover, they often comment that because they are not poor (*garib*), it is not necessary to charge their clients. Curers, however, are allowed to receive donations (*dan*) and in practice do so, though many state that to keep them would also be sinful. Consequently, *bhagats* often stress that whatever money is offered to them is later deposited in the donation box at the temple of Balaji.

But, despite the apparent piety of healers, pilgrims have mixed opinions about them. In fact, a number of those who travel to Mehndipur to take part in healing rituals at the shrines refuse to consult *bhagats*. Some pilgrims comment that, if they were to attend the séances conducted by these practitioners, they would simply be wasting their time; for only Balaji is able to cure their diseases and end their affliction. Also, since the majority of the pilgrims whom I interviewed said that they had previously consulted curers in their home villages or towns without gaining any benefit, a number of them claimed to have no faith (*vishvas*) in *bhagats*. Some pilgrims even express greater scepticism, seeing curers in Mehndipur as being barely distinguishable from other types of occult practitioner who not only remove but equally inflict mystical harm. This, I believe, is likely to have been the reason why some of those who actually attended one particular *bhagat*'s *darbar* did not want to accept *cay* (tea) from the latter. The healer in question often asked patients and their carers to take a small glass of the sweet liquid refreshment. The fear of having someone's *sankat* transferred to them was probably why these clients insistently refused the offer. According to many pilgrims, in certain instances sickness or adversity can only be removed by means of transference. In such cases, a spirit that is exorcised from one person's body is held to enter the body of a second person, who then begins to experience the illness, disease or misfortune that formerly afflicted the first. It is a process that is often said to be facilitated by means of food or drink, the item that is consumed being the medium or object by which this takes place.

On the other hand, many pilgrims find the *bhagat*'s *darbar*s extremely beneficial and complementary to temple healing rituals. Indeed, for these individuals, *bhagat*s are saints (*sant*s) and are accorded a great deal of respect. A number of patients, who periodically journey to the pilgrimage centre, even travel to Mehndipur specifically to attend these séances, arranging their itinerary to coincide with a specific healer's publicised visits to the village. And some of them also testify that they have only gained improvement or relief from *sankat* with the help of such practitioners.

To be sure, the role Mehndipur healers play in helping their clients to gain relief from supernatural malaise or *sankat* appears to be a crucial one, as I shall attempt to demonstrate in this book (especially in chapter 5). But I now turn to focus on supernatural affliction itself and concentrate in the next chapter on key patterns or features of such affliction, particularly patterns of causation, attribution and vulnerability.

2

SUPERNATURAL MALAISE AND KEY PATTERNS OF AFFLICTION

Causation, attribution and vulnerability

Introduction

With specific reference to the case study data I collected in Mehndipur, this chapter explores the way in which numerous problems, including, for instance, physical and mental illness, family tensions, loss of profits in business enterprise, failure to gain employment or to find a suitable marriage partner, are ascribed to supernatural agency. I will argue that the process of identifying the particular supernatural agent considered to be responsible for causing adversity is often closely connected with certain events, such as the untimely death (*akal mrityu*) of a family member, friend or neighbour, the cessation of ritual performance at specific shrines or temples, leaving the house or commencing certain tasks at inauspicious times, and journeying outside the home village or town. However, the manner in which these and many other events are linked with particular supernatural beings to which illness (*rog/ bimari*) and misfortune (*abhagya/durbhagya*) are attributed is extremely complex. For example, although women are typically held to be susceptible to possession or affliction by capricious spirits, a particular woman who is suffering from infertility (*banjhpan*) or from acute abdominal pain (*pet dard*) may not always invoke this explanation. She may be considered to have been bewitched by an angry neighbour with whom she is constantly arguing about shared land on which the livestock of their respective families graze; or she may be thought to have mistakenly consumed ensorcelled food offered to her husband by a jealous business rival. On the other hand, she may consult a local healer, such as a *bhagat* or a *tantrik*, and accept his pronouncement that her affliction is caused by an angry ancestor spirit (*pitri devata*) whose requests for particular offerings, such as food or clothes, have been ignored.

Yet while the relationship between certain events and the identification of the afflicting malevolent agent is a complex interpretational one both for Hindus themselves and for the anthropologist, a number of important patterns can be found, as I will show. Indeed, I will demonstrate that, in a large number of cases, depending on whether one is male or female, married or single, certain incidents preceding malaise tend to be singled out for particular attention while other events are ignored. For example, when a woman is suddenly afflicted, having earlier gone out into the street to urinate, perhaps in a place close to a temple, shrine or holy tree, such as the *pipal* tree (*ficus religiosa*) or the banyan (*ficus bengalensis*); or having left the house at twelve noon, an inauspicious (*ashubh*) time of day; or having traversed the crossroads (*cauraha*) at one of the exit points of the village or town, perhaps while eating milk sweets (*dudh mithai*); or having dropped a morsel of food in the street and later consuming it – these types of incident occurring prior to the onset of illness are commonly emphasised or considered to be intrinsically connected with it. For it is during such events that women are said to become vulnerable to attack from *bhut-pret*, the souls of the departed that are stranded between the human world (*manushya-loka*) and the world of the ancestors (*pitri-loka*).

The finding that female pilgrims interviewed in Mehndipur were disproportionately afflicted by these spirits is also examined in this chapter.[1] Drawing upon insights derived from Bruce Kapferer's (1991) investigation of spirit possession in Sri Lanka, I argue that women frequently become the prey of these beings because they are viewed as being particularly at risk from their malevolent attention. In other words, their susceptibility is essentially a function of cultural typification (cf. Kapferer ibid.: 128 and *passim*).

Another major cause of supernatural affliction discussed in this chapter (and in chapter 3) is sorcery (*jadu-tona*).[2] In Mehndipur and throughout north India, it is widely believed that a person can become the object of *direct* or *indirect* (i.e. a diverted) sorcery attack. In the former case, person A is said to be harmed by his or her enemy, person B. In the latter case, by contrast, person C, who is an essentially innocent victim, is injured; and this is thought to occur because B may try to get at A by afflicting C, or because the third party in the triad is harmed inadvertently. Now, with respect to pilgrims interviewed in Mehndipur, sorcery was suspected or identified as the cause of adversity equally by both men and women, though married persons claimed to be the object of direct attack far more than single persons. The widespread notion or common perception that married persons are especially predisposed to harm or injury in this respect, as compared with single persons, appears to be one of the main reasons the former typically accused their enemies (*dushman*) of resorting to sorcerous practice to which illness and misfortune were ascribed. But a large proportion of unmarried persons at the pilgrimage centre were also said to be victims of sorcery. In many cases, however, they claimed to be the object of indirect attack. In fact, it was often stated that a single person had been afflicted, not by a personal foe, but by an enemy of his or her parents. This suggests that, if one is married, one not only perceives oneself and one's spouse to be at risk from sorcery, one may also view one's children as being vulnerable, which, in turn, perhaps influences the way in which the single person sees him or herself as being potentially prone to this type of mystical attack. And this, I contend, explains why unmarried individuals who alleged that they had become victims of occult practice often believed that the enemies of their parents were responsible for causing them harm or injury.

In addition to the troubles and tribulations created by *bhut-pret* and sorcery, the ancestors may also cause adversity. It is a common belief that any member of the family may be affected by their malevolent behaviour and that any type of illness or misfortune may be caused by them. The general belief that no specific category of person is exceptionally at risk from their malevolent attention was also reflected in the actual cases of malaise ascribed to their anger or wrath (*kop*) which I documented in Mehndipur. A phenomenological approach, therefore, is adopted, not only to analyse why certain individuals in Mehndipur stated that they were possessed by ghosts or were the object of direct or indirect sorcery attack, but also to account for the finding that no particular category of person invoked ancestral wrath as the agency of supernatural affliction.

This approach, as I will show, provides a critical perspective for analysing these patterns of affliction as well as for understanding the susceptibility of those who are drawn into the orbit of healing practices in Mehndipur. Indeed, it enables exploration of the issues I address in this chapter (as well as the ones addressed throughout this book) to be reoriented, as I will also show; for the kind of phenomenology I espouse moves away from psychologism and other forms of rationalism in which much anthropological discussion of these issues is grounded. Approaches utilised by writers like Bourguignon (1965), Freed and Freed (1964), Kakar (1982), Obeyesekere (1970, 1977, 1984) and Spiro (1978) – writers who engage in speculation about the inner psychological states of those who succumb to the kinds of affliction I describe – thus sharply contrast with the approach adopted here. For the phenomenological perspective I engage is predicated on the view that the actions, behaviour and orientations of Mehndipur pilgrims are to be seen from the standpoint of *their* social world – a standpoint that not only privileges the authority of pilgrims' discourse about their own social and psychological realities, but one which discloses the groundedness of these realities in shared, common sense, taken-for-granted conceptions and beliefs.

Such an approach, of course, is seen by some scholars (e.g. Bourdieu 1992: 25 ff.) to have limitations or is viewed by other writers (e.g. Foucault 1994: xiv) in a wholly negative light for being unsuited, for instance, to historical or structural concerns or forms of analysis. However, whatever limitations may be ascribed to phenomenology it does not assume an epistemology superior to those whose knowledge it aims to disclose. It does not insist on dominating the materials to which it attends; nor does it seek to subordinate the native voice to any other authority except its own. This is one of the chief merits of the approach I engage, one that enables full recognition to be given to the native voice.

Mehndipur pilgrims

Now, as indicated in the early pages of this book, when pilgrims are questioned about their purpose for visiting Mehndipur village, some comment that they have made the journey to offer worship (*puja*) at the village's shrines or to have a *darshan* (literally, a 'viewing') of the deities whose images are displayed in them. However, the vast majority of pilgrims say that they have come to Mehndipur because both allopathic remedies (a term which describes Western medicine (cf. Leslie *et al.* 1976)), and traditional systems of healing, including *ayurveda, yunani, jhar-phuk* (sweeping and blowing), and many other local remedies,[3] have not cured the diseases from which they are suffering. Pilgrimage to the village's healing shrines, principally to the temple of Balaji, in fact, is often seen as providing the only possible hope that sufferers have of overcoming illness and adversity. For many sick pilgrims, then, the temples in Mehndipur are a place of last resort. Moreover, because Western and traditional medicine has either failed to work, or has been ineffective in completely removing illness (whether the pathology is physical and/or psychological), it is almost invariably viewed as having a supernatural cause.[4]

Ailments that are ascribed to the work of supernatural agents in fact are clearly distinguished by pilgrims from ailments that are said to arise as a result of factors such as faulty diet or faulty regimen; and when an illness does not respond to allopathic medicine and/or to a variety of traditional therapies, this itself is taken as a sign that supernaturals are likely to be involved. The logic of attribution here, however, should not be seen as some kind of *unscientific* lapse in native thought, as involving a flight into the *irrational* (cf. Leslie *et al.* ibid.). For this would not only be a misrepresentation of pilgrims aetiological conceptions; it would also be a refusal to consider them in terms of their own authority; and this is critical, as I will show.

To examine how illness or adversity comes to be attributed to the supernatural and how this is typically linked to a particular event preceding the onset of disease, I now provide six case studies recorded in the field. These cases, which are characteristic of their types, fall into three indigenously distinguished categories, namely, 1) possession by capricious spirits; 2) sorcery, which may or may not result in spirit possession; and 3) possession or affliction by ancestor spirits.

Possession by capricious spirits

(i) Sonu[5] was a 35 year old woman from Lucknow in Uttar Pradesh. She was brought by her husband to the temple of Balaji in Mehndipur for the first time one year before I interviewed the couple. The woman informed me that for three years she had been suffering from pain throughout her entire body (*puri sharir dard*), particularly headaches (*sir dard*), as well as lethargy and weakness (*bharipan aur kamzori*). Shortly after the problem began, she said that she consulted a physician, but the medicine prescribed failed to provide any relief. Both Sonu and her husband commented that this was bewildering. They could neither explain why the illness had started nor why it refused to respond to medical treatment. However, they added that, after pondering on the matter for some time, they began to suspect the possibility that the illness might have a supernatural cause. But which type of malevolent being could be responsible? When could it have attacked her? What might be its motive for causing the affliction?

Sonu and her husband stated that, while reflecting on these and other questions, they recalled that the malaise began quite suddenly one night after returning home from a nearby suburb of the city. They had been to a temple dedicated to the goddess Kali, a temple which they often visited in order to offer worship to the deity. On the night in question, the couple said that they did not return home immediately. They decided to purchase *lassi* (yoghurt) from a shop situated at the crossroads (*cauraha*) where their home suburb adjoins the neighbouring one in which the temple of Kali is located. Because they had taken the milk-drink at this inauspicious place, an event that immediately preceded the onset of the illness, they maintained that there was no longer any doubt about the nature of the complaint or its cause: it was clear that Sonu had become possessed by a capricious spirit (*bhut*); and this, they stressed, became more apparent when the same incident was repeated again just two months after the illness started; for immediately following it the woman's condition was said to worsen.

(ii) Asha, an 11-year-old girl from Pattel Nagaur in Delhi, began to have headaches (*sir dard*) and abdominal pains (*pet dard*) only three months before being brought to Mehndipur. I was informed by her parents that she had received a thorough medical examination, including both X-rays of the affected parts of the body and a blood test. But nothing abnormal had been detected. They said that the medical specialists had commented that there was nothing seriously wrong with the girl and had claimed that she would soon recover. However, I was told that the girl's pains increased day by day and that her condition became progressively worse. Her parents said that they later discussed the problem with a neighbour, who informed them that a local healer (*bhagat*) lived only a short distance from their home. The neighbour was said to have given them renewed hope and encouragement by pointing out that, if the medical experts could neither diagnose nor cure the girl, it was possible that the *bhagat* could help.

Asha was thus brought before the traditional curer. According to my informants, when the healer examined the girl, he started in studied silence. But, after a short while, he instructed her to take a few grains of uncooked rice from a small clay pot resting on a shelf behind him. These were then placed into the *bhagat*'s hand who, after smelling them, proclaimed that Asha was possessed by two ghosts, a *pret* and a *musalman*. The former, he was alleged to have stated, was a disciple of the latter from whom it had learnt how to inflict pain upon its victims. Asha's parents said that the healer told them that these spirits had entered her body while she was picking flowers from the small field behind her school and that exorcism (*bhut-pret utarna*) was required to expel them. But despite the *bhagat*'s attempt to release the girl from their control, they maintained that the exercise ended in failure.

Asha's parents said that they had not at first suspected possession. However, they commented that the explanation offered by the *bhagat* made perfect sense; for the girl often picked flowers from the small field behind her school; and it was on one particular evening when she returned home from school with flowers in her blazer pocket that the pains in her head and stomach first began.

The above events, which are viewed as being causally related to possession by evil spirits, are essentially similar; and they are good examples of the kinds of incident frequently thought to precede spirit possession. As in many other cases which I documented, the woman and the girl become the object of capricious attack because they enter into places where it is said that spirits or ghosts typically prey upon their victims. Here, then, emphasis is put upon *place*. However, when one turns to consider other kinds of supernatural malaise, this is less significant. Thus, regarding sorcery, for instance, whenever this is invoked, it is social *schism* that tends to be stressed. The cases cited below are examples of this type of affliction.

Sorcery

(iii) Sita, a 30-year-old woman from Merat, a large city in Uttar Pradesh, came to Mehndipur for the first time thirteen months before the interview with her was recorded. She informed me that she had taken the 450 kilometre journey on a number of occasions with various members of her family and often resided in the village for three or four months at a time. When I interviewed the woman, however, she was alone. She stated that for the past three years she had been suffering from dizziness (*cakkar*), headaches (*sir dard*), aches and pains in her hands and feet (*hath aur pair me dard*) and a feeling of weakness (*kamzori*) in the body. Sita had consulted a number of doctors and magico-religious curers (*tantriks*) but said that her condition had not improved. She had also gained no respite from the illness while dwelling in Mehndipur either, though she claimed that her health could only be restored by Balaji, the reason she continued to take part in the daily rituals in the main healing temple.

The illness, Sita commented, began shortly after a dispute about property. I was informed that the woman's husband and her husband's elder brother jointly owned a small field on which they cultivated seasonal vegetables. However, when the produce was sold in the market, the small sums of cash that were made often became the subject of fierce arguments between the wives of the two men. Sita's husband's elder brother's wife (*jethani*) allegedly wanted a larger share of the proceeds. But my informant told me that she was unwilling to agree to this; so the wife of the eldest brother divided the field into two parts. Yet, according to Sita, this did not solve the problem. On the contrary, it compounded it; for Sita claimed that her *jethani* wanted a larger portion of the land. In the end, however, Sita said that she reluctantly agreed to the arrangement.

Now, three or four months after the wall dividing the field had been erected my informant said that she became sick. And when she unearthed from her portion of the land a small clay pot, containing a fragment of coal, a few grains of salt, black mustard seeds and three iron nails, as well as pieces of her sari and hair, these objects, she stated, confirmed that the illness had been caused by sorcery (*jadu-tona*). She believed that a *jind*[6] (a Muslim spirit) had entered her body, which intended to end her life by making her progressively weaker, just as the pieces of sari and hair were buried in the soil to become completely ruined by a process of decay and decomposition. Moreover, there was no doubt in Sita's mind who had done this. She stated that her *jethani* had paid an occult practitioner or *tantrik* (sorcerer)[7] to perform the wicked deed. Her *jethani* allegedly wanted Sita to die. But this was not to happen instantly; for the former was said to want the latter to suffer tremendous pain and misery first, which is why the particular method of sorcery designed to achieve this had been used. As far as the afflicted woman was concerned, if her *jethani* had not been so greedy, the squabbles that erupted between them would never have occurred and she would not have become the victim of sorcery.

(iv) Vinod was 26 years old when he became sick. He informed me that for four years he had not only been suffering from constant headaches (*sir dard*), he easily became angry (*gussa a gaya*) and would often assault (*mar-pit karta hai*) anyone who came near him. He had been treated by medical experts in a mental hospital in Agra as well as by local healers (*tantrik*s and *pir baba*s) in Merat, the city where he was living. However, his health and behaviour did not improve. His parents said that they began to fear that their son would perhaps never get well. But after learning from a neighbour how hundreds of people are miraculously cured every day in Mehndipur from all kinds of disease, they became more hopeful. Vinod's parents stated that they knew that the god Balaji could cure their son and were confident that the deity would listen to their appeal for help. This is why they had come to the healing shrines in the village.

Before he became ill, I was informed that Vinod's family were dwelling in the lower rooms of a large house in which the owner also resided. For a number of years their relationship with him was said to be friendly. But this was soured and became bitter when they were told one day that they had to leave the house. The landlord wanted to let the rooms that they were occupying at the time to another family willing to pay 400 rupees (approximately £8.88) for the accommodation, an increase of one third on the rent he had formerly received each month. Because Vinod's family neither had the financial resources to pay the extra 100 rupees every month, nor the desire to do so, they maintained that they had no alternative but to move out.

According to Vinod's parents, it was shortly after vacating the rooms when their son first started to have severe headaches and to become extremely violent in his behaviour towards others. The affliction, they commented, had been caused by sorcery (*jadu-tona*). Because Vinod's parents had had a number of vexed arguments with their former landlord before leaving his house, they said that the latter attempted to inflict harm upon them by employing the services of an occult practitioner (*jadu-tona karne vala*). From the sorcerer *materia medica* was allegedly obtained and placed into a bowl of curd, which was later given to them. But, since only Vinod consumed this, only he was affected by it. In their view, Vinod's malaise could not be attributed to any other cause. The fact that he had been the only one to eat the curd, a gift which in itself was said to be incongruent with their former landlord's deplorable behaviour towards them, was ample proof that he had been harmed by sorcery, and that the landlord, who had become their enemy (*dushman*), was the one responsible for afflicting him.

Unlike events that often precede sorcery accusations, namely, disputes and conflicts, the incidents which are thought to be causally related to affliction by ancestor spirits usually involve some kind of unforeseen provocation on the part of their living descendants. In the examples below, an ancestor spirit causes illness or suffering because it is either neglected or because its request for help in achieving its desired goal is ignored.

Possession or affliction by ancestor spirits

(v) Nirmila came to Mehndipur from the city of Lalitpur in Uttar Pradesh because she had a stomach disorder, a disorder that caused her to experience much abdominal pain (*pet dard*). The 52-year-old woman informed me that she had had the complaint for three years. Although she had received treatment at an allopathic clinic near her home, she stated that her symptoms still remained and that this was the reason why she came to the pilgrimage centre. The illness, I was told, was caused by an ancestor spirit (*pitri devata*) and that this had recently been confirmed by a Lalitpur magico-religious curer (*bhagat*) whom she had consulted. In a divinatory séance, the *bhagat* was said to have informed the woman that the ancestor spirit afflicted her because she had stopped offering it worship at the family shrine. Since she had neglected it, the ancestor spirit became angry and attacked her.

Nirmila told me that she had stopped worshipping the *pitri devata* because her son had prevented it. According to the informant, her son was adamantly opposed to the practice. He had received a college education and considered it to be a foolish, 'superstitious' tradition. Nonetheless, because she had neglected to worship the ancestor spirit, she was convinced that she had aroused its anger and that this was the reason why she had become sick.

(vi) For more than a year Ramdas had been suffering from lethargy and weakness (*bharipan aur kamzori*) and had constant head pains (*sir dard*). The 56-year-old man said that he had not consulted a medical practitioner, though he had been treated by two local healers (*bhagats*) in Badaiwa, his home village, situated in the district of Sivpuri, Madhya Pradesh. However, when their attempts to cure him failed, he told me that, despite being old and frail, he decided that it was necessary to take the 350-kilometre journey to Mehndipur.

Ramdas claimed that he was possessed by a *pitri devata*, the same ancestor spirit that had also afflicted his brother ten years earlier. He informed me that the reason it was acting malevolently was because it wanted *mukti* (release or liberation).[8] It had previously entered the body of his brother in order to communicate that it wished to be reborn.[9] But the sibling was said to have ignored this. The latter did not go to the shrine of any god or goddess to beseech a deity to grant the *pitri devata*'s request.[10] However, after some time his brother recovered, and the ancestor spirit allegedly entered the body of Ramdas. It appeared in his dream (*svapn*), instructing him to go to the temple of Balaji. For without the aid of the god, Ramdas stated that it would have to remain in its existing form for an unforeseeable length of time. Only Balaji could ensure its immediate release from the ancestral realm.

As far as Ramdas was concerned, the affliction could only have been caused by his family's *pitri devata*. He said that this became apparent to him within a few weeks of becoming sick. For it was the very same illness from which his sibling had suffered a decade earlier. Ramdas was, therefore, not baffled or puzzled as to why he was unwell; neither was it necessary for him to consult an expert in the art of divination, such as a *tantrik*, to discover what the ancestor spirit demanded. Because it had appeared in his dream, he claimed that he knew what it required and what he had to do in order to regain his health.

Establishing the link between illness or misfortune, a given event, and a particular malevolent agent is often extremely problematic, as a number of the case examples I have just outlined illustrate. This is one of the main reasons why many Hindus consult those who are skilled in the art of divination. However, a number of patterns can be found, as indicated earlier, patterns which in Mehndipur are clear and discernible. Thus, for instance, the first two case examples cited above (Sonu's and Asha's afflictions) are typical of the spirit possession cases that I recorded in that emphasis is put upon *place*: whenever illness was actually ascribed to possession by capricious spirits, from which women are specifically held to be at risk, events such as consuming a milk drink at the crossroads on the edge of the town or suburb or wandering into an open field were typically singled out by pilgrims. And this, perhaps, is to be expected, since it is widely believed that these are the places where spirits or ghosts usually attack their victims. In addition, in actual cases where sorcery was stated to be the cause of illness or misfortune, pilgrims often claimed that conflicts with particular individuals preceded affliction. Sita's case is a good example of this. Indeed, because married as opposed to single persons are held to be targeted by their enemies, they are more likely to see conflicts occurring prior to the onset of illness as being linked to sorcerous acts carried out against them by the latter. This is perhaps the reason Sita is quick to accuse the relation with whom she had recently quarrelled of being responsible for causing her affliction. Moreover, it is perhaps understandable why the parents of Vinod, who is unmarried, also invoke sorcery to explain their son's sickness. It will be recalled that the parents believe that they themselves are the ones whom their former landlord wishes to injure by occult means. When Vinod falls sick then, it is assumed that he inadvertently or indirectly becomes the victim of the landlord's cunning sorcerous plot. However, it should further be noted that, whereas spirit possession and sorcery are associated with gender and marital status respectively, affliction by ancestor spirits is essentially unconnected with these factors. But in order to substantiate this and other claims which have been made regarding the issue of vulnerability, I first give the quantitative data which I collected at the pilgrimage centre.

The Mehndipur data set

As indicated in the Introduction to this book, on the basis of opportunity and willingness of pilgrims to provide information, semi-structured interviews were conducted over a period of six months at the temple of Balaji in Mehndipur. Of the 734 patients and/or their accompanying carers whom I interviewed, the vast majority were domiciled in northern India. A little under three-quarters of these informants came from towns and cities while a little over a quarter came from villages large or small,[11] a particularly uneven distribution that is even more pronounced when compared with the population at large, since almost three-quarters of India's population is rural.[12] Fifty-one per cent of the patient sample was female. Male as well as female sufferers came from different socio-economic backgrounds, though most were high caste, and they were predominantly middle class (cf. Kakar 1982: 281, n. 6).[13] With regard to education, excluding those patients who were either illiterate or who possessed degrees and other similar qualifications, the average age at which formal school terminated for men (in some cases, however, this was still in progress) was 14 years. For women the average age was 13. A hundred and forty six (40 per cent) of the men had received college education and 92 (25 per cent) had degrees or other higher qualifications. The corresponding figures for women were 55 (15 per cent) and 44 (12 per cent) respectively. Ninety-seven per cent of males and 69 per cent of females in the sample were literate, extremely high levels when compared with national and regional percentages.[14]

The most common types of ailment I recorded in Mehndipur were headaches, dizziness, bodily aches and pains, loss of appetite, lethargy and weakness, depression, irritability and various kinds of mental illness, though a number of the interviewed informants stated that they had cancer, heart or respiratory disease, tuberculosis, haematemesis or some other serious illness.[15] Ninety per cent of male and 88 per cent of female sufferers had previously been treated in clinics or hospitals. Thus, the overwhelming majority of them had received, and in some cases were still receiving, Western medical treatment. A large number of them had also consulted local healers, such as *tantriks*, *mantriks*, *bhagats*, *vaidyas* and *pir babas*, before journeying to Mehndipur. Sixty-one per cent of male and 64 per cent of female patients claimed or were said to have received traditional forms of treatment from these practitioners. Many of those in the sample had been sick for a considerable length of time, though some for only a few months or weeks. One woman, for instance, had been suffering for over thirty years. But the person who had been afflicted for the longest period was a man. He had been ill for more than fifty-one years. The median length of time of affliction for both sexes, however, was six years.

Regarding various categories of supernatural malaise, more female than male interviewees stated that their ill-health was caused by capricious demons and ghosts. Thirty-five per cent of women as compared with 26 per cent of men invoked this explanation.[16] On the other hand, there was no significant disparity between the sexes concerning the attribution of illness or misfortune to sorcery. Half of both female and male respondents said that they were injured or harmed by occult practitioners, though those who were married more frequently than those who were unmarried claimed to be directly afflicted. Sixty-eight per cent of married persons as opposed to 28 per cent of single persons, in fact, accused their enemies of directly harming them by means of sorcery.[17] Men and women in more or less equal numbers also stated that they were afflicted by ancestor spirits. Seven per cent of both sexes stressed that their ailments would never have started had they not unwittingly angered their ancestors; and 0.5 per cent of men and 0.3 per cent of women made the same claim regarding deities.[18] There were relatively few in the sample who ascribed suffering to supernatural agency while simultaneously being uncertain of its nature; only 0.3 per cent of men and 1 per cent of women said that they were perplexed about the matter. A larger number of respondents, however, were unsure whether their malaise was caused by supernatural or mystical agents. Thus, 10 per cent of men and 8 per cent of women maintained that they had no knowledge about how and why they became sick. Finally, although a significant percentage of women were uncertain about aetiological matters, none of them stated that their illness could be attributed to factors such as faulty diet or faulty regimen. Six per cent of men in the sample, by contrast, did explain ill-health in such terms and rejected the notion of supernatural causation.[19]

The data obtained from interviews with Mehndipur pilgrims give rise to a number of questions. First of all, why did more women than men claim to be possessed by capricious spirits? To explain the vulnerability of women to spirit possession many South Asianists (e.g. Freed and Freed 1964; Gellner 1994; Harper 1963; Jones 1976; Kakar 1982; Obeyesekere 1970, 1977, 1984; Opler 1958; and Mayaram 1999) have utilised the *deprivation hypothesis*, whose most notable proponent is the anthropologist Ioan Lewis (1966, 1978, 1986). In general terms, these writers argue that women are not only coerced into submissiveness in a repressive, male-dominated society such as India but are often unable openly to air their grievances or other mental frustrations which they experience in their everyday lives. Consequently, in order to exact demands and to gain attention from their menfolk, as well as to express their anxieties, they succumb to spirit possession and enter into the orbit of exorcist practice.

But the arguments put forward by deprivationists, arguments which involve speculations about the inner psychological states of those who get afflicted, are problematic (cf. Boddy 1989; Freeman 1999; Kapferer 1991; Parry 1994; Shaara and Strathern 1992; and Skultans 1987a, b.). One of the major difficulties with them is that they are predicated on the Western rationalist notion that women's vulnerability to spirit possession or their resort to exorcist practice is a matter of *choice*. Women in South Asia, however, are prefigured in their cultural identity as being particularly vulnerable to possession by spirits or ghosts. It is not surprising, then, if they are more frequently afflicted by them, as Kapferer (1991) argues with respect to his findings in Sri Lanka. For the belief that women are prone to attack is a social fact, which is likely to have an important influence upon their behaviour and the way in which they interpret illness and adversity. Indeed, it is for this reason that a phenomenological approach is particularly useful, as it provides an alternative way of analysing, not only women's susceptibility to spirit possession, but also other types of supernatural affliction involving both men and women. From the phenomenological perspective Hindu perceptions of vulnerability are critical. Before examining them, however, it will be useful to provide an overview of the theoretical orientation adopted here.

The phenomenological perspective

The phenomenological approach I utilise emanates from the philosophy of Edmund Husserl and from the sociology of writers such as Alfred Schutz, Peter Berger and Thomas Luckmann.[20] The importance of phenomenology to the understanding of spirit possession has already been demonstrated by Bruce Kapferer, who was the first anthropologist to engage it systematically for this purpose. The focus of phenomenology, as the term itself denotes, is the science of appearance or perception. According to Husserl, before one can begin to examine the nature of perception, it is first necessary to 'bracket-off' or 'suspend' belief in what he calls the 'natural attitude', that is to say, the attitude of common sense consciousness that arises from 'natural cognition' (Husserl 1964: 18). For Husserl, consciousness is always consciousness *of* something, and, because it is purposive agency, it is also consciousness *for* something. Concomitant with this is the view that consciousness can be understood in two senses: as *noesis* and as *noema*. The first of these terms refers to pre-reflective consciousness or the stream of thought, which Bergson calls 'inner time' or 'durée' (cf. Schutz 1970: 210). The second, by contrast, denotes reflective thought and is a function of the intellect.

Thus, when one is emerged in one's stream of thought one cannot distinguish between what has been and what is now taking place. There is no apprehension of the self. However, when one grasps oneself reflectively, the very awareness of the stream of consciousness presupposes an inevitable turning back against it. One creates an artificial division. And such a division reveals that reflective thought is always dominated by the past tense, since this perception is only possible by examining what has already taken place. Pre-reflective thought, on the other hand, is atemporal. In the language of Bergson, one simply 'grows older' and 'fuller' (ibid.: 186–7).

Now, the world of everyday life can be understood in exactly the same manner. It also has a noetic component as well as a noematic aspect. As Berger and Luckmann have pointed out, '(t)he man in the street does not ordinarily trouble himself about what is 'real' to him and about what he 'knows' unless he is stopped short by some sort of problem. He takes his 'reality' and his 'knowledge' for granted' (1967: 14). It is only when he is confronted by the strange or the alien, that he sees his reality noematically. In the routinised taken-for-granted world of normal daily life sociological apperception remains absent. Everyday life functions in a fundamentally noetic mode. The natural attitude is never questioned.

However, on the other hand, one can also talk of the *epoché* of the natural attitude. Schutz writes:

> Phenomenology has taught us the concept of phenomen-ological *'epoché'*, the suspension of our belief in the reality of the world as a device to overcome the natural attitude by radicalizing the Cartesian method of philoso-phical doubt. The suggestion may be ventured that man within the natural attitude also uses a specific *'epoché'*, of course quite another one than the phenomenologist. He does not suspend belief in the outer world but on the contrary, he suspends doubt in its existence. What he puts in brackets is the doubt that the world and its objects might be otherwise than the way it appears to him. We propose to call this *epoché* the *'epoché* of the natural attitude'.
>
> (ibid.: 229)

Yet this is not a self-conscious affair in the same way that the natural attitude is never self-consciously constructed. 'It does not require additional verification over and beyond its simple presence. It is simply 'there', as self-evident and compelling facticity' (Berger and Luckmann 1967: 37). Moreover, suspension of doubt underlies the very notion of typification itself, a term Schutz adopts to designate the taken-for-granted idealisations which structure daily life.

In addition to the method of 'bracketing-off' the natural attitude, Husserl contends that the act of thinking and the object of thought are internally related. Although one cannot be certain about the independent existence of things, in Husserl's view, one can be sure of how objects appear immediately in consciousness:

'(i)n perception the perceived thing is believed to be directly given. Before my perceiving eyes stands the thing. I see it, and I grasp it. Yet the perceiving is simply a mental act of mine, of the perceiving subject' (Husserl 1964: 15–16). Objects are, therefore, not regarded as things in themselves but as things posited or intended by consciousness. Consciousness 'is not only the meaning-apprehending but meaning-giving agency. It not only attends to objects, it 'constitutes' them' (Kultgen 1975: 372).

The notion that consciousness is 'meaning-giving agency', which orients itself in the world in a purposive manner, is also central in the writings of Alfred Schutz. Following Husserl's phenomenological initiative, together with ideas drawn from the sociology of Weber, Schutz (1967) maintains that social action is the meaning which the actor bestows upon it, that is to say, the meaning it has for him. However, as Natanson points out in the introduction to the first volume of Schutz's *Collected Papers*, 'Dr. Schutz thinks of the subjective interpretation of meaning as above all a typification of the common-sense world, the actual way in which men in daily life do interpret their own and each other's behaviour' (1967: xxxv). Thus, although one's action is subjectively motivated, it is fundamentally rooted in social life and may not be considered apart from it. 'Man's specific humanity and his sociality are inextricably intertwined. "Homo sapiens" is always, and in the same measure, "homo socius"' (Berger and Luckmann 1967: 69). One is born into a world that exists before one's birth. In view of this, as Schutz (in a way reminiscent of Durkheim) points out, the social world is 'handed down to me by my friends, my parents, my teachers and the teachers of my teachers. I am taught not only how to define the environment ... but also how typical constructs have to be formed in accordance with the system of relevances accepted from the anonymous unified point of view of the in-group' (1967: 13–14). And, according to Schutz, this includes 'ways of life, methods of coming to terms with the environment, efficient recipes for the use of typical means for bringing about typical ends in typical situations' (ibid.: 14). Thus, when one encounters a person acting in the social world, one is aware that one must view the other's action as essentially meaningful; and this presupposes that his action means something to him as well as to oneself. It is because the meaning of action is shared by *both*, then, or rather perceived in this manner, because it is taken for granted by *us*, that the world is typical as well as intersubjectively possible.

Supernatural affliction: a phenomenological approach

One's beliefs and ideas about the world, as well as one's place within it, therefore, are fundamentally connected with perceptions that emerge and develop intersubjectively, since they are rooted in the natural attitude, the everyday world of common sense. In the Hindu world, because women are viewed as being particularly vulnerable to possession by capricious spirits or ghosts (*bhut-pret*), the perception itself is likely to influence the frequency with which they are drawn into the orbit of exorcist practice. It is understandable, then, why more women than men interviewed in Mehndipur were said to be afflicted by spirits. Similarly, the reason why fewer men accounted for illness or adversity in terms of spirit attack and often attributed it to other types of supernatural agency may equally be analysed phenomenologically. For perceptions concerning susceptibility seem to be central here also.

Now, women are held to become possessed by capricious spirits for a number of reasons. Firstly, they are ritually more impure than men. Every month during their menses they become unclean (*ashuddh*) for three or four days; and after giving birth they remain in a polluted state for approximately twelve days, the twelfth day being the one on which the Brahman pandit usually enters the home to perform the *nama-karana* ceremony during which the baby receives its name. On both occasions impurity is terminated by taking a bath (*snan*). But, despite the fact that the ritual bath puts an end to their temporary pollution, they must wait a number of days to perform this. Men, by contrast, who become temporarily unclean by inadvertently coming into contact with a polluting object, such as a dead animal, can terminate this immediately in the same customary manner. Moreover, with respect to men, contamination is essentially external. This is not so in the case of women. Rather it is internal. Here the impure object is the body itself (cf. Nicholas 1981; Yalman 1963). It is the very substance of the female organism and its natural processes which are the source of contamination. The spatial opposition of externality-internality is a particularly apt metaphor, therefore. For while men are conceptually separate from the object of pollution, women by virtue of their sex never can be.

This, in part, explains why spirits or ghosts are said to prey upon them. It is held that these malevolent beings exhibit undue interest in unclean substances. As Crooke graphically points out, spirits 'eat filth, and drink any water, however impure' (1911: 602). By being unclean vessels, women's bodies are thus attractive to them, just as places such as the cremation or burial site (*masan*) as well as toilets have a magnetic hold on their attention (cf. Babb 1975: 205; Berreman 1963: 112; Daya 1990: 8; Maitra 1986: 83; Majumdar 1958: 234; and Singh 'Sher' 1961: 228). On the other hand, evil spirits are believed to be attracted to women because they are often beautiful (*sundar*) (cf. Harper 1963: 175) and because they are fond of wearing scent or sweet-smelling perfume as well as beautiful apparel. Women, moreover, are considered to have strong fleshly appetites. They are often said not only to have an excessive desire to consume rich, expensive foods, such as pure ghee and milk sweets (*dudh mithai*), but delight to engage in various sexual practices.[21] Consequently, because their minds are often filled with greed and with carnal thoughts, *bhut-pret,* which are equally gluttonous, lustful creatures, are partial to them.

But women are also held to be disproportionately afflicted because they are *weak* (*kamzor*) (cf. Kakar 1982: 84; Skultans 1987a: 661). As many Hindus often comment, 'Women have a weak heart; so spirits severely attack them.' (*Aurato ke kamzor dil hota hai; islie bhut-pret us par jyada hamla karte hai.*) Since they are considered to be weak and particularly fearful (*bhayanak*) of these malevolent beings, they are perceived as being exceptionally vulnerable. Men, by contrast, are viewed as being *strong* (*prabal*); they have inner strength which women do not possess. They are thus considered to be resistant to the capricious attacks of *bhut-pret*; and this equally helps to explain why it is thought that the latter tend to refrain from choosing male victims. Because men are seen as being less predisposed than women to this type of affliction, it is hardly surprising that fewer men in the Mehndipur sample actually ascribed illness and misfortune to it. It appears, therefore, that female vulnerability to spirit attack is essentially a function of cultural typification, a function of the way in which women are seen *as women* to attract the malevolent attention of spirits or ghosts.

Yet, although men are stronger than women, the former are commonly said to be just as susceptible as the latter to the mystical forces that sorcerers may unleash. Irrespective of gender, caste, class wealth or age, any person who becomes the object of their destructive power is thought to be unable to escape harm or injury. Regarding sorcery, however, despite the fact that men and women are said to be equally powerless in the face of this mystical force, married persons are widely viewed as being predisposed to direct attack. This is because after marriage it is thought that they are more likely to enter into fierce conflict with other household members or with close relations, who may then employ the services of occult practitioners to harm them.

Indeed, in Rajasthan, as elsewhere in India, it is said that when a woman leaves her natal home and takes up residence in her husband's village or town, her relationship with her affines frequently becomes tense or schismatic. Thus, if she is the wife of a junior member of the household, for example, her *jethani* (her husband's elder brother's wife), who is often seen as being a tyrannical figure, may be extremely hostile towards her and may subject her to a great deal of mental and emotional torture, pain and misery. In such circumstances the wife of the subordinate husband is essentially powerless. If she does not readily obey her *jethani* or respect her authority, she may well receive a beating or suffer other forms of abuse. Similarly, her mother-in-law (*sas*) may also be cruel towards the new member of the household, particularly during the first few years of married life before she has successfully weaned a child or if promised dowry is not immediately forthcoming. On the other hand, a newly married woman may be exceptionally favoured by the mother-in-law, as, indeed, may any other female affine in the group. This may then lead to jealousy (*jalan*) on the part of those wives who are less favoured. Jealousy may equally arise when one of them is unable to rear children, especially if the woman is senior. For a woman's standing in the home is largely determined by her fertility or ability to raise offspring. In the case of the latter female, this may erode or weaken the woman's superior status vis-à-vis other wives. It is these kinds of problems or tensions that women frequently associate with acts of sorcery carried out against them. Thus, a woman may accuse a despotic *jethani* or *sas* of inflicting harm upon her by occult means; or the former may be denounced for using sorcery to gain illegitimate or unjustified revenge against the older women who, in her view, have treated her oppressively; or a female member of the household who cannot raise children may resort to sorcery in order to inflict injury upon any or all of the fertile women in the home, including the mother-in-law herself.

When a man enters into marriage, it is said that his relationship with immediate and extended family members often degenerates into conflict too. He may find that elder male siblings, for example, suddenly begin to treat him contemptuously, seeing him no longer as one who is to be protected by them but rather as a rival, as one likely to make an equal claim to their parents' land, property or wealth. Moreover, after a man acquires this, other close kin relations, particularly aunts and uncles[22] who are senior in status, may become envious, especially if the transfer renders them economically inferior or poorer. After marriage a man may also discover that he can no longer assist his siblings, his aunts and uncles or even his friends with respect to financial aid as he had perhaps formerly done. Because he has a new responsibility to maintain a wife and, eventually, children as well, he may refuse to offer cash loans or gifts to them, resulting in animosity, enmity or perhaps a complete rupture in their relationship. Furthermore, if he treats his wife generously, lavishing gifts upon her, such as expensive saris, perfumes and scented soaps, other male and/or female kin may become jealous or angry, the former because they are perhaps unwilling or unable to be as generous towards their wives, the latter because they have not been treated as favourably.

These are just some of the tensions and conflicts that are often said to arise after marriage, tensions which are frequently viewed as leading to sorcery. Thus, if members of kin are the first to be suspected or accused when sorcery is invoked to explain illness or misfortune, this, perhaps, is to be expected. It is an essentially common sense, taken for granted assumption that married persons are directly at risk from this type of mystical attack, and that it is usually close relations who are responsible for harming them by occult means. It is not surprising then that married as compared with single persons in the Mehndipur sample more often denounced members of kin for launching a direct attack upon them with the aid of black magicians, and saw kinship rivalry or enmity as the motive for this.

In addition, as indicated earlier, married persons frequently suspect sorcery when their unmarried sons and daughters suddenly become sick. Although they are the ones who often expect to be injured or harmed by it, a jealous or angry relative may be suspected of attacking a person's offspring in order to create problems for the parents as well as their children. For it is said that by afflicting a person's son or daughter with disease, the malicious relative can cause great suffering and misery to both, not to mention the financial loss that parents may incur as a result of this. This, to recapitulate, is perhaps why single persons interviewed in Mehndipur who invoked sorcery typically accused an enemy of their parents of resorting to occult practice, rather than a personal foe. The view that a relative may harm a person's unmarried son or daughter is often expressed by parents. This in itself is likely to influence the way in which single persons see themselves as being potentially susceptible to this type of malevolent force; and it may also account for the finding that, in actual cases, uncles and aunts as well as other close relatives allegedly in conflict with the parents of unmarried informants were usually denounced for committing acts of sorcery against the latter.

The reason why a number of my informants attributed suffering to ancestral malevolence is equally comprehensible from the phenomenological perspective. As indicated earlier, it is often stressed that the ancestors may afflict any individual, irrespective of sex, marital status or other such factors. The belief that no one is exceptionally at risk from their malevolent attention is widespread. Because this belief is particularly prevalent, it is not surprising that no specific category of person interviewed in Mehndipur found it necessary to undergo ritual curing as a result of being afflicted by them. Indeed, as the data collected at the pilgrimage centre show, men and women in the sample equally claimed to be harmed in this respect. Here, therefore, it appears that there is also a close relationship between belief or perception and vulnerability to supernatural malaise.

Conclusion

I have shown that in the Hindu world the attribution of illness or misfortune to a particular supernatural or mystical agent is often linked to a specific preceding event with which it is held to be causally related. But this does not appear to be a contingent or arbitrary phenomenon. For certain categories of individuals tend to be viewed as being susceptible to different types of supernatural malaise. Thus, women are perceived to be particularly predisposed to affliction by capricious spirits or ghosts. This, I have argued, is why incidents such as traversing the crossroads at exit points from the town or village or wandering into an open field are commonly emphasised when they become the object of supernatural harm. For these are the kinds of places where capricious spirits are widely believed to prey upon their victims. Moreover, because married rather than unmarried persons are thought to be specifically prone to direct attack from sorcery, I have argued that it is under-standable why the former often see disputes or quarrels with others as preceding such an attack. The tendency to view single persons as being indirectly at risk, especially from the malicious attention of parental enemies, is also marked; and this is why whenever it is alleged that they have been injured or harmed by occult practitioners, conflicts between their parents and the latter's enemies are frequently emphasised by them. On the other hand, where factors such as gender and marital status appear to be insignificant with respect to vulnerability events connected with malevolent ancestor spirits may be stressed, events such as neglecting to offer them worship (*puja*).

The arguments put forward in this chapter are predicated on a phenomenological interpretation of affliction. This approach has been adopted because supernatural malaise appears to be frequently linked with perceptions rooted in cultural typifications. The view that certain individuals are exceptionally predisposed to possession and to direct or indirect attack from sorcery seems to influence the extent to which the former invoke the latter to account for adversity, and this is reflected in the Mehndipur findings presented in this chapter. Similarly, the belief that anyone may be harmed by ancestor spirits is also reflected in actual cases of affliction ascribed to them, as I have shown.

To be sure, I have shown that a phenomenological approach is useful, not merely because it facilitates understanding of susceptibility to affliction, but also because it provides an alternative to the kinds of approach that confine themselves to the authority of discourses developed within the Western rationalist tradition. As indicated in this chapter, much anthropological discussion of susceptibility to supernatural malaise (or appeal to practices designed to alleviate it) is concerned with choice, which involve speculations about the inner psychological states of sufferers. It is grounded in a rationalism that manifests a psychologism to which phenomenology is opposed. Whereas the former denies the authority of those taken for granted beliefs or cosmological conceptions to which I have attended, the latter attempts to disclose its import; and it is phenomenology which enables the full force or value of that authority to be recognised.

Now, the phenomenological approach I have outlined in this chapter – an approach that shapes and orients the analysis provided in it, as throughout this book as a whole – is engaged in the next chapter to explore sorcery beliefs and practices in more detail, as well as to examine other forms of mystical agency, namely, witchcraft and the evil eye, which, though distinguishable from sorcery in certain respects, are conceptually linked to it. In the next chapter, further analysis of sorcery in particular is required for a number of reasons, an important one being to redirect debate as well as to address certain misunderstandings on the part of many scholars concerning the role played by healers or diagnosticians in the production of sorcery fears and accusations. The active role diagnosticians sometimes play in actually initiating sorcery fears and accusations in fact is an issue that has often been ignored but a critical one to which I now turn.

3

SORCERY, WITCHCRAFT AND THE EVIL EYE

Introduction

This chapter examines sorcery in more depth and also explores belief both in witchcraft, which, as we shall see, is distinguishable from sorcery and the evil eye. Sorcery, as demonstrated in the previous chapter, is a mystical force to which illness and misfortune are often attributed following rifts or ruptures in social relations. However, although specific conflicts and tensions may be said to precede direct or indirect sorcery attack, the forging of links between a particular conflict, sorcery attack and adversity is a process that requires further examination; for, while sorcery suspicions typically emerge in circumstances of perceived risk, in some cases diagnosticians may actually initiate them, as I shall show.

I will demonstrate in this chapter that prior to consultation with occult practitioners, sorcery suspicions are not always immediately present in the thoughts of those who seek guidance and help from them. During séances and consultations, then, it may not be assumed – *pace* Fuller (1992: 236), Gough (1958: 450) and Parry (1994: 237) – that Indian diviners merely concretise their clients' existing suspicions or, alternatively, simply allow them to acquire moral sanction and support for public denunciations that they wish to make. Undoubtedly, such situations are a common occurrence. But, in some instances, occult specialists are actively involved in producing the suspicions. A diagnostician may invoke sorcery to account for illness or misfortune, just as he may attribute this to evil spirits or to other supernaturals. When sorcery is identified as the cause of adversity, clients may be quite genuinely shocked or surprised, having assumed that some other malevolent being, such as an unknown, angry deity, has harmed them. The revelation may sometimes lead on to accusations, but it would be quite fallacious to suppose that these are always dependent upon actual prior sorcery suspicions. The very fact that a diviner invokes sorcery may be sufficient in itself to produce denunciations. Thus, I will argue that the diagnostician may play a central role as initiator of suspicions as well as accusations.

In this chapter, witchcraft accusations are also discussed. These, however, are extremely rare (cf. Babb 1975: 205–6; Lambert 1988: 191). Because one seldom hears of witchcraft, emphasis is placed on sorcery. Moreover, I examine the statements of a number of respondents in Mehndipur who claimed to be unaware of the identity of those who had allegedly harmed them by means of sorcery. Although informants sometimes insisted on the claim, it cannot be treated as unproblematic for reasons that will be given. But, in certain cases, it may have been genuine, and I contend that this is not implausible because it is widely believed that sorcery is frequently used to cause suffering, death and destruction. From a phenomenological perspective, given that sorcery is thought to be particularly prevalent, this may be a sufficient reason for suspecting it in situations of misfortune, even if those responsible for performing it cannot be identified. Indeed, because the practice of sorcery is considered to be widespread, I contend that this is an equally important reason why diagnosticians or occult specialists are able to plant the seeds of suspicion that may later lead to sorcery accusations, despite sorcery itself not being immediately present in the thoughts of clients prior to a consultation.

Besides sorcery and witchcraft beliefs, as well as belief in the evil eye, this chapter also analyses the key links between all these forms of mystical agency, though important differences between them, especially between sorcery and witchcraft, are examined as well. I adopt standard anthropological usage in employing the latter two terms, following Evans-Pritchard (1937). This terminology is used because in Mehndipur and throughout north India (as in parts of the Sudan and many other societies), the sorcerer is thought to cause harm by using magical techniques (cf. Fuller 1992: 237); the witch, by contrast, is believed to achieve this by means of innate forces (cf. Lambert 1988: 190). Thus, as Lambert points out, the sorcerer causes adversity 'only at particular times' whereas the witch is 'always ... dangerous' (ibid.).

Furthermore, while it is said that the second may often be unaware of the effect her malevolent powers have upon others, the first is always conscious of them. For, unlike the witch, the sorcerer must perform special rituals as well as utter spells and incantations (mantras) to injure his victims. The witch, on the other hand, succeeds in doing this by the mere fact of her existence, the very person she is being the source of her destructive potential. In rare instances, however, it is thought that a witch may equally use spells, as I shall illustrate. This may suggest that use of terms derived from Evans-Pritchard's writings on the Azande is not only inappropriate but also semantically problematic (cf. Crick 1976: 109 ff.).[1] Nonetheless, as Lambert argues, 'analytic distinction between witch ... and sorcerer ... seems justified since the two types of person and the kinds of influence they exert over others are indigenously distinguished. Not only are different terms used to describe them, but the person categories ... they occupy, (and) the powers they hold ... are clearly separated' (1988: 190–1).

The sorcerer, as indicated earlier, is commonly known as a *jadu-tona karne vala*, i.e. one who performs destructive magic. But *tantrik, mantrik, pir, auliya* and *sayana* are sometimes used as synonyms. This may seem peculiar, since these terms also denote Hindu and Muslim specialists who are frequently employed for curing purposes or for counteracting mystical harm. However, it is understandable why these nouns may have negative as well as positive connotations: occult practitioners are widely thought to be ambiguous figures, as I will also show. For one who is able to remove supernatural harm is, by the same token, believed to be capable of inflicting it; and one who has the power to bless equally is said to possesses the ability to curse. The term used by many of my informants to distinguish the witch from the sorcerer – a term that is well known in Rajasthan particularly – is *dakan*, though, unlike the sorcerer, she is not considered to be ambiguous. It is said that she cannot choose to give blessings or to use her powers for beneficial purposes. Because her nature is inherently evil, the *dakan* is always malevolent. Moreover, the widely held belief that she typically injures people by gazing at them (her malevolence often emanating unconsciously from the eyes), means that conceptions about the witch are closely related to conceptions about the evil eye (*nazar*). Indeed, I will demonstrate that these and other parallels show that witchcraft and the evil eye are not merely understood to be connected but are part of the same complex of beliefs. Sorcery is linked to these less closely. But, since all three forms of mystical harm can only be directed by human agents (and because these particular forms of supernatural attack are also often viewed as being motivated by envy or jealousy), it is contended that they are fundamentally interrelated.

Sorcery suspicions and accusations

The belief that a supernatural agent is likely to be responsible for causing a person to become sick is almost invariably the reason why an ailing individual goes to visit a traditional healer or diagnostician. Thus, supernatural malaise is usually suspected by the sick person before he or she seeks help from a healer. However, the actual identity of the malevolent agent may be completely uncertain prior to consultation with an occult specialist, as is shown, for instance, by Asha's possession presented in chapter 2. What is also particularly striking is that when a diagnostician is consulted, the client may initially venture a firm opinion as to the presumed cause of his or her ailments, only later to have this completely overturned by the healer.

Now, the observation that a client may not be sure which malevolent being has afflicted him or her before consulting a healer, as well as the finding that the latter may ignore or dismiss the former's opinion or tentative hypothesis regarding the supposed identity of the agent responsible, made me aware that diagnosticians often play an extremely influential role in shaping or moulding their clients' aetiological conceptions. Indeed, the way in which a client may behave in response to the diviner's oracle may have important repercussions and may even be socially disruptive or damaging – a state of affairs for which diagnosticians, in some measure, are clearly accountable; and this is perhaps nowhere more telling than in sorcery cases. For, as the case cited below illustrates, these practitioners not only initiate sorcery suspicions on some occasions but accusations as well.

Mr Gupta, a wealthy factory owner from Ashok Vihar in Delhi, first went to Mehndipur in September 1990. When I met him two years later, he informed me that he made periodic journeys to the village with his wife, staying at the pilgrimage centre every one or two months for approximately four or five days on each occasion. His wife was receiving special treatment from a healer (*bhagat*). This, he stated, is why the frequent journeys were necessary. She was suffering from body pains (*sharir dard*), severe headaches (*sir dard*) and, occasionally, from pyrexia (*bukhar*). Her husband commented, however, that her health had greatly improved and believed that she would soon fully recover. According to Mr Gupta, the woman had become sick because of sorcery (*jadu-tona*). His own elder brother (*bara bhai*) was the one responsible for causing the affliction. When asked how he discovered she had been harmed by sorcery, I was informed that the *bhagat* had told him this. Mr Gupta then explained the matter in more detail.

He pointed out that the reason he first came to Mehndipur was not to escort his wife but rather to bring his 13-year-old son. For over three years the boy had been suffering periodically from fever (*bukhar*), a condition, it was stressed, that was often life-threatening. His son had been examined by many doctors and had tried numerous medicines. He had even been treated by leading experts or specialists at the famous All India Institute for Medical Sciences (AIIMS) in Delhi. But still the problem had not been solved. Mr Gupta's brother-in-law (*sala*) and a friend advised him to take the boy to Mehndipur. Initially, however, he said that he was not inclined to do this. He emphasised that this was not because he lacked faith in the healing power of Balaji as such, but because he had no belief in popular 'superstitions'.[2] Being a university graduate, he refused to accept that spirits could enter a person's body or that someone could be mystically harmed by *tantrik*s and other occult practitioners. He claimed that only the illiterate and ignorant village folk held such beliefs. Nonetheless, he decided that the boy's welfare must take precedence over his own pride; for it was possible that his son might benefit from a visit to the temple of Balaji.

On the day that Mr and Mrs Gupta took their son to Mehndipur, the former said that the latter's fever symptoms were particularly pronounced. But, despite having made offerings (Darkhast and Arji) at the main healing shrine, there was no change in the boy's condition. Acting on the advice of fellow pilgrims, the following day they consulted a *bhagat*. The curer examined the patient and informed Mr and Mrs Gupta that he was suffering because of sorcery. The *bhagat* also asked if anyone else in the family was sick. Now, for many years Mrs Gupta had been afflicted by the ailments already mentioned. However, I was told that she had never considered them to be particularly extraordinary. That is to say, although they were extremely troublesome and often debilitating too, she had never imagined them to be caused by supernatural forces. But because the *bhagat*'s line of questioning was persistent and emphatic, she decided to tell him about the illness. As soon as the details had been disclosed, the healer was said to attribute this to sorcery as well. According to the *bhagat*, the person who had harmed the boy had also attacked the mother. Yet this was not a recent happening. The healer claimed that the person responsible for afflicting them had performed the wicked deed many years earlier.

To end the *sankat*, the *bhagat* stressed that it was first necessary to transfer the boy's illness to the mother. In this way it would be easier to control. This was carried out in the *bhagat's darbar* later that day. A few hours after the ritual was completed, Mr Gupta said that his son began to improve, and by evening the fever had fully abated. But, although his son had recovered, the mother of the boy started to experience severe head pains. Her body temperature had increased as well. Bewildered by what was happening, Mr Gupta stated that he hurried to the *dharmshala* where the *bhagat* was residing. The healer, however, told him not to worry, since this was to be expected. The healer also instructed him to bring the woman to the next *darbar*, which was to be held the following morning. This is precisely what Mr Gupta did, and he maintained that his wife's health dramatically improved during the séance. Nevertheless, as indicated above, even two years after the event, it was still necessary for his wife to make periodic journeys to Mehndipur.

Now, because the boy miraculously recovered from fever – an ailment that had not returned since he was treated by the curer – Mr Gupta said that he put his faith in the *bhagat*. He came to accept the very beliefs that he had earlier repudiated and ridiculed. Despite once rejecting the idea that a person could be mystically afflicted by occult adepts, the explanation provided by the healer was adopted by Mr Gupta. As far as he was concerned, his son had become sick and his wife continued to suffer because *jadu-tona* had been employed. But why had sorcery been used? Furthermore, who could have done this? Mr Gupta stated that for a considerable length of time he found it impossible to answer these questions. He was unable to think of anyone who might be responsible for this or what the motive could have been. But he added that the key to the mystery had been provided by the *bhagat*, who, it will be recalled, said that many years had passed since the attack was made. Thus, remembering a major dispute that had occurred between Mr Gupta and his elder brother eleven years earlier, the former commented that he finally realised that it could only have been the latter who had caused his wife and son to become ill. He alleged that sorcery had been practised because of a quarrel about inheritance. After the death of their father, Mr Gupta's brother took full control of the family business and refused to share ownership of it with the junior sibling. The argument that arose because of this was eventually resolved; for Mr Gupta stated that he decided to withdraw claim to a portion of it. Yet, since a dispute had taken place, Mr Gupta maintained that this must have been the reason his brother resorted to sorcery, even though it was the elder brother who actually benefited from the clash.

This case study shows that Mr Gupta views the suffering of his wife and son, the quarrel with his brother, and the latter's sorcerous attack as being inseparably connected. But it is equally apparent that these links are only made because sorcery is invoked by the diagnostician. The *bhagat's* role in the whole interaction process, then, is far from being passive. Indeed, it is precisely because he ascribes the ailments of the woman and the boy to this mystical force that a sorcery allegation later emerges. If the healer had not been consulted, it seems doubtful that an accusation would have been made, or that Mr Gupta would have connected his wife and son's ill-health to a past dispute with his elder sibling. Before visiting the healer, Mr Gupta clearly has no prior suspicions of sorcery. In fact, to be more exact, before journeying to Mehndipur where he meets the *bhagat*, the notion of supernatural affliction does not even enter his thoughts except for purposes of ridicule. Similarly, his wife previously has no suspicions of sorcery regarding her own illness; and it is only in response to the healer's questions that a supernatural cause is contemplated by the woman. The idea that the malaise is related to her son's sickness is never considered prior to meeting the healer either. It is difficult not to conclude, therefore, that the *bhagat* is actually responsible for initiating the sorcery accusation. In addition, this case equally shows that to accuse a person of causing harm by magical or mystical means is not always an expression of current social tensions or conflicts, as some scholars have assumed.[3]

The invocation of sorcery in cases such as Mr Gupta's is not particularly exceptional or extraordinary. Indeed, the seemingly arbitrary link that a diagnostician may make between illness and sorcery is apparent from the dialogue below between Ramjilal, a senior shrine functionary in Mehndipur, and the father of a sick young woman, a dialogue which was recorded during the early stages of my fieldwork.[4]

PATIENT'S FATHER: Oh Maharaj,[5] please look at my daughter, and tell me what this affliction (*sankat*) is.

RAMJILAL: What is the nature of the sickness (*bimari*)? What illness does she have?

PATIENT'S FATHER: She suffers from fever (*bukhar*), headache (*sir dard*) and insomnia (*anidra*). She wanders away from the home and during her menses (*rajodharam*) becomes extremely unwell.

RAMJILAL: (after pausing briefly) Your daughter is possessed by a Masan, the spirit of the graveyard. This is because of sorcery (*cauki*). Someone has put something into her food. Does she have any other symptoms (*lakshan*)?

PATIENT'S FATHER: Yes. Although her periods are heavy (*bhari*), sometimes they are irregular (*aniyamit*). And when she urinates, she experiences a burning sensation (*jalan*). She also stays in the toilet for excessive lengths of time.

RAMJILAL: These things show what I have said is true (*sac*). It is confirmation (*pramanikaran*). All these troubles are caused by an Aghor Masan, a spirit that is controlled by a *tantrik*. I will give you a mantra.

During the discourse between Ramjilal and the patient's father, the priest states clearly and unequivocally that the young woman's malaise is caused by sorcery (*cauki*). He claims that she is possessed by a Masan (a spirit that is often said to be sent by a sorcerer to attack his victims) because someone has put ensorcelled substance into her food. But, as I subsequently discovered, this was the first occasion that Ramjilal had seen the patient. Thus, it was not possible for him to know if any specific conflict or schism had preceded the illness, or whether the patient or her father suspected anyone of wanting to harm the young woman. It is evident from the dialogue itself that there is no mention of quarrels or disputes, and the priest does not ask a single question about the patient's relations with other family members or with neighbours. No attempt is made to elicit information regarding sorcery suspicions and none is volunteered. Even though they may be absent, then, it would appear that a diagnostician may still ascribe illness to sorcery. This, as I have shown, may eventually lead to allegations being made. It would be erroneous, however, to assume that they are always dependent upon prior suspicions, since, in certain contexts, the diagnostician or diviner evidently plays an important role in generating them.

Having demonstrated that diagnosticians may initiate sorcery suspicions and accusations, it is important to emphasise that some of my respondents in Mehndipur were unwilling to level accusations against specific individuals, even though they were convinced that they had been harmed by sorcery. Of the 365 persons who attributed their ailments to sorcery, 94 of them (26 per cent) stated that they were unaware of those who had afflicted them (see Table 3 in Appendix 6). Not knowing the identity of those who had harmed them was the reason why many interviewees said that they were unable to denounce their attackers. But, as indicated earlier, this claim cannot be treated as being unproblematic. In some cases, pilgrims may have deliberately concealed such information to avoid discussing the matter with a foreign researcher. Some pilgrims may equally have not disclosed it because they were unwilling to voice their suspicions, or because they had no particular wish to indict certain individuals publicly. In addition, since the only accounts that I had access to in Mehndipur were self-reported, this was a limitation that prevented me from discovering whether such an assertion had any real validity at all. Nonetheless, in certain cases, those invoking sorcery who insisted that they did not know the identity of their attackers may have been genuine in making this claim. One reason for supposing this stems from the observation that in Mehndipur, as in other places of pilgrimage, an individual can very often engage freely and openly with others about sensitive matters, such as sorcery. This, of course, would almost be inconceivable in the home village or town where face-to-face relations have a powerful constraining hold upon social action and behaviour, as Favret-Saada (1980) has shown in respect of witchcraft suspicions in rural France. Since pilgrims are able to speak relatively freely about their fears and suspicions and, in fact, often choose to do so – not least because discussing them is a way of reducing what may be a tremendous burden – it is likely that a number of those claiming to be unaware of those responsible for harming them by means of sorcery provided an honest or faithful testimony. Two cases where ignorance of an attacker's identity is alleged are given below.

(1) A young, unmarried businessman from the city of Kanpur in Uttar Pradesh came to Mehndipur because for six years he had been sick. He informed me that he suffered from constant headaches (*sir dard*), pain in the lower limbs (*tang me dard*) and dizziness (*cakkar*). These ailments were partially relieved by medicine prescribed by an allopathic practitioner. But, because he had not been fully cured, he said that he decided to visit the famous temple of Balaji.

When the interview with the 26-year-old Brahman was conducted, the respondent had only been in Mehndipur for two or three days. It was the first time that he had been to the village, though he had known about the healing shrines for many years. The informant stated that he had not seen any of the priests or healers at the pilgrimage centre regarding his illness; neither had he previously visited an occult practitioner in the city where he was residing. Nonetheless, despite the fact that a diviner or diagnostician had not been consulted, the respondent believed that he had been harmed by sorcery (*jadu-tona*). When questioned about who had attacked him, however, he appeared to be completely puzzled. He said that he was unable to name the person who had done this. The informant suggested that sorcery was probably used against him by a rival businessman, but there was no one in particular whom he suspected. He maintained that he generally had an amiable relationship with other competitors in the area of the city where his shop was located. To accuse one of them, then, would be unjustified and unwarranted. But, if the Brahman businessman did not suspect one of these individuals specifically, why was sorcery invoked? In response to this question, the informant stressed that competitors often used this mystical force in order to attack one another. Perhaps someone was envious of his success and wanted to harm him. He claimed that this was the most likely reason why he had become sick, even though he had no notion of who had caused the affliction.

(2) A 22-year-old man from Mohari, a large village in the district of Aligarh, Uttar Pradesh, was brought by his father to Mehndipur because he was suffering from amnesia (*smriti lop*). The patient was frequently troubled with stomach pain (*pet dard*) too. According to his father, although a traditional diagnostician had not been consulted, the young Rajput had previously received treatment in a mental hospital in Agra and in Mathura. Yet, despite having spent a considerable sum of money on this, I was told that there had been no marked improvement in his condition.

My informant said that the illness itself began suddenly approximately six months earlier. The patient, however, had since been unable to complete his education, and for most of the time it was necessary for him to remain in the home. His father maintained that he was ill because he had been afflicted by *jadu-tona*. It was alleged that this had been practised by one of the students at the institution where his son had been studying. The motive for this was jealousy (*jalan*). Formerly, his son had had an excellent memory and was one of the most intelligent individuals in the entire school. This, according to his father, was undoubtedly why he was harmed and why it was the young man's mind that became the specific object of attack. Yet, while the father believed that his son had been afflicted by sorcery, and that it must have been a jealous student who was responsible for this, he denied that he possessed any knowledge of the attacker's identity. He did not know which particular student had performed the wicked action. He said that it was, perhaps, carried out by someone who had been in his son's class. But even of that he could not be sure; for the young man's academic ability was known to most students throughout the school. It was possible, then, that he was not only attacked by someone from another group but by someone who was younger or at a junior stage of development. But, although the informant stated that he did not know who the attacker was and that the whole matter was a source of bewilderment, his conviction that sorcery had been used remained firm.

Whether either or both of the above informants actually suspected particular persons of practising sorcery – information that they may have been unwilling to communicate to me – I was unable to discover or discern. However, they may have been genuinely unaware of the identity of the possible perpetrators, as each of them had insisted. And, as noted earlier, this is not implausible precisely because sorcery is generally held to be prevalent and widely used: this in itself may be a sufficient reason for suspecting it – a point that Favret-Saada, whose study of witchcraft in the Bocage already mentioned, has also stressed regarding the attribution of misfortune to the supernatural by French peasants (1980: 6 ff.). From this point of view, then, it is understandable why sorcery may still be seen as the cause of adversity, even if those who may have performed it cannot be identified. While certain categories of individuals tend to be viewed as being directly or indirectly at risk from sorcery, as I demonstrated in chapter 2, there may also be occasions when anyone may suspect it after being stricken by illness or misfortune. Thus, if a person suspects sorcery and simultaneously claims to be unaware of the individual who may have harmed him, this may not be seen as involving some kind of inconsistency. In terms of the cultural logic, there is no inherent contradiction between invoking this mystical force to explain suffering and claiming not to know who the perpetrator is. Moreover, precisely because the practice of sorcery is itself held to be widespread or prevalent, it is not surprising that diagnosticians or healers may actually initiate sorcery fears or suspicions in certain cases, as I have also indicated – suspicions which had not developed in the minds of clients prior to a consultation but which nonetheless become pronounced as a result of the consultation process. Indeed, given the alleged frequency of sorcery practice, it is equally understandable and not at all surprising to find that diagnosticians may generate sorcery suspicions with apparent or relative ease. The diagnostician's ability to do this, therefore, appears, once again, to be a function of a key common sense assumption, the widely held belief in the prevalence of sorcery practice; and it seems likely that this, too, is central whenever an individual claims to be a victim of sorcery as well as to be unaware of the perpetrator's identity.

The sorcerer

Turning now to the human agents who are thought to possess special powers to injure or harm others, I focus first of all upon the sorcerer.

As indicated in the introduction to this chapter, this occult practitioner is said to attack his victims by means of destructive magic. In Mehndipur, *jadu-tona* is the term my informants commonly used to denote it. According to many of the respondents, including both healers and their patients as well as other individuals who were not suffering from any kind of affliction, magical or supernatural power (*siddhi*) can generally be acquired by anyone; but, to obtain it, it is necessary for the aspirant to perform *sadhana* (ritual practices or methods). It is said that this usually involves lengthy recitals of mantras, a practice that is almost invariably accompanied by austerities, such as depriving oneself of food or sleep. One particular form of *sadhana* that sorcerers are widely held to undertake involves capturing and learning to control a departed spirit, a *bhut* or a *pret*.[6] It must not be assumed, however, that the individual who successfully completes this will always use his power for malevolent purposes. For it is thought that some occult practitioners with a reputation for curing and for counteracting mystical harm rather than inflicting it may equally acquire, as well as gain control of, spirits by performing this *sadhana*. It is said that these practitioners, of course, would employ a ghost as an aid or as a helper in a manner resembling a *bhagat*'s use of a *dut* (a helpful messenger spirit), which I demonstrate in chapter 5.

Regarding the *sadhana* itself, this must be undertaken in a graveyard (*masan*) during the hours of darkness. According to one healer who claimed to have done this – a healer who sometimes journeyed to Mehndipur from Ajmer (but who did not operate as a practitioner at the pilgrimage centre) – the ritual is ideally performed from twelve midnight until two o'clock in the morning, the period when ghosts are particularly active. This curer commented that an individual who wishes to capture and master a spirit must first exhume a corpse (*lash*), preferably one that has recently been buried. This is because the spirit remains close to the site of the body for at least three days following death. Since it hovers in the vicinity of the grave, it can easily be seized when the appropriate mantras are used. Although any corpse can be exhumed for purposes of the *sadhana*, the healer stated that sorcerers usually prefer to take the corpse of a baby or a miscarried foetus (cf. Lambert 1988: 178–9).[7] I was told that the main reason for this is because the spirit of an infant, known throughout the Rajasthani region as a *kacca-kalava* (ibid.: 173), has no knowledge or understanding of righteousness or unrighteousness. Because a sense of what is right and wrong has not been inculcated, the Ajmeri curer informed me that the sorcerer can easily train it to perform acts of wickedness. Whereas the spirit of a deceased man or woman might object to carrying out a particular command, I was told that the *kacca-kalava* would have no qualms or misgivings about it. Thus, for the latter, to terminate the life of someone would be essentially no different to performing a mundane task, such as finding an item of lost property. That is to say, it would simply have no feelings of guilt or remorse about doing this.

Now, when the sorcerer has removed the body of the infant from the grave, he may call upon and later seize its spirit with the aid of mantras alone. But, on some occasions, an additional ceremony may also be required. The details of this, which were given to me by the above mentioned Ajmeri healer, are as follows. To conduct the ritual, the sorcerer first obtains thirteen litres of milk and a number of other food items, namely, wheat flour, sugar and ghee. The milk is used to bathe the body. When this has been completed, the milk is heated and left to cool. Afterwards, the informant said that this automatically becomes sour (*dudh phat hota hai*) due to being contaminated or polluted by the corpse. The sorcerer then adds the other food items to it and prepares two balls from the mixture. These balls (which remind one of the *pinda* offerings used to unite a *pret* with its ancestor spirits in the traditional Sanskritic *shraddha* ceremony)[8] are placed at the head and feet of the corpse. Following this, the sorcerer uses a mantra, and the ghost of the infant returns to the body. While it is in this reanimated state, the sorcerer utters another mantra to bring the spirit fully under his control. Finally, after accomplishing this, the ghost is removed from the body and the corpse abandoned or discarded.

However, I was told that to gain control of the spirit in the way that has just been described may take a considerable length of time. For, while it is possible for some sorcerers to achieve this by only performing the ritual once, others need to repeat it. Nevertheless, it is widely believed that as soon as a sorcerer has captured and trained one ghost by means of *sadhana*, he can easily acquire others. It is frequently said that he can send the familiar spirit to the places where *bhut*s and *pret*s congregate in order to recruit them into his service. A sorcerer, then, may command a countless number of spirits. These may not only be used for injuring or harming someone: they may be employed for many other purposes too, such as finding the hidden location of buried treasure, for gaining prestige as a seer or as a fortune-teller, and for acquiring other types of esoteric knowledge. Moreover, even when spirits are used to attack people, it is said that the sorcerer can target individuals who are particularly affluent. In this way, he can also become extremely wealthy. Thus, it is thought that sorcerers sometimes afflict rich people simply to extort money from them. When a person is possessed by a spirit, he or she frequently has no alternative but to consult an occult practitioner. Yet I was often told that it may not be known to the former that the latter has specifically engineered the attack. By doing this, the sorcerer is believed to acquire large sums of money, which he is able to demand from wealthy clients.

But the sorcerer is thought to harm his victims not only by using his familiar or some other spirit. He is held to achieve this by other means as well. Generally, while all the types of sorcery that he performs are known as *jadu-tona*, in Mehndipur *muth* is a word that tends to be used in cases where it causes sudden or instant death. *Cauki* is also used interchangeably with the term *jadu-tona*, though it is often viewed as being a particularly powerful form of destructive magic. Indeed, it is sometimes claimed that, although anyone can practise mild forms of sorcery (*halki jadu-tona*), only a person who has acquired special powers (a *siddha*) is able to afflict his victims with *cauki*. It is said that mild or weak forms of destructive magic are performed simply by using mantras, which are easily obtained from cheap paperback books and pamphlets available in town bazaars as well as in the market places of many villages. Sorcerers may also use these particular mantras, though it is believed that most of the spells they cast are secret. Nevertheless, when the occult adept, as opposed to the lay-person or non-specialist, uses widely known, harmful mantras, they are considered to have a far greater damaging effect. For magical words are always charged with power when they are spoken or written by him.

This may be illustrated briefly with reference to an interview with the healer from Ajmer referred to earlier. During the interview that took place with this particular curer – a Brahman by caste from the village of Pushkar close to the city of Ajmer – the occult specialist emphasised the magical potency of mantras. While discussing the topic, I asked if he could copy the words of a destructive mantra on to a blank piece of paper, explaining that this would be extremely helpful to my research. The request was made specifically because the healer showed me a few examples of this type of spell in a book that he owned. However, he flatly refused to do this. The curer stated that he would not object if I were to copy a harmful mantra from his book. This was perfectly acceptable to him. The reason he refused to do it, he claimed, was because the mantra or spell would have a negative effect upon me and upon others who came into contact with it.

If an occult practitioner uses a harmful mantra, then, whether it is spoken or printed, it becomes extremely potent. When the sorcerer utters this, the spell is thought to travel through the air in order to reach its target. It is widely viewed as being a kind of invisible arrow that moves at an incalculably high speed, and that nothing (except for an additional spell to counter this) can prevent it from striking its victim. It can travel any distance and hit any object against which it is directed. In some instances, however, particularly if the purpose of the mantra is to kill someone, informants in Mehndipur stated that a sorcerer may take certain precautions to ensure that it does not strike the wrong person. It is held that this may occur on some occasions for a number of reasons. It might happen, for example, because the intended victim is out of the home when the spell is cast. In this case another member of the family could be inadvertently harmed. Someone could also be indirectly injured or killed because he or she has the same forename as a particular relation whom the sorcerer is instructed to attack. To attempt to prevent this kind of mistake being made, it is said that the sorcerer might ask his client to supply important information. He might not only want to know when the client's enemy is likely to be present in or absent from the home; he might also insist on being given the enemy's full name and title, as well as any abbreviated or 'pet' names by which he or she is known.

A mantra that is written rather than uttered and sent through the air is also thought to maim or kill the wrong person occasionally. This method, therefore, is equally subject to error. Ordinarily, the procedure for attacking an enemy, however, is uncomplicated. According to a number of my informants in Mehndipur, after the sorcerer has printed the mantra, his client takes the paper on which it is written and puts it into food or drink. The paper is later removed and the ensorcelled substance offered to the victim. Alternatively, it is claimed that food is sometimes taken to the sorcerer so that he can literally blow the spell on to it. Certain objects may equally be treated in this way and then added to food afterwards. It is said that the objects typically used for the purpose include bones (*haddiya*) taken from the cremation ground (*masan*), the flesh of an owl or crow (*ullu ya kauva ka mas*), the victim's hair (*bal*) and nail (*nakhun*) pairings, iron (*loha*), black mustard seeds (*rai*), salt (*namak*) and lemon (*nimbu*). And it is generally believed that a person is only inadvertently harmed when this type of sorcery is practised because he or she mistakenly consumes the ensorcelled food.

But an object that has a spell placed on it may not always be prepared for consumption. It is widely held that the sorcerer sometimes buries it in the soil close to the victim's house or puts it under the foundations of the dwelling. But, on some occasions, he may actually bury it at the place where the dead are cremated. Whenever this is undertaken, an effigy of the victim may also be made. Some of my informants stated that this is usually fashioned from a piece of cloth (*kapra*) or a garment belonging to the person who is to be harmed or slain. It is said that mantras are also uttered over and blown onto it by the sorcerer before it is put into the earth. But, in some instances, a piece of paper bearing a mantra and the victim's name may be buried with the effigy.

Another magical technique that the sorcerer is thought to employ involves sending objects through the air. It is claimed that these remain unseen but implant themselves in the victim's body, causing pain, sickness or even death (cf. Lambert: 1988: 202). My informants commented that *mung dal* and *urad*, a green and a black pulse, are typically used for this purpose. Once again, however, the sorcerer essentially performs the destructive work by means of mantras, since he is believed to employ magical words both to ensorcel the grains of pulse and to propel them through the air.

Other types of *materia medica* that the sorcerer is commonly said to use are roots and herbs (*jari-buti*). There are many different varieties of these, and their harmful effects are also thought to vary. A number of my informants claimed that these are sometimes administered by the sorcerer to kill a person as well as to cause minor physical problems, such as a stomach or a head pain.[9] The sorcerer is considered to use roots and herbs for other purposes too. It is said, for example, that they may be given in order to hypnotise a person or to make someone become quarrelsome or feel constantly irritable and melancholic, though sometimes they may be administered to make a person become mad or insane. The sorcerer's knowledge of these medicines is believed to be secret. It is held to be acquired from a guru, a preceptor who bestows it upon his disciple together with knowledge of spells and other types of destructive magic. But, as with all the other objects that the sorcerer uses to strike his victims, *jari-buti* are generally considered to be effective because mantras are placed on them. While it is sometimes stated that certain roots and herbs are able to kill a person, for instance, without a spell being uttered, most are said to be practically worthless without it. Moreover, even when it is possible for a sorcerer to give someone the *materia medica* that has not been cursed, it is held to become far more potent and effective when it has.

According to my respondents in Mehndipur, the length of time that a person suffers as a result of being harmed by a sorcerer usually depends upon the type of sorcery used. My informants stated that clients sometimes instruct an occult adept to afflict an enemy only for a specific number of days or months or, in some cases, for a certain number of years. The occult specialist may be requested to do this for many reasons. I was told that some clients, for example, may simply want to punish someone for a misdemeanour or may wish to retaliate against an individual for being offended or insulted by him or her. Indeed, in some instances, this is perhaps the only way that they are able to gain retribution for these minor offences (as in situations where larger ones are committed). In all these cases, however, it is thought that essentially mild forms of sorcery are employed. For it is said that the victim not only recovers at some predetermined point in time but that the ailments and diseases he or she is afflicted with are also usually minor.

If a more destructive kind of magic is employed, by contrast, it is held that the victim frequently suffers from a painful disease and eventually dies as a result of it. The length of time that he or she is sick may or may not be protracted. When *cauki* rather than *muth* is used, it is often said that the victim does not die instantly. He or she may be ill for many years, though the affliction sometimes lasts for only a few months. Typically, the disease that seizes the victim becomes progressively worse. The individual who is targeted by the sorcerer gets sicker and experiences more and more pain as each day passes. This is thought to continue until the destructive magic finally terminates the life of the victim. Where a person is struck by *muth*, on the other hand, he or she may die within one or two days; but, in most cases, it is said that this occurs within a matter of hours. In general terms, it is believed that one can detect that *muth* has been practised from the manner in which a person suddenly expires, since the victim usually has a violent heart attack and/or chokes on blood that is held to gush uncontrollably from his or her mouth.

When one is afflicted by sorcery, however, one can always turn to, or seek help from, healers – from curers found, not only in particular pilgrimage centres like Mehndipur, but in towns and villages throughout the length and breadth of India. If a curer has the power to counteract a curse, it is thought that the one who is afflicted will recover, irrespective of the type of destructive magic that has been employed. But it must be emphasised that healers themselves are ambiguous figures. As indicated earlier, this is because anyone who is able to remove a spell is thought to be equally capable of casting it. Moreover, since some occult practitioners cure the sick with the help of a familiar spirit, they are automatically held in suspicion. For it is this very spirit that the sorcerer is often said to employ to harm someone. Some healers in Rajasthan also treat their patients with roots and herbs (*jari-buti*), the very medicines which sorcerers sometimes use to strike their victims. Healers are ambiguous for a number of other reasons as well. An exorcist, for instance, may be said to afflict one person deliberately in order to cure another. Pilgrims in Mehndipur frequently mentioned this. A typical case is that of a man who was known at the pilgrimage centre as Ravan, so named because of the ferocity he displayed during trance (*peshi*). This patient informed me that he became ill shortly after the wife of a former friend was cured by a *tantrik*, an occult adept who operated in the town where the patient himself was actually domiciled. Apparently, the occult practitioner transferred the woman's *sankat* to Ravan. I was told that the malevolent spirit that was removed from her body thus entered his, causing the affliction from which he had been suffering for over five years. While an exorcist is able to heal the sick, then, he is often considered to do this at the expense of others. Because of this, he may be feared and abhorred as much as he is, perhaps, praised or shown respect. An occult adept may purposely injure or harm a person for other reasons too. Thus, a Muslim Baba who sometimes visited Mehndipur informed me that he often used his supernatural power to afflict people.[10] Although this occult specialist claimed not to practise in Mehndipur itself, he stated that many individuals came to his home in Ajmer city, asking him to do this. According to the Baba, however, those whom he attacked always deserved the affliction meted out. He illustrated this with an example. He pointed out that a poor man might be coerced into working many hours a day for only a few rupees. The tyrannical employer might also refuse to allow him to take time off work, even during periods of sickness or when a needy friend required his help. Should such an oppressed individual come to him seeking retribution, the Baba stressed that he would willingly inflict injury upon the uncharitable, despotic employer.

From the point of view of the exploited worker, the occult specialist may appear to be acting justly. But it is unlikely that the employer would interpret the Baba's behaviour in this way. On the contrary, he would typically see the Baba as practising destructive rather than beneficial magic. Similarly, although the woman cured by the *tantrik* may view the practitioner as being a great healer, from Ravan's perspective, he is a malevolent or evil sorcerer. Whether an individual who possesses supernatural power is considered in positive or in negative terms, therefore, frequently depends upon whether one is blessed or cursed by him. More importantly, perhaps, a practitioner may be seen by one person at a certain point in time as performing helpful magic and, at a later stage, as practising sorcery. This is because it is held that the occult adept, for instance, may cure someone from a particular ailment but afflict the same person with a different one a day or so afterwards. A number of pilgrims in Mehndipur claimed that he usually does this to increase his income, the afflicted individual having to pay once again for treatment necessitated by it. Nonetheless, whatever the motive happens to be, it is clear to my informants that an occult practitioner is essentially ambiguous; and this is perhaps inevitable, since one who is capable of controlling supernatural harm is likely to attract suspicion when a person is suddenly smitten by illness or disease.

The witch

Unlike the sorcerer, the witch is never ambiguous. As mentioned in the introduction to this chapter, this is because she is never thought to use her mystical powers for beneficial purposes. According to Mehndipur pilgrims, these powers are only ever employed to injure or harm others. Indeed, in Mehndipur, as in the wider Rajasthani region, it is believed that the *dakan* always causes adversity because her nature is inherently malevolent. It is said that she becomes a witch from the moment of birth. While some of my informants claimed that she is full of vice due to having an inauspicious *nakshatra*,[11] i.e. by being born at an inauspicious (*ashubh*) time, others stated that she becomes a witch as a result of consuming impure (*ganda*) substances during childhood (cf. Lambert 1988: 197), particularly faeces and urine. In addition, it is sometimes said that she may be further corrupted or made wicked because her body is never washed and/or because she enjoys wearing dirty clothes and sits in filthy places. Some informants commented that she may become possessed by an evil spirit during childhood as well; and the malevolent ghost that is considered to enter her body is also known as a *dakan*.[12] But, whether she becomes a witch for any, or for all, of these reasons, her blood is held to become contaminated. Thus, it is believed that the witch has dirty blood (*khun ganda*). It is by virtue of this that she is seen to be inherently wicked, a quality that causes her to harm people, irrespective of whether it is done consciously or unconsciously. Like the Zande witch described by Evans-Pritchard, therefore, the *dakan* creates adversity because of a particular substance in her body, i.e. polluted or impure blood.

Concerning other aspects of the organic nature of witchcraft, it is sometimes claimed that a witch can be identified by means of certain physical signs and characteristics. I was told that she may have long or abnormal teeth as well as large lips. It is said that saliva may also exude uncontrollably from the corners of her mouth, and, in some cases, that there is a long straight line down the centre of the witch's tongue, which stretches from the back to the front of it. Most important of all, perhaps, she is held to have peering eyes, which may sometimes be red in appearance. Indeed, some witches are thought never to blink or to close their eyes.

With respect to behavioural patterns and characteristics, the *dakan* is stereotypically aggressive and bad tempered. She is viewed as being quick to harbour a grudge and is said to be easily angered. The witch is also a mean, greedy, envious or jealous individual who hates to see anyone prosper or enjoy good fortune (cf. Babb 1975: 206; Carstairs 1983: 15 and *passim*; Crooke 1907: 262; Epstein 1967: 154; Fuller 1992: 238; Lambert 1988: 191). Thus, in Mehndipur – and throughout the surrounding region – notions of the witch's demeanour are evidently similar to those found in many other societies, including, it might be added, medieval England and Europe.[13] For it is these anti-social tendencies and traits by means of which this mystical evil-doer is universally identified. Indeed, north Indian folk beliefs about the witch's ability to transform her human appearance into that of an animal, as well as the belief that she is often a member of an unholy fraternity, are equally widespread cross-culturally. Regarding the latter some of my informants commented that witches meet from time-to-time on the cremation ground, where they dance naked together and where they may also hatch a plot to injure a particular individual or group of individuals. Moreover, I was told that the ritual to reanimate a deceased infant, which sorcerers are held to perform, is carried out by witches from time to time too. But, in contrast to sorcerers, witches are not said to revive it for purposes of harming others but rather to play with and/or to nurse the child. All these events are thought to take place during the hours of darkness, during the period when ghosts and other fiendish creatures are active.

So far the male counterpart of the witch has not been mentioned. The main reason for this is that the wizard is rarely heard of in Mehndipur (or anywhere else in north India). Yet, while this is the case, some informants claim that wizards do exist and that, in certain situations, they may afflict people as well. The standard indigenous term that translates the English word for wizard is *daki*. It is believed that the wizard, like the witch, may be young or old, rich or poor. Sometimes the *dakan* and the *daki* are said to live together as husband and wife. When they do so they may work in tandem and jointly select their victims. The witch, however, is viewed as being far more venomous than the wizard. Whether they operate as a team or independently of each other, the former is always more malevolent. Many informants told me that the witch is quick to strike her victims and attacks people indiscriminately; whereas the wizard does this usually when his anger is aroused. Thus, it is said that '(T)he witch tyrannises everyone' (*Dakan sabhi logo ko satati hai*); but '(T)he wizard oppresses people when they provoke him' (*Jab daki ko log bharkate hai, tab vah un logo ko satata hai*). Witchcraft, then, as Babb points out, is essentially a feminine phenomenon: what is '(m)ost striking is the distinctly feminine overtone that seems to pervade witchcraft lore' (Babb 1975: 203).

Now, the witch may injure or harm people in a number of different ways. In Mehndipur informants claimed that the main weapon she uses to attack her victims is *nazar*, the malign gaze. It is thought that the witch may cause someone to become sick and/or die merely by glancing at the individual. Similarly, it is believed that she can cause any object to decay or to be ruined by looking at it too. Because the witch is inherently malevolent, whatever she looks at is negatively affected by the gaze. No-one who comes into contact with her eyes is able to benefit from the experience, since the witch is unable to bless anyone. In this regard she is thought to have no control over her malign power, which constantly emanates from her eyes.

On some occasions, the witch may also use spells (mantras) to attack people. While this only occurs rarely (indeed, none of my informants in Mehndipur claimed to have been harmed by witchcraft of any kind), one sometimes encounters Hindus who testify to being afflicted as a result of a witch's spell. Thus, on one notable occasion when I had to make a journey from Mehndipur to the city of Ajmer during the early months of fieldwork, I met a Hindu at a shrine in the city who told me that his own daughter had become mentally ill because a witch had put a curse upon her. I discovered that his 21-year-old daughter had been sick since she was a young girl. She was said to be perfectly healthy before her thirteenth birthday but that, soon afterwards, she started to talk and laugh to herself. Although she was taken to a number of psychiatrists, her condition was said not to have improved. In fact, her father stated that it had significantly deteriorated. For, despite having become a young woman, her general behaviour remained extremely childish: she often played as well as fought with small boys and girls in her neighbourhood. According to the young woman's father, she was attacked by a witch during infancy. He alleged that it was done by a woman with a reputation for harming people by witchcraft in the community where they lived. The young woman's father commented that the *dakan* came to his home one day when his daughter was only a baby and asked for an item of clothing to be given. The request, however, was refused. Because of this, the *dakan* was said to mumble or mutter a curse. As far as the afflicted young woman's father was concerned, it was this spell that caused his daughter to become sick, even though the illness did not actually manifest itself for many years.

But the witch may also harm her victims by possessing them. Whenever she does this, her body is held to appear still or lifeless (cf. Lambert 1988: 198). It is said that she is physically unable to move and that her body remains motionless until her spirit returns to it. In the case of a deceased witch, however, it is believed that her spirit can enter a person's body and stay there indefinitely. She may do this to cause illness or disease. On the other hand, as indicated earlier, the *dakan* may possess a young girl or an adult woman to corrupt her, to pollute her blood. In doing this, the female host also becomes a witch. But, in some instances, it is held that the female who is transformed into a malevolent creature may not always be aware of what has happened. Thus, it is believed that a particular female may harm others by means of witchcraft without being conscious of it, without actually realising that she is a witch.

If a person innocently shares food or drink with a witch, he or she may be at risk from attack. Again, it is thought that the witch may be unaware of causing affliction by partaking of whatever is offered to her, as may the individual who donates it. A person is considered to be susceptible because the food or drink becomes tainted or contaminated. This happens precisely because the witch touches or comes into contact with it and the person who then shares a meal with her may get sick or die shortly afterwards.

Although anyone can be harmed by witches, women and children are widely believed to be particularly vulnerable. Of the two, however, the latter are seen as being exceptionally at risk; for witches are said to be especially attracted to them. They are thought to take great pleasure and delight in preying upon a woman's offspring. But, according to some informants, the witch may kill a child on some occasions in order to resurrect it in the graveyard. By doing this, she is able to take it for herself. Some informants also maintain that, to terminate the life of a child or, indeed, of anyone else, the *dakan* may consume the victim's liver (*kaleja khati hai*) and other vital organs. Thus, the person whom she attacks in this way becomes more and more sick, and often extremely thin as well, until death finally occurs. But, while the *dakan* may afflict an individual with a serious, life-threatening disease and/or kill someone, she is frequently believed to cause people to develop minor ailments. The ones that are said to be particularly common include the following: loss of appetite (*bhukh na lagna*), vomiting (*vaman*), a feeling of uneasiness (*becaini*), or lethargy (*bharipan/susti*), and all children's maladies (*bacco ki bimari*).

To counteract witchcraft, various apotropaic objects and substances can be used. But when a person has actually been afflicted by the *dakan*, it is often necessary to consult a healer. One of the standard techniques that an occult practitioner may employ to remove the harm allegedly caused by a witch is *jhar-phuk* (sweeping and blowing), a technique that is also widely used in north India to exorcise (*utarna*) evil spirits. Sweeping the patient's body with a fan of peacock feathers (*morchal/morpankhi*), as well as blowing helpful mantras on to the sick person, are believed to nullify the malevolent force. On some occasions, however, it is said that the healer may cure a person by focusing upon the witch rather than the patient. Thus, to free someone caught in the *dakan*'s clutches, an occult adept may utter a mantra and send it through the air. Here, it is thought that the magical words uttered, not only seek out the witch and undo the harm she has caused, but also that they immobilise her vehicle (*vahana*), preventing the witch from making a second journey to the victim's home later.

Confronting the *dakan* in person is held to be another way of counteracting witchcraft. When a particular woman is suspected of bewitching someone, I was told that she may be asked to lick up the victim's spittle (*thuk*). If she does this it is said that the sick person will recover because the destructive force is automatically removed. But it is clear that the action also incriminates the woman. It is tantamount to making a confession of guilt. Moreover, once a woman admits to being a witch, there may be future reprisals. As a known witch, she could be held responsible for illness or misfortune experienced by others in the community and subsequently beaten or even murdered for this, as Carstairs has shown (1983: 14 ff.). On the other hand, I was told that a woman who is suspected or accused of witchcraft may refuse to lick up the victim's spittle, which could also result in a beating. But this kind of confrontation is rare. To be sure, while some individuals may privately suspect a particular woman of being a witch, they are seldom eager to denounce her publicly. There are at least two reasons for this. First, it is thought that the witch could retaliate against her accusers, employing mystical powers to avenge herself upon them. Second, a woman who is accused of witchcraft may actually report this to the secular authorities. If she were beaten or killed, the police and the courts could then take legal action against her attackers (cf. Epstein 1967: 139 ff.). Indeed, it may be noted that this is exactly what happened in a notable incident reported by Carstairs (1983: 22 ff.). Thus, the threat of legal proceedings being initiated, as well as the fear that the witch might afflict a person for levelling an accusation against her, undoubtedly prevent many people from voicing their suspicions.

The malign gaze

In Mehndipur and throughout north India, the fear that anyone (especially women or witches) can create adversity by means of the malign gaze (*nazar lagna*) is prevalent. In fact, the belief that a person is capable of injuring someone and is able to spoil or destroy an object simply by looking at it is common in many societies besides India. Although it is not universal (Dundes 1981: 259), this widespread belief is always connected with envy or jealousy (ibid.: 263). The Hindi term for this negative emotion is *jalan*, from *jalna* (meaning literally, 'to burn'); and in north India jealousy or *jalan* is assumed to be present when the evil eye is cast: that is to say, the latter is assumed to be dependent on it. Whenever anyone is the object of envy, then, he or she is viewed as being at risk from injury or harm. Similarly, if someone's property is coveted, this is also susceptible and may be completely ruined or destroyed by the onlooker's *nazar*. According to Pocock, one tends to be harmed by the evil eye of 'those with whom one is, in most other respects, equal, or has reason to expect to be' (1973: 28). He claims that the envy of a person who is a social equal but marginally less fortunate than oneself, therefore, is particularly feared, and that this individual is likely to be suspected of causing illness or misfortune attributed to the malign gaze.

But sometimes there is also great disparity between the victim of *nazar* and the one who causes the affliction. The two are not necessarily from the same *jati* or sub-caste, and, in some cases, there is a large difference between them in terms of economic status. Thus, in Mehndipur, informants claiming to be sick because of the evil eye were high caste and/or affluent in relation to those who were allegedly responsible for afflicting them. Although I was unable to conduct an in-depth interview with any of the three respondents who stated that they had been harmed by *nazar*, in each case my records show that there was considerable inequality between the victim of the malign gaze and the one who allegedly cast it. Two of the informants were Brahmans. The husband of the first was a taxi driver from the city of Kota, Rajasthan. The second woman's spouse was a shop worker. Both of these women stated that they became ill following an encounter with an untouchable female. The first said that a sweeper (*bhangi*) asked her for money. The request was refused, and soon afterwards she developed a cough (*khansi*), had pain throughout her entire body (*puri sharir dard*) and would sometimes temporarily lose consciousness or faint (*murccha*). The wife of the shop worker claimed that she suffered from loss of appetite (*bhukh na lagna*) and vomiting (*vaman*). The ailments started after she refused to give soap (*sabun*) to a woman from one of the scheduled castes. The third respondent was a Rajput. Her husband was a fairly wealthy businessman who owned a large shop and also supplied many others with milk sweets (*dudh mithai*), which he manufactured. She was afflicted because she would not give fruit (*phal*) to a poor (*garib*) woman who came begging at her door. As soon as the beggar was dismissed, the businessman's wife stated that she started to suffer from headache (*sir dard*), a feeling of weakness (*kamzori*) and extreme tiredness (*thakavat*). According to all three of the informants, it was the evil eye of the inferior females who caused their malaise, the reason why they had come to the pilgrimage centre.

However, it appears that few individuals who are afflicted by *nazar* travel to Mehndipur. This is perhaps because it is easily counteracted. It is often said that one can remove it by reciting a simple mantra or by having *jhar-phuk* performed over one's body or over one's property. Compared with sorcery or spirit possession, then, it is generally held to be less problematic to treat. Whenever treatment is required, it is also relatively inexpensive. Moreover, it is widely believed that *nazar* may be averted by wearing a charm (*tabiz*) or some other protective object. Property can similarly be protected by suspending from a door lintel a small cloth containing mantras. Alternatively, it can be safeguarded by hanging up a few green chillies (*hari mirc*) and a lemon (*nimbu*), as well as by placing mustard seeds (*sarso*) at the property's entrance/exit points. All these particular objects or devices for counteracting the evil eye are said to work effectively.

Interestingly, it is held that the evil eye often causes adversity without the envious person realising that he or she has cast it. Belief in the malign gaze, therefore, partly resembles belief in witchcraft, since a person can unconsciously injure or harm another with either of these mystical forces. In addition, it is thought that one may unwittingly injure oneself by means of *nazar*. It is said that admiring one's own reflection in a mirror, for example, or feeling proud about one's appearance after putting on fine clothes can be extremely dangerous; for one may lose one's health because of this or, like the Greek tragic figure, Narcissus, even one's life (cf. Elworthy 1895: 12; Guirand 1959: 185).

But, while anyone may be afflicted by the evil eye, it is children and infants who are considered to be most at risk. Because of their health and beauty, and because women particularly desire and cherish them, it is said that they often attract *nazar*. Yet, in many cases, it is believed that the child becomes sick, not because an admirer deliberately wishes to harm it, but because admiration itself, which is always a potentially negative force, causes the malaise. Indeed, I was told that women can even harm their own babies when they are too affectionate towards them (cf. Pocock 1973: 27). On the other hand, women who are childless (and who also may be suspected of being witches) are considered often to injure or kill babies intentionally with the evil eye. These women are said to do this because they are full of resentment and bitterness. Since they have been deprived of offspring, which, as Babb points out, 'represents the very centrepiece of the mother's identity as a complete woman' (1975: 101), their jealousy becomes particularly venomous and can be targeted at any infant upon which they gaze, though pregnant women are held to attract it as well.

Links between mystical forces directed by human agents

Before turning to the conclusion, I briefly examine a number of important links between sorcery, witchcraft and the evil eye.

The first point to make is that all these types of mystical attack are fundamentally interrelated because they are directed by human agents. In this respect, they are opposed to, or different from, divine as well as demonic forms of malevolence.

However, moving beyond this rather elementary observation, what is particularly striking about informants' accounts of affliction by sorcery, witchcraft and the malign gaze is the moral overtone that seems to pervade them. The sorcerer, for example, is typically condemned because he flouts the moral rules, codes and conventions. But, as pointed out earlier, although he is often said to breach them and may be accused of using his supernatural powers to extort money from his clients, on some occasions, his destructive magic may be viewed as upholding moral norms rather than subverting them. His ritual practices, then, may be considered just, despite the negative consequences that they have for certain individuals. Whether his behaviour is seen as benevolent or malevolent depends, in part, on how one is affected by it as well as on the circumstances that lead to its employment. For, as I have shown, if one is injured or harmed, one may be quick to condemn the destructive magic; on the other hand, if this provides a way of gaining retribution, it may be viewed in positive terms.

It must be emphasised, however, that, in the main, sorcery practice is considered seriously reprehensible from the moral standpoint, not least because it is essentially rooted in, and fueled by, envy, jealousy and greed. Indeed, that envy or jealousy is seen as being central here – as a major motivation for resorting to sorcery practice – is not only evident in many of the kinds of case to which attention has been drawn in this chapter; but it is a particularly prominent feature of the whole corpus of sorcery cases I documented in Mehndipur: in the vast majority of cases reported to me at the pilgrimage centre alleged victims of sorcery stated that envy or jealousy was the principal reason why their enemies had used sorcery to harm them.

Given that envy or jealousy is commonly claimed to be the motive for launching a sorcery attack, it is evident, too, that conceptions about sorcery are linked to conceptions about witchcraft, as well as to conceptions about the evil eye. Indeed, with regard to witchcraft, this form of mystical attack is frequently thought to occur because of envy or jealousy, as I have indicated. Witchcraft, therefore, is also morally reprehensible. To be sure, because it is said that the witch's actions and intentions are directed by envy or jealousy (the witch, it will be recalled, is not only thought to be a particularly jealous individual who hates to see anyone prosper, but one who always endeavours to reverse or undermine the welfare and good fortune of others), she is seen as an enemy of the moral order and of the good society – an enemy who should not be tolerated in any shape or form. It is thus small wonder that suspected witches may be subjected to harsh punishments – severe beatings which, as in some reported instances, may even result in death (cf. Carstairs 1983).

In a similar way, and for similar reasons, *nazar*, the malign gaze, is condemned. As in typical cases of witchcraft or sorcery affliction, *nazar* is held to be deeply rooted in, or motivated by, envy and jealousy. *Nazar*, like witchcraft and sorcery, is thus considered to be a heinous breach of moral rules, codes and conventions, a subversion of acceptable moral practice.

Now, although all these mystical forces are connected (in the sense that they are often said to be motivated by envy or jealousy and to have important moral underpinnings, as well as in the sense that they are all held to be directed by human agents) the relationship between witchcraft and the evil eye is particularly close. There are a number of reasons for this. First, as previously noted, one who causes affliction by means of witchcraft or *nazar* is often thought to be unaware of doing this; whereas sorcery, by contrast, can never be performed unconsciously. Second, witchcraft typically manifests itself in terms of the malign gaze. This is because *nazar* is believed to be the main weapon of the *dakan*. Third, both are linked because they are essentially feminine forms of supernatural attack. While any man or woman may harm someone with witchcraft or the evil eye, it is mostly women who are held to do so. Concerning the former, this is evident from the ethnographic data I have provided. In the case of the latter, it can be deduced from the fact that babies and infants are seen as being particularly prone to *nazar*, which is almost invariably ascribed to the envy of certain women. In addition, women themselves are also believed to be vulnerable to *nazar*, even though they are said to be affected less frequently than children. Again, it is other females who are thought to cause the affliction, females who are usually jealous because they are barren or less fertile than those whom they harm. Furthermore, since some of these females may be suspected of being witches as well, the close relationship between witchcraft and *nazar* can easily be detected. Both are evidently part of the same belief complex to which sorcery is related less intimately. But, as I have stressed throughout this chapter, because sorcery, witchcraft and the evil eye are considered to be human or, rather, *extra*-human forms of mystical attack, and because each of these forms of mystical harm is also thought to involve envy or jealousy, there is a clear conceptual link between them.

Conclusion

In Mehndipur and throughout the surrounding region, sorcery, witchcraft and the evil eye are greatly feared. However, while one person may be accused of harming another by means of any of these mystical forces, I found that sorcery allegations in Mehndipur were particularly prominent, as indicated both in this chapter and in chapter 2. Perhaps one reason for this is that those who are harmed by witchcraft or *nazar* rarely travel long distances in search of cure or relief from sickness and disease. In Mehndipur, none of my respondents claimed to have experienced adversity as a result of the former, and only three individuals attributed illness to the latter. It is equally important to note that, while people are never eager to accuse a suspected witch of attacking them (it is thought that this could not only anger her, but lead to mystical reprisals), those harmed by witchcraft are also, perhaps, less likely to be found in pilgrimage centres, such as Mehndipur, because witchcraft may be suspected as being the cause of malaise far less frequently than sorcery. Moreover, those afflicted by the evil eye may seldom embark on a long journey to Mehndipur or to other healing shrines far from their homes because *nazar* does not appear to be treated as seriously as sorcery. *Nazar*, in fact, is often said to be easily counteracted by *jhar-phuk* or by reciting a simple mantra, as I have indicated.

Finally, although one often hears that illness or misfortune has been caused by sorcerers (indeed, half of the interviewed informants in Mehndipur claimed to have been afflicted by them), I have demonstrated in this chapter that diagnosticians or diviners are responsible for initiating sorcery suspicions as well as accusations on some occasions. However, it must be emphasised that clients do not always accept the pronouncements of diagnosticians; neither are the former simply passive participants during séances. A client may reject the diagnosis given by an occult practitioner and consult a number of other specialists until he or she is satisfied with the explanation provided. And this may occur not only when the diagnostician invokes sorcery but when adversity is ascribed to other supernatural agents or forces as well. During consultations, a client may equally supply the specialist with particular information, and may even give names of persons who have possibly afflicted him or her by means of sorcery, culminating in a pronouncement that the client wishes to hear. Undoubtedly, clients do this when they suspect particular individuals of harming them with the aid of black magicians. Nevertheless, as I have shown, some clients have no prior suspicions of sorcery before consulting a healer. Yet, after visiting a diagnostician, accusations sometimes follow. It is evident, therefore, that in some instances diagnosticians play an important role in generating them. And this, as I have stressed, is perhaps to be expected: given that sorcery practice itself is held to be prevalent or widespread, it is understandable that diagnosticians are not only able to plant the seeds of sorcery suspicion, but also to initiate the accusations that may follow.

4

HEALING AND THE
TRANSFORMATION OF SELF
IN EXORCISM

Introduction

In the previous chapter, I not only discussed sorcery accusations and the observation that diagnosticians may sometimes initiate or generate them, but supernatural affliction was further explored in terms of the three major themes introduced in chapter 2, namely, causation, attribution and vulnerability. Some of the strategies for coping with illness and misfortune were also examined in chapters 2 and 3, and in the former I stressed that these are often pluralistic, as many of the case studies cited show. In other words, those who are suffering from illness or disease frequently try a number of approaches in order to regain their health, involving experts in the field of traditional and Western medicine as well as those who are adept in occult science (*tantra-mantra vijnan*). However, when illness is viewed as having a mystical or supernatural cause, I indicated that a special ritual is usually required, either to counteract the malevolent force responsible for this, or, in the case of possession, to remove the offending spirit. Indeed, because possession is often thought to occur when spirits attack a person capriciously, as well as when a person is harmed by other supernatural agents or forces (cf. Henry 1977; Opler 1958), such as sorcery, exorcism is frequently performed.

This chapter thus focuses upon exorcism at Balaji temple, the main healing shrine in Mehndipur, and it explores the role of emotion in it. Emphasis is placed upon the role of emotion in exorcist rituals at Balaji temple, not merely because it is frequently displayed in them, but because it is seen as being critical to the curing project. Moreover, this chapter draws upon the literature on modern Western psychotherapies and endeavours to establish that much of what takes place during therapy is essentially similar to what occurs during exorcism, and that by understanding the first it is possible to illuminate the second and vice versa. Indeed, in both it is argued that the individual at the centre of the ritual process deidentifies with, or dissociates him or herself from, pathological states of being and from negative aspects of emotion and learns to reidentify or reconstruct the self (his or her physical and psychological condition) in accordance with positive feelings and conceptions – a process, it may be noted, that is reminiscent, in part, of the one Lévi-Strauss (1979) has helped to shed light on in his justly celebrated (though equally controversial) comparison between psychotherapy and shamanic curing.[1] In psychotherapy and exorcism, as in other healing traditions, the process by which the self is thought to be transformed, enabling the patient to recover, is always shaped by shared concepts and beliefs into which the individual or ailing person is socialised (cf. Dow 1986; Zatzick and Johnson 1997); and this may involve, or be facilitated by, emotional experience, the activation of emotion, which Kapferer (1979) argues often occurs in healing ceremonies. (On this point also see McCreery 1995: 160.) Kapferer's argument that emotion is frequently produced in the kind of curing practice I explore, in fact, underpins much of the analysis this chapter provides, as does his more recent argument (Kapferer 1997: 259 and *passim*) that emotional experience is a physiological and psychological process as well as a sociological one.[2] Importantly, however, whether emotion is actually present in exorcism and psychotherapy, as this chapter suggests, or whether it is absent in the curing process, this is considered in the Indian context, as in the Western one, to be essential.

However, while it is contended here that fruitful comparison between exorcism and psychotherapy can be made, I, like Kapferer (1991), am critical of a psychoanalytic approach to exorcist practice. This chapter provides a critique of the *hysteria thesis* put forward by Sudhir Kakar (1982), the Indian psychoanalyst who was one of the first researchers to conduct a study of exorcism at Balaji temple in Mehndipur. I reject his Freudian explanation of both spirit possession and exorcist rituals at the pilgrimage centre. One of the main reasons for this is the fact that he does not take adequate account of the cultural construction of illness and cure.

Self and emotion

Before turning to exorcist practice at Balaji temple or to a comparison between exorcism and psychotherapy, it is necessary not only to examine how emotion is conceptualised in India and the West, but also to consider the notion of the self or personhood.

One of the major themes in much of the anthropological literature on the self, particularly when comparing Indian with Western conceptions, is the issue of autonomy. Mauss (1985) maintains that in India, as in other non-modern societies, the individual is not an autonomous, independent agent in the sense which these terms apply to modern man; for while in the West the human subject is held to be singular, unique and bounded, having become both 'a basic fact of law' (ibid.: 14) and a 'conscious moral (being)' who is 'free and responsible' (ibid.: 18), in India, by contrast, personhood is not thought to be indivisible (ibid.: 13).

Dumont (1980: 8–9; 1992: 9–10) and many other scholars (e.g. Kakar 1981: 37; Marriott 1976: 111; Marriott and Inden 1977: 232) have also been concerned with the same issue, arguing that individualism and the concern for individual autonomy are devalued in Indian society. Thus, for Dumont, whereas individualism as a value is fundamental or cardinal in the West, in India individual autonomy is irrelevant (except in the context of renunciation)[3] because personhood is fused with the social whole; and hierarchy not equality is the structuring principle in all social relationships.

However, Dumont's holistic approach has been criticised recently for ignoring the apparent evidence of autonomy or independence of persons in India (cf. Cohen 1994: 14–15; Mines 1988: 568 ff; Morris 1994: 92–95.). Cohen, for example, states that it is necessary to criticise Dumont for failing to distinguish between individuality and individualism (1994: 14–15); and the former, he stresses, is universal because all human beings have a sense of 'I' or self-consciousness (ibid.: 4–10).[4] Thus, he writes:

> Two mistakes follow from this ... The first is the denial to non-Western cultures of concepts and values of individuality ... The second is the axiomatic dichotomisation (Dumont) makes between individualistic and holistic sociologies and ideologies.
>
> (1994: 14–15).

But Dumont never denies that the human subject possesses a self-consciousness; and in *Essays on Individualism* (1992: 1) he points out that the inspiration for his work is Mauss, who asserted that 'India appears to ... have been one of the most ancient civilisations aware of the notion of the individual, of ... consciousness' (1985:

13). Cohen, I believe, is also in error for not recognising that the task of anthropology, as Dumont and Mauss conceive of it, is concerned as much with the *difference* between societies as it is with what they have in common (Dumont 1980: 426.n.2, 1992: 2 ff.). By stressing the latter and by ignoring the former, then, Cohen is unable to mount a convincing attack upon Dumont.

In *Anthropology of the Self*, Morris (1994), like Cohen, also asserts that 'undue emphasis ... (has been) placed on the hierarchical-collectivist view of the Indian person' (ibid.: 95). However, he criticises Dumont mainly for neglecting to consider the 'spiritual' conception of selfhood in India and for 'ignoring the implications of certain key religious conceptions that imply a spiritual totality' (ibid.: 92). He writes:

> In ordinary everyday contexts the Indian person tends to see his or her self identity largely in terms of kin relations and caste membership ... Yet fundamentally ... the 'self' is identified not with the body nor the social but with a spiritual realm.
>
> (ibid.: 93)

But Morris' approach and the one that Dumont develops appear to be complementary rather than being completely opposed (not least because Dumont himself also stresses religious conceptions in respect of social relationships and social organisation). Indeed, for Dumont, the main form of social organisation in India, caste, is simultaneously a religious construction. Moreover, since Morris states that Hindus ordinarily tend to view themselves in terms of kin relations and caste identity, he clearly acknowledges the prevalence of a holistic ideology in the Hindu world, an ideology which sharply contrasts with Western individualism, as Dumont has shown.

Nonetheless, the Hindu distinction between the 'phenomenal self' and the 'inner self', which Morris has drawn attention to, is clearly important, both when comparing Indian with Western conceptions of the self and in relation to the argument developed in this chapter. He says, '... two selves are recognised in Hindu thought – a material or phenomenal self, and an "inner self"' (1994: 79). In fact, in the six orthodox systems of Hindu philosophy, which have had a significant impact on the development of Hindu thought generally, this distinction has been fully worked out, as Morris has shown. In his analysis of these philosophical systems or schools, he points out that, while the inner self is 'identified with spirit' (which is conceptualised as being 'formless, immutable and absolute') (ibid.), the material or phenomenal self, on the other hand, is not: '(the physical body), the mind, cognition, the entire psychological aspects of life are seen in philosophical terms as material conceptions, as part of the phenomenal world of change and karma' (ibid.: 78).

In addition, as Kakar (1982) and others (e.g. Marriott 1976, 1989; Waghorne and Cutler 1985) have also stressed, unlike the notion of the self in the West where mind and body are held to be separate, in Indian thought they are conjoined. Thus, 'the subtle body', Kakar writes, 'is more than the psyche and in fact becomes the locus of identity of body and mind, the subject of both physiological and psychological predicates' (1982: 240).

In very broad, schematic terms, then, differences between Western and Indian conceptions of self are considerable (cf. Freeman 1999: 173–74). Now, in the Indian context, because the phenomenal or lower self (body-and-mind) is the central focus of healing rituals, such as exorcism, it is this conception of the self (as distinct from the inner self or the social self) with which I am concerned. Generally speaking, while the inner self in Hinduism is a transcendental or soteriological concern, the phenomenal self, by contrast, is a pragmatic or worldly one, a distinction that has also been fruitfully utilised by other South Asianists (e.g. Mandelbaum 1966; Babb 1975: 178 ff.; Gellner 1989: 129 ff.). Indeed, since the phenomenal self (hereafter referred to simply as self) is the focus of exorcism, which is performed for pragmatic purposes, for curing the body and mind, it is clearly similar to psychotherapy in the West since psychotherapy is not only concerned with the mind but the body also, as is evident in the treatment of psychosomatic disorders, for example. Moreover, as I also hope to demonstrate, in exorcism and psychotherapy, transformation of the self (despite differences in the way it is viewed) is seen as being critical to the actual healing project; that is, healing is not simply thought to necessitate self-transformation, a change in the physical and psychological condition of the patient, in a certain sense it *is* the very transformation itself. In both types of healing milieu, emotion is also considered to be central and to play a fundamental role in producing the desired changes that enable the patient to recover. But, while emotion is held to be essential, an indispensable feature of the curing process (and this, I argue, is another important similarity in respect of the two healing systems), emotion, like the self, is not conceptualised in India and the West in quite the same way, though the Indian theory of emotion, which was explicitly developed in the sphere of aesthetics in connection with the theory of *rasa*,[5] and the way emotion is conceptualised in modern Western psychotherapy do not constitute completely opposing viewpoints. Indeed, Lynch (1990a: 17) perhaps has this point in mind when he states that the concept of emotion in *rasa* theory only 'differs in *some* ways from Western theories of emotion' (my italics).

Briefly outlined, the Western common-sense view of emotion, as Lynch (ibid.: 4 ff.) has shown, essentially resembles the physicalist model, a particular theory which was largely developed by Descartes in the first half of the seventeenth century. In line with common-sense, the physicalist theory holds that emotion is a passive phenomenon. Here, then, as Lynch observes:

> (Emotions) are 'things' that happen to us, we are 'overwhelmed' by them, they 'explode' in us, they 'paralyse' us, we are 'hurt' by them, and they 'threaten to get out of control'. Emotional action follows a hydraulic metaphor of forces welling up inside of us or of psychic energy about to explode.
>
> (ibid.: 5)

In addition, another equally important feature of the physicalist theory or the common-sense view is that emotion is irrational as well as natural, which is precisely why it can perform an important excusatory function (Lynch ibid.). Thus, in the West, as Heelas has noted:

> We (often) say 'my emotions got the better of me' and 'I fell into a blind rage' ... (M)any emotions are not only naturally experienced as affecting the self – the way in which we conceptualize them also provide excuses for the rational self when it goes awry.
>
> (Heelas 1981: 50)[6]

In India, by contrast, it is often said that the emotions have their seat in the mind or the heart (*manas*), as Lynch (1990a: 19) has stressed, which is part of the subtle body, the locus of identity both for the mind and for the gross body (ibid.). This, in fact, was a view frequently expressed by a number of healers (*bhagats*) and temple functionaries in Mehndipur with whom I discussed the subject of emotion. Moreover, as Lynch rightly notes, the idea that the mind or *manas* is 'the centre of reason and judgement as well as emotion' (ibid.), is not only prevalent in India, but in 'Hindi (the) words *bhava* and *bhavana* mean emotion as well as idea and thought' (1990b: 102). This particular conception of emotion, which is also one of the main features of *rasa* theory, has no correlative in Western thought whatsoever. Furthermore, in India, as Lynch suggests, 'because (it is often said that) the emotions are not separate from (or) lower than reason, it is probable that they do not carry the same excusatory function as some Western ones' (1990a: 19).

But the classical theory of *rasa* is not merely concerned with the emotions but also their activation by means of the aesthetic. Lynch says:

> (T)he major purpose of dance, drama, ritual and poetry is ... catalytic. Aesthetic forms ought to activate an emotion ... in participating members of the audience ... The play, the poem, the dancer, and the myriad elements composing them act as catalysts ... to the various inherent emotions and create a sympathetic emotional response ... in the audience. The critic or cultivated member of the audience responds in such a way that his or her emotion is transformed into a purely aesthetic, transcendental, and universal one, a *rasa*.
>
> (ibid.: 17–18)

Thus, according to *rasa* theory, the experience of a primary emotion, such as love, which is generated by means of the aesthetic, simultaneously provides an experience of divine bliss (cf. de Bary 1964: 253 and *passim*; Hiltebeitel 1987: 356; Lynch 1990a: 18). And this is why medieval *bhakti* movements, as Lynch observes, particularly cultivated aesthetic forms and expression as the fundamental mode of religious experience itself: '*Bhakti* (devotion) was conceived and meant to be experienced as an emotion in which the devotee experienced bliss' (1990a: 18).[7]

Although in *rasa* theory participation in drama, dance or ritual is ultimately a 'cultivation of the emotional taste for divinity and supreme self-realization' (ibid.), aesthetic activation of the emotions also produces a transformation in the mind and body (the phenomenal self) because they are inseparable from them (ibid.: 18–19),[8] and this is a central motif in exorcism too, as I now attempt to demonstrate. Indeed, as mentioned above, since activation of the emotions in Western psychotherapy is thought to produce changes in the self as well, fruitful comparison between the two healing systems – with a specific focus upon emotion – can be made.

Possession trance and the role of emotion in exorcism at Balaji temple

At the Balaji healing temple in Mehndipur exorcism is believed to be transformative. Those who take part in exorcist rituals here are said to undergo radical physical and mental change, an ontological transformation which enables sufferers to overcome ill-health and disease. In the healing rituals at the shrine, possession trance is held to facilitate this, and in a manner reminiscent of the way in which drama, etc. create a powerful experience of affect according to the classical Indian texts on aesthetics, it is also viewed as having an intense charging effect with respect to the emotions. The indigenous term that translates the English word for trance is *peshi*, though this legal term, literally meaning a *hearing*, is used in two senses in the context of a healing ceremony: it refers to the statement (*bayan*) that afflicting spirits make during their *appearance* at Balaji's court (*darbar*), as well as to dissociation, the actual state of trance in which *bhut-pret* (ghosts or spirits) speak through those whom they have possessed. The signs of *peshi* are typical and well defined. The patient's body first begins to sway rhythmically. This is known as *jhumna*, literally, 'to move as if one were intoxicated, as a drunkard'. It is followed by a violent shaking of the head. Those who are possessed may then begin to roll on the ground inside or immediately outside the temple of Balaji, making loud wailing noises, as spirits receive punishment (*saza/dand*) from the deity. They may strike the earth with their hands; beat their backs against the temple walls; plunge their heads into the pit where the image (*murti*) of Bhairava is located while raising their legs into the air; pile heavy stones on to their torsos; or swing their heads and arms into the flames and thick black smoke emitted from kerosene fires.

According to healers and priests, as well as patients and their carers, emotion is generated or activated during the ritual performance. These informants often stated that as soon as the possessed are seized by spirits a strong feeling of tension (*tanav*) is experienced. Prior to the commencement of a healing ceremony, afflicting spirits may be dormant or inactive; for it is thought that *bhut*s and *pret*s may occasionally take rest and sleep, or even leave the body for short periods of time. However, during exorcism, it is said that they are forced to *appear* and are compelled to give an account of their evil deeds. While spirits are held captive in this way and receive punishment from the gods, I was told that the possessed frequently experience a choking sensation (*gala bhar ana*), a contraction of the muscles in the throat, and/or a sense of being bound-up (*bandha*); and informants commented that these are the reasons why tight-fitting garments are loosened before, and some-times during, the ritual, and why a woman's hair must be untied. The unpleasant physical sensations as well as the concomitant mental turmoil, which the possessed are held to experience, are viewed as signifying the presence or activation of *tanav*, the emotional charge itself. Thus, from the point of view of my respondents, those seized by spirits are not passively involved in the ritual action, merely acting out a dramatic performance; rather they are gripped by a powerful emotion, and this is seen as being critical to the curing project.

Indeed, in the dialogue below between Ramjilal (a temple functionary who is frequently consulted by Mehndipur pilgrims), a male patient and his spouse, the affective nature of the exorcist process may also be detected.

PATIENT: Baba,[9] I'm unable to sleep (*sona*) at night. I can't take rest (*aram*).

RAMJILAL: Have you had *peshi* ? Did it come?

PATIENT: No. I've been here three days, Baba, but still have not had *peshi*.

RAMJILAL: Today you'll get peace (*shanti*). You'll receive *peshi* in Pretraj's court (*darbar*). But first you must make a food offering, requesting Baba to give it. (Addressing the patient's spouse) Take him to the temple, to Pretraj's *darbar*.

PATIENT'S SPOUSE: Oh Maharaj, other pilgrims (*yatriya*) have told us that *bhut-pret* give the statement (*bayan*) in *peshi*.

RAMJILAL: Yes. The spirit will say why it attacked and why it is causing trouble. Pretraj will give it punishment (*dand*) if it doesn't go.

PATIENT'S SPOUSE: How long will this take?

RAMJILAL: If you have faith (*vishvas*), your husband will have release (*mukti*) this very day. The *bhut* may try to resist, but it's no match for Pretraj. In *peshi*, it'll be punished. He (the patient) will experience (*anubhav karega*) the spirit being bound (*bandha*) inside him. Don't be alarmed. This is necessary. Without *peshi*, peace is not possible. But have faith. He'll have *peshi* today. Do what I have told you.

It is evident from the dialogue above, a dialogue I tape-recorded at Ramjilal's home, that *peshi* has to be experienced before the patient can recover from spirit malaise. In fact, this is said to be necessary for everyone afflicted by spirits. The use of the term, *anubhav*, which denotes both experience and feeling, not only indicates that the experiential is stressed or considered to be fundamental; it also suggests that feeling is recognised by the shrine functionary as being a characteristic feature of *peshi*. Moreover, because patients are held to regain their health as well as to get relief from suffering by trancing, it is clear that this allegedly charged experience is seen as playing a vital role in the curing ceremony. Hope – an emotion that is perhaps present in any healing context – is clearly important too; and the encouraging remarks that Ramjilal often makes when consulted by an ailing person, such as the male patient above, are one of the ways in which this is fostered. It is equally apparent from the dialogue that illness and cure are understood in terms of a particular idiom, a local system of health care management into which pilgrims to Mehndipur are socialised. Indeed, a number of pilgrims, such as the patient who consults Ramjilal, are initially unable to trance but learn to do this later, especially after observing others who have become proficient in the art of trancing (cf. Boddy 1989: 134 and *passim*; Crapanzano 1977: 15).[10] Such behaviour, therefore, is not incoherent; neither is it some type of erratic activity. Rather, as Humphrey and Laidlaw point out (1994: 235), trance as well as the organisation of emotion in exorcism are socially directed. In other words, they are culturally patterned and predictable forms of behaviour and experience (cf. De Heusch 1981: 152; Freeman 1999: 151–52; Gold 1988a: 96); and, at some level, this means that participants are aware of their actions as well, as Janice Boddy has suggested (1989: 354 and *passim*), though such awareness is not always made explicit in discourse about trance. Regarding trance itself and the display of emotion in exorcism, as well as the observation that trancing is learned, conscious behaviour, as opposed to being chaotic or erratic, I now examine the *arati* ceremony in Mehndipur, a ritual dedicated to the worship of the deities at Balaji temple in which large numbers of pilgrims possessed by spirits participate.

In terms of the actual procedure of the ritual, *arati* at the temple of Balaji is not essentially different from the way the ceremony is performed everywhere else in India. It takes place twice daily, at dawn and at dusk. Approximately thirty minutes before the ceremony begins, the possessed are brought from their lodging houses (*dharmshalas*) to the temple by their relatives and friends, who are the principal carers. Large bowls are provided by the priests for the collection of *laddu* balls, a sweet food prepared from gram flour, sugar and ghee, which sufferers are also later told to consume. These balls are held to become infused with the power of Balaji and also to facilitate the *peshi* experience as well as to enable the possessed to receive divine healing. When they are gathered up and taken inside the temple, the congregation start singing hymns (*bhajans*) in praise of the shrine's deities. Soon afterwards the *arati* begins. The head priest (*pujari*) approaches the image of Balaji with a lamp (*dipak*) in his right hand and a bell (*ghanti*) in his left hand. He is accompanied by other priests, one of them blowing a conch shell (*shankh*), the others beating *jalars*, a gong-like instrument. The possessed then start to sway and to shake violently, and in the midst of the assembled crowd, small circles are formed around those seized by *bhuts* and *prets*.

Suddenly, as is often the case at *arati*, one member of the assembly will raise his or her voice and shout, *Bolo jay Baba ki* ('Speak of Balaji's victory'). The crowd invariably responds by repeating the refrain. This is followed by loud clapping and the rhythmic chanting of couplets (*dohas*). The one who has taken the initiative then typically cries out:

Jor se bolo
(Speak loudly [with force])
All: Jay Baba ki

Jay Baba ki
All: Jay Baba ki

Bhai bolo
(Brother speak)
All: Jay Baba ki

Bahin bolo
(Sister speak)
All: Jay Baba ki

Mere Baba
(Balaji, my Lord)
All: Jay Baba ki

Pyare Baba
(Beloved Balaji)
All: Jay Baba ki

Ek, do, tin, car
(One, two, three, four)
All: Baba tere jay, jay kar
(Balaji, Your victory is already established)
Balaji darbar lagao
(Balaji, let the court begin)
All: Un dushto ko mar lagao
(Punish those who are wicked)

Jay Baba ki
All: Jay Baba ki

The refrain, *jay Baba ki* ('victory of Balaji'), steadily increases both in volume and in tempo. This causes the afflicted to become more and more exaggerated in their movements: some start to pummel themselves with clenched fists, some begin writhing on the floor at the feet of their tormentors. At this point, those patients who have not received *peshi* are often caught by the hair, by the neck or by the shirt collar and dragged towards those who are in a state of violent seizure. The voice that initiated the chanting may then be replaced by another:

Jay Baba ki
All: Jay Baba ki

Bhairav Baba
(Lord Bhairava)
All: Jay Baba ki

Pretraj Baba
(Lord of Ghosts)
All: Jay Baba ki

Divan Sarkar
(The 'chief minister' of Pretraj)
All: Jay Baba ki

Kundivale
(Lord of the tank)
All: Jay Baba ki

Bhangivara
(Purifier of unclean spirits)
All: Jay Baba ki

Samadhivale
(Lord of Samadhi: Ganesh Puri/Ganga-Nath)
All: Jay Baba ki

Peshi dede
([Lord] give peshi)
All: Jay Baba ki

Jhumna peshi
(Swaying peshi)
All: Jay Baba ki

Jay Baba ki
All: Jay Baba ki

Many of those who had not entered into trance previously, now begin to do so. Initially, however, some of them seem rigid, even mechanical in their behaviour, though this soon becomes freer and more spontaneous in appearance. The noise and pace of the chanting increases still further. Relatives of those who have just begun to experience *peshi* draw closer towards their loved ones, as do other members of the assembly, and shout the words, *jay Baba ki,* directly into their ears. This usually produces the desired effect: the seizure intensifies.

Under this barrage of attack, demons and ghosts are said to become weaker in their ability to inflict harm upon the possessed. Indeed, they themselves are thought to become the object of affliction. As the *bhut*s and *pret*s receive stern punishment from Balaji, then, fiendish screams of pain and anguish issue from the mouths of those who are seized by spirits. These malevolent beings, however, often remain defiant during *arati*. Even while being punished for the adversity they have caused, they are typically abusive towards the healing deities but, ultimately, are forced into submission. Defiance, abusiveness and submission are the three major themes that emerge during the trance performance. When the possessed enter into *peshi*, these themes surface immediately.

Thus, on one particular occasion, a possessed woman uttered the following words, which I tape-recorded:

> Oh Baba, come close to me! Baba, we will sit together. You will drink liquor (*sharab*) with me. Oh Baba! Why do You beat me (*marta hai*)? Don't touch me. I am very dangerous (*khatarnak*). You say that I will be sent to Bhangivara. But I won't go. You may send me anywhere except to that place. I will not go to Bhangivara. If I must go, let it not be today. I will go the day after tomorrow. On no condition will I go today. Oh Baba! I will go. I will go to Bhangivara. I will go alone. Baba, release me. I will stay in Your court (*darbar*). Release me, Baba.

As the spirits speak out during *peshi*, the *doha*s chanted by the audience become much harsher in tone. For, according to Mehndipur pilgrims, although demons and ghosts promise to cease acting malevolently and to remain in the court or temple of Balaji, they do not always honour this vow. It is said that they are often deceitful (*chali*) and full of tricks. Therefore, by intensifying the attack upon spirits at this stage in the ritual – when *bhut*s and *pret*s are held to be at their weakest ebb – pilgrims claim that it is easier to gain a more secure hold upon them. The spirits are thought to become more amenable and less difficult to control, making it possible not only to get them to capitulate, but also to expel them from the body. Beseeching Balaji to punish the spirits, a member of the assembly thus typically cries:

Ghotevale
(Wielder of the club [Balaji])
All: Jay Baba ki

Bhut maro
(Beat the spirit)
All: Jay Baba ki

Bahut satana
(Oppress [it] greatly)
All: Jay Baba ki

Ise jala de
(Burn the spirit)
All: Jay Baba ki

Jay Baba ki
All: Jay Baba ki

In response to the increased assault, those experiencing *peshi* begin
to shake more wildly. Their movements become even more
accentuated. Dramatically, this is the high point of the ritual.
Now, as indicated earlier, when *arati* begins, many of the possessed
are automatically seized by spirits and, as the chanting progresses,
a number of those who formerly had not received *peshi* start to
trance. But in the final stage of the ritual the frenzy and violence
of the experience reaches a climax. Unable to withstand the severe
punishment meted out by Balaji, spirits are thought to surrender
themselves to the monkey god, which is signalled by their
agreement to trouble mankind no longer. They are thus driven
out of the body, leaving many of those who had been afflicted by
them lying exhausted on the ground. The chief priest then turns to
the congregation and throws holy water (*jal*) upon them. As this is
performed, all those gathered at the shrine shout, *Bol sacce darbar
ki jay* ('Tell the truth: Victory to the court'). The ceremony comes
to a close. Blessed food (*prasad*) previously offered to the deities is
distributed and, after receiving it, patients are returned to their
dharmshalas.

In the ritual that I have just described, it seems that those who
enter into a state of trance are always conscious of themselves at
some level. At all times they are able to converse with carers and
with temple functionaries, though conversations are frequently
subject to later amnesia (cf. Kakar 1982: 67). During acts of self-
inflicted punishment, participants are careful to avoid seriously
injuring themselves. I have attended *arati* in Mehndipur on over a
hundred separate occasions but never once saw a single person
suffer severe injury. Moreover, I have seen women stop trancing for
short periods of time during exorcism in order to feed a distraught,
suckling child. And from the account of the ceremony given above,
it is also clear that the behaviour of participants is highly controlled
and regulated: *peshi* starts when the ritual commences; it usually
intensifies only in response to particular *cues* (the chanting of
dohas); and it is terminated as soon as *arati* is completed.

Those who are drawn into the orbit of exorcist practice
frequently testify to being aware of the way in which they are
affected during exorcism as well. In addition to unpleasant physical
sensations already referred to, many participants maintain that
they are conscious of losing all control over the body. It is often

stated by the possessed that as soon as they are seized by *bhut*s and *pret*s it is impossible to stop the body from shaking. In other words, they are cognisant of the violent jerking movements but have no power to halt them. Furthermore, participants not only frequently say that they experience a feeling of tension (*tanav*) during trance, as indicated earlier, many of them also claim to feel anger (*gussa*). At the pilgrimage centre, this is attributed to the wrath of the spirits possessing them. Because these malevolent beings are forced to *appear* in Balaji's court and must promise to stop being trouble-some, they are said to become enraged, and patients are thought to experience this emotion directly. That is to say, the anger of the spirits is not simply viewed in an abstract manner, it is believed that the emotion itself is activated.

Because the possessed are expected to feel vexed during the possession trance, as well as to experience tension when the spirits are held to be subdued by Balaji, it is understandable why participants of exorcism often claim that these emotions are actually generated. Similarly, it is also understandable why participants maintain that they experience physical and mental changes while trancing too. For in Mehndipur sufferers not only learn the local expression of illness or distress (*sankat*), which informs and shapes the way they explain and conceptualise it, but the treatment that they receive has a local expression too, which they also learn; and this is clearly central in the accounts that patients give when reporting on trance and the efficacy of exorcist ritual, as one would predict. Thus, conceptualising illness in terms of spirit attack or the supernatural, as well as responding to it appropriately through ritual, are evidently a collective project. Ideas about illness and ceremonial curing in Mehndipur are socially or culturally directed, as in any healing system. This is apparent from the testimonies of those who claim to have received divine healing in the village, as the two cases below illustrate.

1. Ravi, a 39-year-old lorry driver from Delhi, came to Mehndipur for the first time two years before I interviewed him. He was educated up to the age of 22 and claimed to possess a number of academic qualifications. In almost perfect English, he informed me that he had returned to the temple of Balaji to offer thanks to the deity; for, as he put it, the god had cured him from 'mental disturbance'.

According to the informant, he became sick because a former lover had put ensorcelled substance into a glass of tea, which was given to him because he refused to continue having sex with the woman. Ravi stated that he was married and felt guilty about cheating on his wife; so he decided to terminate the extra-marital affair. But the former lover was said to be much aggrieved by this and used sorcery (*jadu-tona*) to harm him. This, he maintained, was essentially a retaliatory act. Thus, to exact her revenge, it was alleged that the woman had caused him to become possessed by a malevolent spirit, and that it was the *bhut* who was responsible for his mental deterioration, a problem that typically manifested itself in the form of 'depression' and 'mental frustration'.

When Ravi first came to Mehndipur, he stated that he was unable to trance at first, but on the third or fourth day at the temple he suddenly became aware that his body had started to shake. A few moments later, after catching a glimpse of the image of Balaji, he said that he immediately fell into a 'blind rage'. According to the informant, it was impossible to contain the overwhelming sense of anger that he felt welling up inside, and he began to curse Balaji. He commented that during *peshi* he challenged the deity to a fight and also shouted, 'I will kill you; I am stronger and more powerful than you.'

The intense feeling of anger, which Ravi claimed to experience while trancing, emerged on all other occasions during exorcism too. Every time he entered into a state of trance, the informant stated that the emotion was present. Indeed, in his view, it was by actively participating in exorcism that he was cured from the mental disturbance. Balaji, he believed, had removed the afflicting spirit, which had not only been at the root of his illness but the very being which had caused him to act in a belligerent manner towards the deity.

2. Jagannath was a 30-year-old married civil engineer from Rohtak in Haryana who came to Mehndipur because he had been suffering from fever (*bukhar*). He informed me that the ailment was caused by a Muslim demon (*jind*), which had possessed him because his paternal uncle (*caca*) had used sorcery (*jadu-tona*). According to Jagannath, the motive for the attack was jealousy. The relative was envious of the success that the young man had had in his career, and this was the reason why the former allegedly harmed the latter.

However, when questioned about these matters, Jagannath was not feeling sad or depressed, since Balaji, he claimed, had cured him of the ailment the previous day. Indeed, when I visited the informant at his home five months later, he commented that the fever had not returned, that he had clearly made a full recovery. During the interview with Jagannath in Mehndipur and in Rohtak, I was not only told that the malevolent spirit had been exorcised but that he had also received a *dut*, a helpful spirit which Balaji had sent to guard him against further potential attack by spirits or sorcerers.

Now, Jagannath stated that the *jind* was expelled when he had *peshi* at Balaji temple. But, while the informant said that he experienced anger in trance, he stated that it was tension that he felt most, and that this emotion was particularly pronounced throughout the exorcism. The feeling of tension, which he singled out as being prominent in the curing ritual, was attributed to Balaji's restraint of the spirit. And, according to Jagannath, it was immediately after the *jind* had been expelled from his body – thus ending his sickness – that the healing deity sent the *dut* to protect him.

Both of the above cases show that Ravi and Jagannath report on their experience of trance, as well as the alleged efficacy of exorcist ritual, in a manner typical of all those who are familiar with, and who use, the local Mehndipur discourse. This means that the claim made by the two informants, and by many other ritual participants, carers and temple functionaries, namely, that the emotions are activated during trance, cannot be treated as being unproblematic. In addition, it cannot simply be assumed that emotional display in exorcism is indicative of genuine emotional experience either. For, as I have shown, trance and emotional display are structured and regulated in the ritual performance. Regardless of whether emotions in fact are produced, tension and anger in the *arati* ceremony are undoubtedly collective expressions, as well as customary and conventionalised forms of display (cf. Durkheim 1926: 397 and *passim*).

However, in 'Emotion and Feeling in Sinhalese Healing Rites', Bruce Kapferer emphasises that

> (E)xpressive behaviour in the performance of (exorcism), while often independent of ... individually felt emotion, strives to produce emotional feeling for ritual participants and strives to link these emotions to the prevailing ritual form.
>
> (1979: 153)

He thus maintains that 'when individuals or groups express (emotion) in the cultural medium of ritual, they often actually feel what they express' (ibid.). This, of course, as Kapferer acknowledges, is merely an assertion (ibid.). But it is also an interesting suggestion. Since exorcism in Mehndipur explicitly aims to activate the emotions by means of trance, an altered state of consciousness which participants are frequently informed will enable them to feel the emergent emotions, as well as certain physical sensations, the curing ceremony may often actually generate them. Yet, if emotions are activated or engaged during trance, and this is not implausible, they are not to be understood as being variously experienced by different individuals, but as Humprey and Laidlaw following Gell (1980) have argued, as being essentially common feelings and states of mind (Humphrey and Laidlaw 1944: 237). Moreover, if *peshi* actually facilitates cure, as my informants stressed, emotion in trance may well be critical in the curing process, a process which enables patients to de-identify with negative states of being (spirit affliction) and to re-identify body and mind or the self in accordance with positive feelings and conceptions (the cessation of spirit malaise). Indeed, the way in which the self is thought to be reconstructed during trance is clearly manifest in the two case studies which I have cited. Before Ravi and Jagannath are liberated from the spirits possessing them, in each case the self is held to be in a negative, sick or demonic state, which takes a particular expressive form in exorcism. Thus, it is ritually represented and, in a sense, also represents itself *as* the *bhut*. This is why Ravi, for example, maintains that he is unable to control the overwhelming sense of anger, which he not only claims to feel, but which he also displays during *peshi*. When the malevolent spirits are removed, the patients' pathological state of being is transformed, since it is thought that the self is freed from affliction or spirit malaise; and this transformation as representation is particularly revealing in the case of Jagannath; for the *dut* that he claims to receive from Balaji does not merely signify that he will be protected from further potential spirit attack but is an indicator of profound ontological change: it signifies that he has been cured or completely released from the spirit that caused his illness.

Exorcism and psychotherapy

An emotional charge, as I have stressed, may well be central in exorcist ritual, enabling transformation of the self or healing to occur. Emotion is also considered to function in certain similar ways in modern Western psychotherapies; and this can be demonstrated. To do this, I now briefly examine some of the relevant literature on them. It will be suggested that there are a number of important commonalties between psychotherapy and exorcism, especially regarding the way emotion or emotional experience is seen as playing a vital role in the curing process. Moreover, in the former, as in the latter, because a great deal of emphasis is placed upon the emotions, they may often actually be generated in therapy too.

In much psychotherapeutic discourse an emotional charge is said to be essential for the successful treatment of patients. Indeed, when analytic therapy first emerged in the latter part of the nineteenth century, the theory of tension-release developed by Freud and Breuer placed particular stress on catharsis. Abreaction, the discharge of repressed feelings through emotional display or expression (Freud and Breuer 1956: 8 ff.), was viewed as the mechanism that facilitated cure. One of the best examples of how it was thought to operate is found in Freud's early writings on hysteria. Commenting on Breuer's treatment of Anna O, a 21-year-old patient who was allegedly suffering from the complaint, he writes:

> It was actually possible to bring about the disappearance of the painful symptoms of her illness if she could be brought to remember under hypnosis, with an accompanying expression of affect, on what occasion and in what connexion the symptoms had first appeared.
>
> (1991: 36)

Freud, of course, soon abandoned the use of hypnosis, replacing the technique with the method of free association and, later, by concentrating on dream interpretation. But it was not only the methods used for treating psychopathology that were to change; stress upon inducing catharsis was later replaced by emphasis upon transference (Brown 1976: 35), the process whereby the patient puts the analyst into the role of the powerful parent as seen by the very young infant (Freud 1949: 38). Analytic therapy, therefore, sought to revive the emotions felt in early life towards significant persons, particularly parents, by means of projection, though, instead of trying to induce catharsis, it attempted to produce an emotional charge to reshape the ego in accordance with positive conceptions of self. According to Freud, transference could thus be utilised, for example, to 'correct blunders for which parental education was to blame' (ibid.: 39). In both its early and later developments, then, emotion in analytic therapy was held to be a basic prerequisite for transforming the self.

In addition to the tête-à-tête approach of classical Freudian practice, group therapy strives to create an emotional charge to reshape or transform the self as well. And by engaging the emotions, group therapy, like individual therapy, also aims to cure a number of mental and physical ailments. The following list cited in Bloch and Aveline (2000: 87) includes the common difficulties that are believed to be successfully tackled in a group:

1 *Interpersonal* – pervasive difficulty in initiating and sustaining relationships ... inability to achieve intimacy, either in friendship or (in) sexual (relationships), discomfort in social situations, and maladaptive interpersonal style (e.g. lacking trust, overly dependent, abrasively assertive).
2 *Emotional* – unawareness of feelings in oneself or in others, inability to express feelings like love or anger, poor emotional control (i.e. explosive and volatile), obsessive (i.e. controlled and rigid).
3 *Self-concept* – blurred identity, poor self-esteem, lack of purpose and direction.
4 *Symptomatic* – anxiety, depression, somatization, poor work or study performance, ineffective coping with stress.

These problems are dealt with and are thought to be resolved during the interaction process; for the patient learns to share difficulties with others in the group by confiding in and, in turn, by providing support for, them. Thus, according to Hobbs, 'the (patient) learns what it means to give and receive emotional support and understanding in a new and more mature fashion' (2000: 291); and this transforms a person's identity: '(t)he self is redefined' (ibid.). In fact, in group psychotherapy, that the emotions must be engaged or stirred for this to occur, for the treatment to be effective, is axiomatic.

In this type of therapy, therefore, as in orthodox Freudian practice, an emotional charge is viewed as being essential for curing the patient or for restructuring the self. Indeed, according to Frank (2000), a prominent American psychiatrist, without this it is impossible to transform the ego. He writes:

All schools of psychotherapy agree that intellectual insight is not sufficient to produce change. The patient must also have a new experience, whether this be related to re-living the past, discovering symptom-reinforcing contingencies in his environment, or becoming aware of distortions in his interpersonal communications. Experiential learning occurs through ... emotionally charged self-discovery, transference reactions, and the feelings aroused by attempts to change the contingencies governing his behaviour.

(2000:12)

Emotion in therapy, then, is seen as facilitating experiential learning, enabling change to take place.

Now, because psychotherapists frequently endeavour to generate emotion, which many patients may be aware of and are expected to feel, it may often be produced, as in exorcism. And, if this is the case, participation in therapy, as in exorcism, is likely to be a truly experiential phenomenon. Indeed, with regard to the latter, informants in Mehndipur often commented that it is not sufficient simply to be present during the *arati* ceremony, to believe or have faith in the efficacy of it, but to be involved *experientially*. This is why entering into trance during exorcism is considered necessary, and why my informants frequently stressed that, unless the possessed received *peshi*, they would not recover from sickness or ill-health. It thus appears that exorcist ritual and psychotherapy have much in common. In both active participation is held to be essential for cure, the accent being on emotional engagement in the two healing systems. In psychotherapy, the production of emotion is thought to re-shape the self – the physical and psychological condition of the patient – by means of *experiential learning*. In an important respect, this is the case in exorcism too; for, in the *arati* ceremony, it is thought that the emotionally charged experience of *peshi* or trance enables those seized by spirits to re-construct a healthy self. Moreover, in exorcism and psychotherapy, emotion in fact could be the dynamic force that actually makes the desired transformation possible, as I have suggested.

However, while emotion in exorcism or therapy is a central feature of discourse about healing or self-transformation, it must be pointed out that in the former case it is the emotion of the invading malevolent spirit in the struggle with the healing deities which patients are often said to experience. Here, then, emotion is, in a sense, thought to be experienced *vicariously*. In therapy, on the other hand, the experience of emotion itself is not merely inextricably tied to a journey of self-revelation but also to the resolution of *internally* constituted states of being. There are thus certain differences between the two healing systems in terms of their underlying cosmological or cultural assumptions. And this is the case regarding conceptions about the actual cause of harm as well. For, in the exorcist milieu, the source of harm – an invading spirit (and, in some instances, a sorcerer who may be said to have sent it or to have control over it) – is, like the agents of cure (the healing deities themselves), *external* to the patient; whereas, in the setting of Western psychotherapy, the source of harm is thought to have its primary locus in the internal world of the patient; and it is upon this which therapeutic attention is focused. But, despite these differences, the similarities I have delineated in respect of the two healing traditions are striking.

By comparing these healing systems it seems possible to identify other important similarities too.

(A) Each is underpinned by a special *rationale*. Regarding all psychotherapies, Frank writes:

> A *rationale* or conceptual scheme ... explains the cause of the patient's symptoms and prescribes a ... procedure for resolving them. The rationale must be convincing to the patient and the therapist; hence it cannot be shaken by therapeutic failure ... The rationales and procedures of all therapies inspire and maintain the patient's *hope for help*, which ... is a powerful healing force in itself ... Hope is sustained by being translated into concrete expectations.
>
> (2000: 11–12)

In the exorcist milieu, illness and cure are explained in terms of conceptions embedded in the patient's world view. The belief that sickness and disease are caused by malevolent beings, which can be controlled by invoking the help of deities, thus gives meaning to the problem of suffering as well as shaping the patient's response to it, as I have indicated. Whenever exorcism is considered necessary, then, the anticipation of cure is likely to be present from the start. For the very belief in the efficacy of the ritual sustains the hope that the patient will recover. In addition, in Mehndipur the expectation of cure is, not only likely to be augmented when sufferers consult temple functionaries (e.g. Ramjilal mentioned earlier), but is also continually reinforced by a large class of ex-patients, who, as Kakar points out, testify that 'cures are neither ephemeral nor hearsay ... (F)ormer sufferers are living witnesses ... that the temple healing really "works"' (1982: 83). Many of these ex-patients journey to the village periodically, particularly when festivals (melas) are held, such as Holi and Dashahara.[11] Others come to give a votive offering (savamani).[12] One pilgrim, who made periodic journeys to Mehndipur since being cured over thirty years prior to the time that I met him, had even written a number of small pamphlets, extolling the powers of the healing shrine. He often gave free copies of these to other pilgrims. In one of them, entitled 'Why Suffering'? (Dukha Kyo?), the author refers to how he himself was cured by Balaji. The relevant extract is summarised here:

> The incident took place in 1961. I was seriously ill, and all the doctors of Allahabad had declared that my illness was incurable. A number of people with whom I was acquainted, however, advised me to go to Mehndipur. For it is a fact that those who are severely sick are miraculously cured there.
>
> Formerly the Agra-Jaipur bus was unable to traverse the sandy route to the temple. And when I came to Mehndipur for the first time, I could not walk the three kilometre journey. I was brought by my wife and our two servants. It was five o'clock on a November evening when we alighted from the bus. The sun was about to set. Our luggage was heavy and there appeared to be no means of reaching the village. I was deeply engrossed in prayer, requesting Balaji to provide help. Then just a short time later, I noticed that a tanga (horse-drawn vehicle) was coming towards us from Mahwa. Two young men were sitting inside the carriage. As soon as the boy holding the reins took the turning for the village, my wife entreated him to take us to the temple. He readily consented to this and agreed to take the luggage also.
>
> After arriving there, we offered him money, but he refused to take it. He said: 'We have travelled eighteen kilometres to get to this place on a pre-paid contract. We shall not charge you anything.' We did not ponder over this matter very deeply at the time. But later, we discovered that the tanga was not owned by anyone in Mehndipur. It had not been transporting cargo either. Moreover, shortly

after alighting from it, the *tanga* completely vanished. Even to this day, I do not know who that *tanga* boy was, why he readily agreed to help us, or why he had come to Mehndipur. I am not only convinced that it was Balaji himself who appeared in the guise of that *tanga* boy at such a critical time; I believe that he prevented me from dying too. For it was at that time that my fever also abated. No one other than Lord Hanuman can perform such a miracle.

Many others who receive divine cure at the temple also testify of similar miraculous events. This encourages others who are sick to maintain their faith in the healing power of Balaji, even though they may have been suffering for many years or may have experienced a recurrence of illness after an initial pronouncement of cure. Indeed, patients at the Balaji shrine who appear to suffer from recurrent or recalcitrant illnesses are frequently said to be possessed by numerous spirits, which may take a lengthy period of time to expel fully. Here, then, an explanation is not only provided for failure to achieve automatic cure; but an assurance of healing itself is apparent; and this gives hope to the afflicted. In exorcism, as in psychotherapy, the feeling of hope thus plays a critical role, a role that is underpinned by belief or faith in the efficacy of the ritual.

(B) Psychotherapy and exorcism may equally be compared in terms of the *feeling of security* that emerges during treatment, and the *feeling of support* that the patient experiences in the healing environment. Carl Rogers, a client-centred therapist, writes:

> Where the client undergoes, in the process of therapy, a real reorganization of self, the relationship to the counselor and to the counseling interview comes to involve a very special meaning of security ... In this sense ... (t)herapy is experienced as supporting, as an island of constancy in a sea of chaotic difficulty.
>
> (2000: 70–1)

And Hobbs, commenting on individual and group forms of therapy, says,

> As in individual ... therapy, the members of a group must perceive the situation they are in as being dependably

sustaining of their selves. They bring to the situation a freight of anxiety, a product of their unsuccessful efforts to relate themselves effectively to other people ... (E)ach member of a group, if he is to profit from therapy, must find in the therapist and in other members of the group a genuine feeling of acceptance. He must find in the group situation increasingly less need for the defences against anxiety which render him so ineffectual in living with others and so unhappy in living with himself.

(2000: 286)

The feeling of security and support that sufferers experience in Mehndipur is generated, not only because of the caring attention they receive from some of the priests, as well as healers (*bhagats*), family members and friends, but also because patients are able to share and discuss problems with one another, a point which patients themselves communicated to me on numerous occasions. But family carers here play a particularly important role, a role that is of major therapeutic value, as the work of Pakaslahti (1996, 1998) based on recent in depth research in Mehndipur also reveals. They accompany patients from early in the morning until late into the evening, providing the necessary assistance the sick require during the rituals in which they must participate. Family carers spend many hours every day reciting sacred literature (*japa*s, *kirtan*s, *mantra*s, or *path*s) on behalf of their loved ones too. Moreover, in many instances, those accompanying the sick actually trance on behalf of their possessed relatives, a phenomenon which Skultans (1987a, b) in her analysis of temple healing in Maharashtra has also commented upon. This is more than a mere expression of empathetic caring, which it, nonetheless, supremely demonstrates; it involves the very transference of the patient's suffering or distress (*sankat*) on to the carer. Thus, it is thought that the spirit that is possessing the former seizes the latter, which is also signalled by *peshi*. There are a number of reasons why a person agrees to have a spirit transferred to his or her body. Some do this simply to minimise the burden suffered by the patient. Others volunteer because those who are afflicted are too old and/or too weak to have *peshi*. Severely mentally handicapped patients do not enter into trance either. Similarly, those who cannot walk, and those who are suffering from paralysis, arthritis, back complaints and other comparable debilitating ailments, often do not have *peshi* because of the ferocity of the physical trauma it typically involves.

It is important to point out, however, that in Mehndipur only a kin member may trance on behalf of a patient. The priests at Balaji temple do not permit non-family members to become the object of demonic transference, though adherence to the rule is also understandable within the wider context of popular religious belief and practice. As I have already indicated, spirit possession is often thought to occur, not only when a person becomes the object of a capricious spirit's malevolent attention, but also when he or she is held to have been harmed by other supernatural or mystical agents, especially sorcerers. And many of those who become possessed as a result of sorcery are held to have been harmed inadvertently; that is to say, the attack itself here is not said to have been directed at the actual victim but at someone else, a person who typically is a member of the victim's kin and who has unwittingly managed to escape injury. In these and other similar instances, then, a family member who agrees to become the object of demonic transference makes sense because the volunteer (or proxy) is also a potential victim of the same attack.[13]

But although any member of the family may assume the role of a proxy, volunteers are typically female. Women usually agree to trance for their sick relatives primarily because it is thought that this may also result in the actual transfer of the illness itself. Pilgrims comment that, if a man were to have *peshi* instead of a woman, and then became sick because of this, he would not be able to continue working. Consequently, the problem affecting the family would be compounded. But trancing for the sick, assisting them during the daily healing ceremonies, reciting sacred verses on their behalf, and remaining constantly by their side engender a powerful feeling of support. Patients equally feel secure, not only because of the care they receive, but also because they are able to share their burdens with others, the latter quite literally through the transfer of suffering or *sankat*. Whether one is treated in the psychotherapeutic or in the exorcist milieu, then, supportiveness and a sense of security appear to be important. In both they appear to have a positive effect and to make the treatment itself beneficial.

A critique of the hysteria thesis

The relationship between psychotherapy and exorcism in Mehndipur has also been explored by Kakar (1982: 57–82). Indeed, many of the parallels delineated above have been discussed and examined by him. But, despite the fact that he makes a number of points resembling those that I have outlined, his central thesis is problematic.

Kakar argues that the possessed have 'much in common with Freud's women patients from the Viennese bourgeoisie', though 'the similarity', he writes, 'does not lie in their symptoms but in their underlying *hysteric personality* which they share' (ibid.: 75). To illustrate this claim, he provides four case studies. The most detailed of these is concerned with Asha, a 26-year-old woman from Delhi of lower middle-class Punjabi parentage (ibid.: 70–75). According to Kakar, Asha's hysteria is evident, not only from her neurotic symptoms, but equally from her trance behaviour. He says:

> Asha, it seems, had become addicted to *peshi* ... If for any reason the *peshi* did not take place for more than two days, Asha's eyes screwed up into narrow slits, her headaches became worse and she inevitably had one of her fits of rage. In a more theoretical formulation, Asha was attempting to exchange her possession symptoms, a pathological reaction to individual conflict, for the ritual trance of *peshi*, a socially sanctioned psychological defence.
>
> (ibid.)

The main difficulty with this analysis, however, is that the cultural construction of illness and cure is neglected. The contention that Asha is 'addicted to *peshi*' because it enables her to cope with the alleged hysterical disorder, and that this is apparent from the symptoms that recur if trance is not forthcoming, fails to account for the fact that these phenomena are a collective response (cf. Claus 1979: 33–34). As indicated earlier, in Mehndipur it is stressed that every patient must have *peshi* in order to recover. Indeed, if trance is not immediately forthcoming, a patient is typically instructed by the temple priests to make a food offering once again, requesting Balaji to give it. The dialogue above between Ramjilal, a patient and his spouse illustrates this. Moreover, even when the patient experiences *peshi*, if he or she does not trance in the temple every day, and if it cannot be sustained during exorcism, the patient is also instructed to give a food offering to the healing deities. The fact that Asha constantly endeavours to trance and claims to experience a return of the symptoms when *peshi* does not take place, then, can not be taken as clear evidence that she is suffering from hysteria or that she has a 'hysteric personality'. The response is both socially constructed and predictable. It is necessary to criticise the explanation advanced by Kakar, therefore, because he is too reductionist. He places too much stress upon the subjective feelings of participants in exorcism.

The reductionist nature of the explanation that Kakar proffers with respect to Asha's illness is also apparent in his assessment of her symptoms. Kakar states that the young woman's malaise began because her sister-in-law used sorcery to afflict her. The spirit that entered her body as a result of this was a particular kind of *bhut*, namely, a Masan, which, it is claimed, is 'a ghost ... whose speciality is the eating of unborn babies in the womb' (1982: 71). Since Asha is possessed by a Masan, which causes her to have stomachaches, Kakar maintains that this is an expression of her 'unconscious pregnancy fantasy' (ibid.: 74). However, although Asha claims that a Masan is possessing her, the interpretation that Kakar provides is problematic. In the vast majority of cases where sorcery is invoked, a Masan is held to enter the body. This is because it is thought that sorcerers control these spirits, which are believed, as Kakar correctly points out, to '(inhabit) cemeteries and cremation grounds' (ibid.: 71). The fact that Asha is held to be possessed by a Masan, then, is neither peculiar nor unusual. The majority of other patients afflicted by sorcery equally claim to be possessed by such spirits, though the types of illness attributed to them may differ. According to my informants, a Masan may cause any kind of malaise. It does not have a particular *speciality* as such, since it affects those parts of the mind and body that it is directed to injure by the sorcerer controlling it. Asha's stomach disorder, which is ascribed to this spirit, may not be taken simply as a sign of hysterical illness because the very attribution itself is culturally produced. It is precisely because sorcery is invoked that the sickness is considered to be caused by the spirit of the cemetery or cremation ground. The problem with Kakar's approach is that he places the accent upon the individual patient's subjective experience and does not take adequate account of cultural understandings. By focusing upon the individual the meaning of sickness interpreted as supernatural, therefore, is lost or distorted. Indeed, because Kakar's approach is firmly grounded in psychoanalysis, he privileges the authority of Western notions of illness and cure rather than the authority of Indian concepts or cultural exegesis – a major weakness, it should be noted, that is also a feature of the work of the frequently quoted scholar Obeyesekere (1970, 1977, 1984), who has adopted a similar Freudian approach to spirit possession and exorcism in Sri Lanka, and who has equally been aptly criticised by Kapferer (1991).

Conclusion

This chapter began by drawing attention to the differences between Indian and Western conceptions of self and emotion. I not only stressed that persons in Indian society are collective beings ideologically and lack individual autonomy (a cardinal value in the West), as Dumont (1980 (1970), 1992) and others (e.g. Mauss 1985) have shown, but also (and more importantly for purposes of the argument developed in the chapter) that Cartesian conceptions of body and mind, as well as emotion, are characteristic of Western rather than Indian thought: in India body and mind are not considered to be separable in strict dualistic terms, and the emotions are also widely held to be intrinsically connected to them, having their seat in the heart or the mind (the *manas*), which is part of the subtle body, the locus of identity for the mind as well as the gross body.

But, while there are fundamental differences between India and the West in terms of the way self and emotion are conceptualised, I have attempted to show that Indian and Western thought converge to a large extent when one compares exorcism with psychotherapy. For both exorcism and psychotherapy are not only believed to produce physical and psychological changes, an ontological transformation, but in both types of healing milieu the desired transformation itself is also frequently said to be effected by engaging the emotions, a theory developed explicitly in much of the literature on psychotherapy and one that equally informs speculation on emotion in the classical Indian texts on aesthetics.

Now, in exorcism and psychotherapy, as in other healing systems, the process by which the body and the mind are thought to be transformed from a negative to a positive state or condition is always shaped by shared concepts or beliefs; and with regard to exorcism, I have demonstrated this by focusing on the way in which pilgrims to Mehndipur are socialised into the local system of health care management, a system in which learned behaviour, particularly trance, essentially dictates how participants act during exorcism as well as how they report on their experience of it. The notion that emotions are generated in trance, an altered state of consciousness which is thought to facilitate cure due to its avowed

111

transformative power, is clearly central in the local discourse. It is thus understandable why participants often claim to experience emotion during exorcism. Nonetheless, because it is thought to be present in the healing ceremony, because exorcism is seen as being emotionally charged and explicitly aims to activate the emotions, I have argued that Kapferer's assertion that the emotions are often actually produced (1979: 153) is plausible. In fact, this may well be the dynamic force that enables healing or physical-and-mental transformation to occur, as in psychotherapy or other healing systems which strive to produce emotional feeling as an aid to cure.

However, although it seems likely that emotion is often generated in exorcism, Kapferer's suggestion that ritual participants are unlikely to be cognisant of this while trancing is problematic. According to Kapferer, when the patient is in a state of dissociation, he or she is emotionally 'under-distanced' (ibid.: 170), a term borrowed from an article by Thomas Scheff (1977), who uses it to denote absence of awareness of intense emotional experience that may emerge in certain types of ritual or drama. Kapferer maintains that it is only when trance is terminated that the patient is fully able to reflect upon his or her condition as it undergoes a process of ritual transformation (Kapferer 1979). But this view is at variance with the claims made by my informants in Mehndipur. As indicated in this chapter, those who are drawn into the framework of exorcist practice not only frequently testify to having unpleasant physical sensations while trancing but an overwhelming sense of anger and tension as well. Indeed, as the two case studies cited earlier show, it is during the actual state of trance itself that ritual participants claim to perceive changes in their physical-and-psychological condition (the phenomenal self), a process in which patients de-identify with pathological states of being and re-identify or reconstruct the self in accordance with positive feelings and conceptions. And, as I have stressed, it may well be this allegedly charged process, a process which patients learn to interpret in the appropriate, socially prescribed way, that enables them to recover from spirit malaise or distress.

5

HINDU PRIESTS AND HEALERS

Introduction

So far I have examined beliefs about supernaturals, different types of mystical attack, issues concerning vulnerability and other related themes, as well as exorcist ritual to which affliction is thought to be amenable. Priests and magico-religious curers, whose help is often sought when illness or misfortune strikes a person, however, have only been given brief mention. This chapter, therefore, focuses on the work of these specialists. With reference particularly to the practices of a senior shrine functionary and a celebrated curer in Mehndipur, I analyse the distinctive (though overlapping) roles that priests and healers play. It is argued that these religious specialists are complementary in two important interrelated ways: (1) in the sense that each of them offers different, non-competitive services to pilgrims – services seen by many pilgrims and practitioners as mutually beneficial to those who are afflicted by spirits or other malevolent supernaturals; and (2) in a hierarchical sense. With regard to the latter, I am broadly in agreement with Parry (1994) who, synthesising the work of Dumont and Pocock (1957, 1959) with the work of Marriott (1955b) and Srinivas (1965), emphasises that the relationship between Hindu priests and healers is a fundamentally asymmetrical one. Like Parry, whose observations of priests and exorcists in Banaras partly resemble my own observations of these practitioners in Mehndipur, I contend that the priest is pre-eminent, that his practices are ritually superior to those of the healer – a relationship of asymmetry that is rooted in common sense understandings at the pilgrimage centre and one that shapes the logic of ritual practice itself.

However, it should be pointed out at the outset that there are some crucial differences between what Parry claims regarding the relationship between priests and healers in Banaras and what I discovered during my own fieldwork. Most important of all: Parry states that in the sacred city of Banaras 'exorcism can only be brought to a successful conclusion with the aid of a Brahman' who in other ritual settings 'can pretend to an autonomy impossible for (exorcists)' (ibid.: 247). Thus, he writes:

> It is ... tempting to conclude that the complementarity between (them) ... exists only from the (exorcist's) point of view. The (priest) can dispense with the (healer); but the converse does not apply.
>
> (ibid.)

In Mehndipur, on the other hand, while there is asymmetry in the relationship between priests and healers – help from the former, for example, is sometimes needed by the latter to carry out curing ceremonies in *dharmshalas*, whereas priests do not require the assistance of healers at the temple to perform the rituals over which they themselves preside – there are contexts in which both kinds of specialist perform religious functions that are mutually interdependent, as I will demonstrate. Moreover, whereas Parry claims priests in Banaras frequently disparage the work of exorcists or healers, in Mehndipur priests have great respect for healers and vice versa, as I will also show. But before analysing the interdependence of the priest and the healer, and the ways in which their practices are complementary, I first consider the major differences between them.

Key differences between priests and healers

In the wider anthropological literature, a dichotomy is frequently made between these two types of practitioner, between the ritual expert, on the one hand, and the curer, on the other, though the latter is referred to by a large variety of terms, such as shaman, exorcist, diagnostician, oracle, diviner, magician and prophet. Indeed, while often stressing the complementary relationship that typically exists between them, these figures are almost invariably viewed in oppositional terms. This can be seen in the treatment of them by scholars such as Allen (1976a: 124, 1976b: 512 ff.); Babb (1975: 178 ff.); Berreman (1964: 53 ff.); Dumont and Pocock (1959: 8); Dumont (1980: 270–71); Inglis (1985: 94); Mandelbaum (1966: 1174 ff.); Mayaram (1999: 103–104); Parry (1994: 226 ff.) and Vitebsky (1993: 22) on South Asia; Beidelman (1971: 376 ff.)

and Evans-Pritchard (1970 [1956]: 287 ff.) on north-east Africa; and Eliade (1964: 4) on central Asia. Moreover, according to Lessa and Vogt, '(t)hese two polar types ... are found in all parts of the world' (1958: 410). A sharp contrast is made between them on a number of grounds, though one of the most important of these concerns religious practices. Broadly speaking, the major difference that is highlighted is that the priest enables men and women to communicate with divinity, while the healer, shaman or prophet brings divine beings into relation with humans. It is this mutually inverse relationship that Evans-Pritchard, for example, has in mind when, comparing Nuer priests with prophets, he says, 'whereas in the priest man speaks to God, in the prophet God ... speaks to man' (1970: 304).

In Mehndipur, this distinction between the two varieties of religious specialist is also found. The Brahman priest here is principally a ritual technician whose key function is to ensure communion between pilgrim and deity, a communion the priest effects through his privileged sacerdotal office and whose presence or ministration, especially when an offering is made, is considered vital, whether the pilgrim who donates it does so specifically to solicit divine help or aid (to achieve a cure, for instance) or for some other purpose (e.g. to express devotion or to offer worship). The healer, on the other hand, typically creates a relationship between deity and pilgrim by means of divine possession, the healer (or a medium with whom he sometimes operates) voluntarily becoming host to a possessing deity. Indeed, at the pilgrimage centre it is believed that healers (most of whom are male and Vaishya by caste) may, not only become possessed by local deities or by minor gods and goddesses, but also that some of them become a conduit of power for the high all-India Sanskritic deities, particularly Hanuman, Bhairava and Kali. It will be recalled (see chapter 1) that in Mehndipur a number of curers in fact claim to become possessed by the monkey god. But, while Balaji is said to enter into the bodies of some of these practitioners, it tends to be *dut*s (helpful godlings or messenger spirits) that possess most curers. Thus, it is generally with the aid of inferior supernaturals that their clients are treated or cured, the *dut*s that possess healers in Mehndipur often being servants of the god Balaji himself. Within the framework of hierarchical concepts and beliefs encountered at the pilgrimage centre, there is an equivalence here between *dut*s and healers, an equivalence that is widely acknowledged by my informants. To be sure, a broader isomorphic structure is found, as the relationship between healer and priest is understood to be correlative with the different orders of divinity these practitioners directly engage: the inferior *dut*s in the case of the healer and the superior deity Balaji in the case of the priest. But these religious specialists are distinct in other ways too. For, while the priest holds office on the basis of hereditary privilege, the healer does not. Unlike the former, the status of the latter is achieved rather than ascribed. Moreover, in contradistinction to the priest, whose authority is grounded in, and legitimised by, Brahmanic tradition, the power or authority of the healer is essentially charismatic (cf. Weber 1968, 1969).

However, despite these major differences, it should be noted that there is also some overlap between the practitioners. A dichotomy between them can thus not be applied too rigidly. One key religious function, where the practices of priest and healer are similar or converge, not only involves the discernment of *sankat* or affliction, but also involves providing help or assistance to sufferers with the management of it. Like curers, senior Brahmans in particular often act as diagnosticians. Indeed, the priests at the pilgrimage centre who do this play an important role in identifying the malevolent forces responsible for causing illness and adversity; and this, in turn, directly influences the advice that they give to their clients, especially regarding food offerings to deities. In a similar way to healers, priests in Mehndipur equally give mantras, special *path*s and *japa*s to those who are suffering from *sankat* as well as furnish their clients with protective amulets (*tabiz*).[1] Most important of all, perhaps, while priests at the Balaji shrine officiate during *puja* (worship) and conduct life cycle rituals at the temple, such as the *mundan* or tonsure ceremony, exorcism has a prominent place in their daily ritual programme, as I demonstrated in chapter 4. During exorcism, however, priests play a sober and largely impersonal role. Unlike *bhagat*s or healers, they never get possessed by deities or by helpful supernaturals; neither do they attempt directly to expel malevolent spirits from those who are afflicted. This specific task is undertaken only by healers themselves. In terms of the distinctions between priests and healers delineated above, this is not only understandable but also, perhaps, to be expected. And it is these distinctions in particular which I now explore in more detail. In order to examine the different religious functions of the priest and the healer in greater depth (as well as the ways in which they overlap), I focus first upon the work of one senior functionary in Mehndipur – the priest Ramjilal whom the reader encountered earlier (see chapters 3 and 4).

Ramjilal: a temple functionary

Ramjilal Puri, the brother of the present *mahant* at Balaji *mandir*, spends most of his time in Udaipur, a small village three kilometres west of Mehndipur. This is where his home is located. Although he has tasks to perform at the main healing shrine – he is partly responsible both for the management of the actual temple itself and for the enormous sums of money donated there, for example – most of his spiritual duties are conducted in Udaipur. Many of those who journey to the pilgrimage centre visit him at his home where the daily consultations, which I attended on over twenty separate occasions, are held. These commence at nine or ten o'clock in the morning and last for two or three hours. On average, approximately ten pilgrims consult him each day, though on some days only one or two individuals walk or take a cycle-rickshaw to Udaipur. However, during periods when festivals are held, particularly the Holi and Dashahara *mela*s, Ramjilal informed me that these numbers increase greatly, and that on such occasions he may see a hundred or more pilgrims daily. Thus, when festivals take place, he said that it is necessary to extend the hours of consultation from two or three to five or six. The priest also stated that he must work in the afternoons as well as in the mornings at such times.

Those who come to see him are given instructions and information about such matters as ritual offerings (especially Darkhast and Arji), when and how often they are to be made, and the food restrictions to be observed by patients. Pilgrims also come to receive special mantras or sacred verses, including *japa*s, *kirtan*s and *path*s, which the relatives of the afflicted are typically told to recite on behalf of the sick. But, as mentioned in chapter 1, the advice provided by priests – and, in this respect, Ramjilal is no exception – tends to be mundane. At the same time, it must be stressed that Ramjilal is not merely an ordinary temple functionary. A number of other senior Brahmans at Balaji *mandir* equally provide consultations, including Ramsvarup, Naresh and Ramji Gosvami, the brother, half-brother and brother-in-law of Ramjilal respectively. Even Kishor Puri, the chief priest, is sometimes available for this purpose. Ramjilal, however, is different from most of these in that a number of pilgrims believe he is endowed with special supernatural qualities (*siddhi*s), though Ramjilal himself claims to be a *shastri* (i.e. one who gives advice or instruction about religious or ritual practice). And the popularity

Figure 4. Ramjilal Puri at the family shrine in Udaipur

Figure 5. Distribution of *savamani* at a *dharmshala* in Mehndipur

Figure 6. The healer Bhagatji outside his private *dharmshala* (with adjoining personal shrine)

he enjoys is undoubtedly related to the fact that he not only has in-depth knowledge of ritual procedure or practice but also because he is thought to have superhuman qualities. With regard to the latter, however, it is important to emphasise that Ramjilal never actually attempts to cure the afflicted. Rather, the magical skills he is considered to display are utilised in the sphere of diagnostics. These skills, coupled with his ability to impart ritual knowledge effectively, are clearly demonstrated in the consultations he holds.

If one focuses upon the way that he conducts himself during interaction with patients, this is immediately evident. The events described below, as well as the dialogues that are provided, are taken from notes and tape recordings of consultations held on one particular morning in January 1993. They show that Ramjilal is

Figure 7. Bhagatji (left, rear) and his medium (right, facing) amongst pilgrims during a séance

frequently sought out by pilgrims both because of his knowledge and understanding of ritual practice and also because of his special diagnostic expertise. The material is presented in the dramatic form in which it was originally recorded.

Ramjilal enters into the family shrine located in one of the lower rooms of his home. Meanwhile, a small group of pilgrims gather in the open courtyard. After praying and meditating for fifteen minutes, the priest emerges and sits on a small mat in the warm sunlight. (He then motions my research assistant and myself to sit beside him.) The first patient approaches Ramjilal. She is accompanied by her father. When both are seated a few feet away from the priest, the young woman begins to rock slowly on her haunches. Her eyes are only half open, and the heavy lids occasionally flicker.[2]

PATIENT'S FATHER: Oh Maharaj, please look at my daughter, and tell me what this affliction (*sankat*) is.

RAMJILAL: What is the nature of the sickness (*bimari*)? What illness does she have?

PATIENT'S FATHER: She suffers from fever (*bukhar*), headache (*sir dard*) and insomnia (*anidra*). She wanders away from the home and during her menses (*rajodharm*) becomes extremely unwell.

120

The priest listens carefully. He remains quiet for a few moments, silently studying the patient. Babu, his assistant, lights a *bidi* (leaf cigarette) for him. Before beginning to smoke it, however, the priest responds.

RAMJILAL: Your daughter is possessed by a Masan, the spirit of the graveyard. This is because of sorcery (*cauki*). Someone has put something into her food. Does she have any other symptoms (*lakshan*)?

PATIENT'S FATHER: Yes. Although her periods are heavy (*bhari*) sometimes they are irregular (*aniyamit*). And when she urinates, she experiences a burning sensation (*jalan*). She also stays in the toilet for excessive lengths of time.

RAMJILAL: These things show what I have said is true (*sac*). It is confirmation (*pramanikaran*). All these troubles are caused by an Aghor Masan, a spirit that is controlled by a *tantrik*. I will give you a mantra.

The man lowers his head.[3] He then places ten rupees under the mat upon which Ramjilal is sitting. Babu is instructed to give him a Bhairava mantra.

As the Brahman assistant leads the patient and her father to one corner of the courtyard, another pilgrim, a middle-aged man from Gwalior in Madhya Pradesh, comes forward.

PATIENT: Baba, I am possessed by my brother's ghost (*pret*). He says that as soon as a shrine (*sthan*) is made for him, I will be well again.

RAMJILAL: If this is the case, a *sthan* shall be prepared for him. He will receive a place. But your brother is fettered by an evil spirit (*bhut*). He must be freed from it. He needs to be liberated. It can be achieved this very day. To do this, offer Darkhast (a small food oblation) and ask Balaji to release him from the *bhut*. Ask Balaji to take your brother into his court (*darbar*). There he will dwell and find release (*mukti*). Now, the cost of the *sthan* will be approximately 100/150 rupees (£2.50/3.00). If you wish you may give the money this morning, and we will make the shrine today.

The patient thanks Ramjilal and is instructed to wait until the other pilgrims have departed. He leaves a small donation, touches the feet of the priest[4] and moves to one side.

121

The next patient brought before Ramjilal is a 27-year-old man. Both his wrists and ankles are chained.[5] The patient is accompanied by his mother. Ramjilal motions the sick man to sit down and, turning to his mother, asks if there has been any improvement in his condition.

PATIENT: (with pride and elation) Maharaj-ji, I am almost completely well. I am much better than before. Please tell me when I will gain full relief (*pura aram*).

RAMJILAL: You say that you are much better. But why are you still shackled with these chains? Why do you feel angry? And why do you still beat people?

PATIENT: The anger has gone. But I still have headaches (*sir dard*) and am always very hungry.

RAMJILAL: (addressing the patient's mother) If he is constantly hungry and eats too much, give rice to Pretraj. Your son, however, must consume part of the food offering (*bhog*). This will diminish his desire to eat continuously, and his appetite shall be brought under control. The feeling of hunger will be reduced.[6] When he is eating the *bhog*, ask Pretraj to remove the affliction (*sankat*).

PATIENT'S MOTHER: (with a tone of desperation in her voice) Oh Maharaj! Will this constant hunger be reduced?

RAMJILAL: (confidently) Just as every pilgrim (*yatri*) receives the blessing of the Lord (Baba) by consuming holy water (*jal*) and sacred ash (*bhabhut*), in the same manner your son will gain relief (*aram*) by eating the *bhog* offered to the deity. Within twenty-to-twenty-five days he will be completely well. However, you must also offer Darkhast on Tuesdays and Saturdays. If you follow these instructions (*adesh*), your son will gain full recovery.

Before the patient's mother has time to ask another question, a woman who is sitting close by suddenly rises to her feet and begins to wail loudly. This continues for a few moments. The female carer accompanying the sick woman stands up and tries to silence her. But she fails.

RAMJILAL: (raising his voice) What do you want? Speak!
WOMAN: Release (*mukti*), Baba. I want release.
RAMJILAL: (addressing the spirit) Who are you? Are you alone?
WOMAN: I am a Cudail.[7] No other spirit is with me.

The woman then starts to cry. Ramjilal asks her to cease weeping. After one or two minutes she becomes silent.

RAMJILAL: Tell me who you are? What is your name? Speak! Are you happy that this woman is in distress (*dukh*)?

The woman does not reply and soon begins to weep once more. After a short while, however, she suddenly starts laughing hysterically.

RAMJILAL: (resolutely) We people will pray to Baba, and he will remove you from this body.

The priest calls to his assistant and tells him to take the woman and her companion to the far corner of the courtyard, where the one who is possessed can cause least disturbance. Babu is also told to instruct them about how and when they must take part in the main temple rituals.

As they are escorted from the assembly, the mother of the young man in shackles also moves to one side. A woman in her early twenties next comes forward. She is guided to a place in front of Ramjilal by her father. Before sitting on the ground beside her, he stretches out his hand and touches the feet of the priest. In response, the latter pats the patient's father gently on the head.

PATIENT'S FATHER: Baba we first came to see you three days ago.
RAMJILAL: That is of no consequence! How is she now?
PATIENT'S FATHER: The girl doesn't speak or cry; neither does she go to the temple from the *dharmshala*.
RAMJILAL: (pondering) H'm. (Rhetorically) What should we do? Tell me, how does she sleep at night?
PATIENT'S FATHER: She sleeps well.
RAMJILAL: What about eating? How is her appetite?
PATIENT'S FATHER: Her appetite is also fine.
RAMJILAL: Any uneasiness (*becaini*)?
PATIENT'S FATHER: No.
RAMJILAL: ... a feeling of heaviness in the head (*sir me bharipan*)?
PATIENT'S FATHER: No.
RAMJILAL: In her actions is she careless or senseless (*hosh-havas kho baithi hai*)?

The young woman's father once more replies in the negative. The priest turns to the patient and, leaning forward, looks into her eyes. The patient, however, remains motionless.

RAMJILAL: (decisively) There is no need to offer Arji (a large food oblation). But some avoidances (*parhez*) must be observed in the home. Babu will tell you about these. Soon your daughter will enter into trance (*peshi*). It will come in the temple. Don't worry. The problem is not so great. She is possessed by a *pitri*. This is the cause of the affliction (*sankat*). Offer Darkhast to Balaji. After this, your daughter must sit facing the image (*murti*) of Baba. *Peshi* then will come.

Ramjilal calls his assistant and tells him to inform the young woman's father about practices to be observed and foods to be avoided by the patient. Following this, the man once more touches the feet of the priest and places five rupee coins on the ground. He and his daughter are then led a few yards away from the congregation.

The last two individuals requiring attention are now gestured to come forward. With the exception of the patient from Gwalior, those who had spoken earlier with Ramjilal depart. One of the two individuals needing help from the priest is a young man in his early twenties. He is with his mother. The other individual is approximately forty years of age and is accompanied by his sister and nephew. The mother of the former patient speaks first.

PATIENT'S MOTHER: Maharaj, my son has almost recovered, but he still laughs too much.

RAMJILAL: What improvement is there?

PATIENT'S MOTHER: By your grace he is much better.

RAMJILAL: If he continues to laugh for unexplained reasons, it is because he is in trance. In *peshi* he will say how he became afflicted and why. He will tell everything in trance. (Offering encouragement) He looks much better. Is he still incontinent? Does he not defecate or urinate in his clothes now?

PATIENT'S MOTHER: No Maharaj. Earlier this was a big worry.

RAMJILAL: This problem will remain only until the Holi festival. After the festival, he will be completely well. Then you can return to your home.

PATIENT'S MOTHER: We have lived in Mehndipur for one year. But we will stay until Holi is over. Before coming here we went to many doctors and hospitals. No good came of this, though it cost a great deal of money. By the grace of Baba, my son has greatly improved. I am much calmer now.

RAMJILAL: Everything will be alright.

PATIENT'S MOTHER: Baba, previously you told us to offer *bhog* to Pretraj in the morning. But at the moment it is too cold to do this.

RAMJILAL: If it is not possible to do this in the morning, you may do it in the afternoon. However, you must remember that it is first necessary to bathe and change your clothes. You should also offer *bhog* to Bhangivara.

The woman lowers her head, leaves two rupees and departs with her son. Babu is now free, and Ramjilal tells him to speak with the man who wishes to have a small shrine constructed for his deceased brother. The two men move a few yards away to discuss the matter. The last patient, who has travelled from Allahabad in Uttar Pradesh, now addresses the priest.

MAN: Maharaj, there are problems (*pareshaniya*) in my business.

RAMJILAL: What kind of problems are there? Are there just obstacles or is the business completely ruined?

MAN: Only obstacles.

RAMJILAL: (after pondering for a few moments) Whatever you have – a shop or a farm – take black mustard seeds (*rai*) and burn them on your property. The smoke from them must also be taken into the home. The problems then will go.

The man thanks the priest, offers a donation of ten rupees and departs with his kinsfolk.

Now, one noteworthy feature of the above consultations is the honour or reverence accorded to Ramjilal by those who go to visit him. It is beyond doubt that the priest is greatly revered and esteemed by his clients, not least from the terms they use to address him, terms such as Maharaj ('great lord') and Baba ('exalted one'). The very fact that these vocative terms are used, not to mention the frequency with which they are uttered, shows that he is highly respected by pilgrims. Yet, in a large measure, it is also evident that he is honoured in this way simply because of the position he occupies in the priestly hierarchy, because of his ascribed status. This is clear because all the other senior Brahmans at Balaji temple are treated and addressed by pilgrims in a largely similar manner.

However, as indicated earlier, Ramjilal is different from most of these in that some pilgrims believe that he possesses extraordinary, supernatural qualities (*siddhi*s). This is precisely why he is considered to be particularly adept in the sphere of diagnostics and an important reason why many pilgrims go to visit him. Indeed, when he is 'silently studying' the patient or 'peering' into the client's eyes, it is evident to his audience that his magical skills are being used. A number of pilgrims in fact informed me that it is by means of these extraordinary skills that he is able to determine which malevolent force or agent is at the root of their affliction. And, in part, it is also because he is thought to have this particular expertise that the advice and instructions he gives are viewed by patients with a profound seriousness.

With regard to the diagnostic work Ramjilal carries out, it is equally clear, as I have further indicated, that there is a degree of overlap between priestly religious functions, on the one hand, and those of healers, on the other hand. For the diagnostic work undertaken by Ramjilal (and other Mehndipur priests) is not unlike that of healers. Nonetheless, distinctions between the practices of these different religious specialists are particularly striking. Not only does Ramjilal refrain from exorcising malevolent spirits during consultations, as well as refrain from becoming possessed by any kind of benevolent *dut* or helpful deity, but he also generally displays a resistance to engage evil spirits in dialogue – the very practices that are prominent in, indeed the hallmark of, the healer's work. Interestingly, there is, however, an occasion during the consultation process outlined above when Ramjilal almost appears to be drawn into the kind of dialogue with spirits one encounters in a healer's séance. It will be recalled that this occurs when the woman possessed by a Cudail spirit starts to disrupt or disturb the consultation process. Yet dialogue with the spirit is not only promptly curtailed by Ramjilal; but he actually instructs his assistant Babu to have the possessed woman physically removed from the company of pilgrims gathered at his home.

The absence or suppression of dialogue with spirits here is both conspicuous and stands in sharp contrast to the work of *bhagat*s in Mehndipur. Indeed, the ability of the latter to cure those who have been harmed by malevolent supernaturals is considered to be critically dependent on negotiation or dialogue with the agents of affliction themselves; and it is these specialists as well as their practices to which I now turn.

Mehndipur healers

In Mehndipur, as throughout the whole region of Rajasthan, it is
believed there are essentially two types of person who cure the sick
by means of magical or mystical agency: one who possesses innate
supernatural qualities, and one who acquires or develops these
later in life. The first variety, however, is thought to be relatively
rare. This individual is considered to have the ability to heal by
being born with exceptional, extraordinary powers. The second is
held to acquire similar attributes in a number of different ways.
Thus, according to healers as well as their clients whom
I interviewed in Mehndipur, a healer may perform *sadhana* (ritual
practices or methods) to develop special powers; he may gain them
after being suddenly and inexplicably possessed by a deity; or he
may acquire them after miraculously recovering from illness caused
by an evil spirit, by sorcery, or by some other kind of malevolent
force. At the same time, it is said that it is possible for an individual
who is born with the gift of healing to increase his *siddhi*s in any of
the above mentioned ways and that an individual who becomes an
adept in the art of curing through possession may also elect to
expand his ability by doing *sadhana*.

One common form of *sadhana* that is frequently undertaken
involves lengthy recitals of mantras (magical formulae or incantations). For example, a sacred phrase or sentence, or perhaps a single
word, such as *Om*,[8] may be used. In order to gain a degree of power,
it is said that an individual might be required to utter a particular
mantra or sacred verse for twelve or more hours a day, perhaps for a
period of four consecutive weeks or even longer. My informants
told me that the practice itself is usually supervised by a holy man
(guru), a person who may also pass on magical skills to the disciple
(*shishya*). Moreover, it is believed that this practice often needs to
be repeated, though using different mantras, for many years to gain
sufficient 'mastery' of them, and that it is only when the practitioner
has become proficient in using them that he can hope to be able to
cure the sick or perform other miraculous works. Indeed, it should
be pointed out that, even after acquiring the power to heal, many
curers stressed that the adept must continue performing *sadhana* to
ensure that his magical skills remain effective. One occasionally
hears that curers in north India (though not in Mehndipur itself)
actually disparage other healers, alleging that they no longer
practise sadhana as regularly as themselves; consequently, the latter
may be said to be weaker or inferior. To some extent, this kind of

criticism is perhaps linked to competition that may sometimes emerge between practitioners. Nonetheless, it clearly shows that the importance attached to *sadhana* is widespread.

Performing it, however, is thought to be difficult. This is because it is typically accompanied by austerities and demands considerable perseverance. Indeed, many healers at the pilgrimage centre told me that they gained occult skills only after a long, arduous period of time. But after an individual engaging in this type of ritual practice achieves his goal, it is widely held that he may use his mantras to summon helpful supernaturals, supernaturals that he can call upon to carry out numerous tasks, which not only include healing the sick, but also finding buried treasure, lost property or a missing person, foretelling the future and so on. Healers in Mehndipur make such claims regarding *dut*s, the supernaturals that are often said to serve a particular deity, especially the god Balaji, but which can be summoned to help them. Interestingly, although it is believed that these benevolent spirits can be called upon by one who has acquired magical powers through *sadhana*, in Mehndipur many practitioners who become possessed by *dut*s commonly testify to being previously afflicted by a *bhut*, a malevolent spirit. With reference to one female medium, this is discussed in more detail below. But before touching upon it further, I introduce the famous Mehndipur healer whom she assists, a charismatic individual whose specialist practices differ significantly from those of Ramjilal and other priests.

Bhagatji: a curer and his medium

Bhagatji, as this healer is respectfully known to his clients, is one of those rare individuals who claimed to possess supernatural powers since birth. He informed me that his exceptional qualities first became manifest when he was very young. Thus, even at the age of seven, he stated that he would often point a finger at an unknown person in the street, declaring that he or she was troubled by a spirit, afflicted by sorcery, or was suffering from some other type of mystical ailment. According to the healer, this not only astonished every member of his household, but the neighbours and many others marvelled at him too, since whatever he proclaimed was always found to be true. When he was nine years old his grandfather (*dadaji*), who was also said to have a reputation for healing, decided to transfer his magical skills to the boy. This was achieved by the 'laying on' of hands. The old man placed his outstretched palms upon the boy's head and uttered a special blessing. From that time onwards, the latter's supernatural powers greatly increased, and he became well known in many parts of Hapur, the city in Uttar Pradesh where he was (and presently still is) living. The *bhagat* claimed that he cured all kinds of people from many types of illness and disease. In addition, he said that he often used to punish *tantriks*, employing occult techniques to injure them because of the harm, misery and grief that they had caused his clients. He told me that he tortured those who practised sorcery until he reached the age of twenty-eight, and that this suddenly stopped because he received a revelation from Hanuman, warning of the hidden karmic dangers that it involved.

According to the *bhagat*, the revelation took place in 1975 when the healer, who is a Kshatriya by caste, journeyed to Mehndipur for the first time. He visited the main shrine in the village only to take *darshan*. However, when he entered the temple, he heard a voice. Balaji told him that, by attacking sorcerers, he was actually accumulating spiritual demerit (*ashubh karma*). The healer thus made a vow to the deity, stating that he would do this no more. He also devoted himself to Hanuman and promised to use his special talents only as instruments in the service of the god. By offering them in this way, the powers that he possessed were further enlarged. Now, following this mystical experience, the *bhagat* returned to Hapur where he continued practising as a healer for another thirteen years, and, although he periodically journeyed to Mehndipur, he never attempted to cure anyone at the pilgrimage centre. But this was to change in 1988, the year in which he claimed to receive a second revelation from Balaji. The *bhagat* said that he was instructed by the god to establish a *darbar* (court) in Mehndipur, and that he obeyed the command immediately, promising Hanuman that for the remainder of his life he would conduct séances in the village for ten days every month.

Nowadays, the *bhagat* journeys to Mehndipur on the twentieth day of every calendar month. During the *darbars* that he holds, however, he never actually becomes possessed by supernaturals himself. He enters into dialogue with both benevolent and malevolent spirits through his medium. He equally communicates with *bhut*s and *pret*s as well as with *pitri devata*s through those who are afflicted. The female medium who assists the *bhagat* becomes possessed voluntarily; that is to say, she is completely in control of the seizures that she experiences. Her role in the *darbar* is a significant one. Some mention should thus be made of how she became involved.

The medium is a Shrivastava Brahman by caste who entered the healing profession shortly after recovering from supernatural illness.[9] She informed me that she became sick a number of years earlier when her husband was killed in a tragic accident. Because he had an untimely death (*akal mrityu*), she stated that he could not get *mukti*. He became a malevolent *pret* and entered into the body of his wife. But when the woman came to Mehndipur, she claimed that she was miraculously cured by Balaji, and that her husband's ghost was liberated. A short while after this she met the *bhagat* and started to assist him during séances. The woman commented that she was able to do this because, after regaining her health, she became possessed by a *dut*, a common occurrence in Mehndipur, as I have indicated. Indeed, as mentioned in chapter 1 and in chapter 4, it is believed that once a person has been cured at Balaji temple, Balaji himself usually sends a benevolent spirit to guard the individual against further attacks from *bhut-pret*. The *dut* that performs the task is often said to be a reformed demon or ghost which has become a servant of the deity; and a person who becomes voluntarily possessed by it is thought to be able to call upon the spirit whenever he or she wishes, though pilgrims, priests and healers stress that it can only be invoked for beneficial purposes, never to cause harm to someone. The medium who helps the *bhagat*, in fact, often becomes possessed, not by one, but by a number of *dut*s (as do many other healers in Mehndipur). And in the *bhagat*'s *darbar*, it is largely through her mediumship that malevolent spirits are captured and brought into the 'court'. However, while she provides valuable help to the *bhagat*, it is the latter individual who cures the sick. I illustrate the way that he does this now, drawing upon the notes as well as tape-recorded dialogues I made during one particular séance.

It is four-thirty in the afternoon. Fifteen women and ten men assemble in the room of the *dharmshala* or lodging hall where the *darbar* is about to begin. The medium is sitting quietly next to a picture of Balaji, which is tacked to the open door of a small cupboard. After a few minutes the *bhagat* enters, lights a small lamp (*diya*) and an incense stick (*agarbatti*) and places them on a shelf inside the cupboard. It is understood that this has now become a temporary shrine. The *bhagat* also takes a *mala* or garland of marigolds and fastens it to the picture of the monkey god. He then begins to sing a hymn (*bhajan*), and a number of the women gathered in the *dharmshala* immediately start to trance. Some of them enter into a physically intense form of *peshi* or trance. The rest of the congregation begin singing and clapping as well. A short time later, Gomati, a 35-year-old woman from Jhansi in Uttar Pradesh, moves towards the *bhagat* who is presently sitting on a mat on the floor. (The healer is less than three feet away from the mat which he has allowed my research assistant and myself to use.) Cataru, her husband, is also sitting on the floor with other members of the assembly.

GOMATI: (pointing to her husband) Make him sit in the court (*darbar*). I want nothing else. Bring Cataru into the court.

A number of those who are gathered together begin to laugh.[10]

BHAGAT: To whom do you refer? Will Cataru sit in the *darbar*?
GOMATI: Yes. He must sit in Balaji's court.
BHAGAT: What boon (*varadan*) do you want? Speak!

Gomati points to a picture of Lord Shiva, which is hanging on the wall close to the shrine.

GOMATI: I don't want his food.
BHAGAT: You tell me your name.
GOMATI: My name is Dharmanand. I am Dharmanand. (Pointing to Cataru once more) He is my son.
BHAGAT: (affirmatively) He is.
GOMATI: I am his *pitri*. But I can do no righteous (*dharmparayan*) work. I am fettered (*bandhan*) by an evil force (*sankat*). Please, free me from it.
BHAGAT: That's enough! Now, you will trouble him no longer. You will stop harming this woman too.

Gomati mumbles something to herself, and the *bhagat* scolds her. He forbids her to talk unless specifically addressed.

BHAGAT: Listen! You will cease troubling Cataru.
GOMATI: (defiantly) Cataru is not my son. (Addressing the *bhagat*) And, as for you, I will take you with me.

The *bhagat* laughs.[11] He stands up. His face is now stern.

BHAGAT: Okay. You take me!

The woman's body starts to shake as violently as it had done when the *darbar* began. One or two minutes later the *bhagat* turns to the medium, who is still seated close to the shrine, and tells her to cut off (*katna*) the *sankat* or evil force afflicting the patient. Following the *bhagat*'s instruction, the medium begins to beat herself on the upper portion of the chest as well as to inhale and exhale rapidly. Moments later she enters into trance, a state of dissociation also known as *peshi*. The spirit that enters her body, however, is a *dut*, a helpful supernatural by which she is held to become voluntarily possessed through the inducement of trance. While she is being seized by the *dut*, the *bhagat* utters a mantra. He then turns to the wife of Cataru and blows the spell onto her. This has a dramatic effect, for the patient falls to the ground. When she collapses, the *bhagat* calls out: *Bol sacce, darbar ki jay* ('Speak the truth: victory to the court'); *Kali Mata ki jay* ('Victory to the Mother Goddess'); *Shankar Bhagvan ki jay* ('Victory to Lord Shiva'); *Vishnu Bhagvan ki jay* ('Victory to Lord Vishnu'); *Balaji Maharaj ki jay* ('Victory to Lord Balaji'); *Bhairava Baba ki jay* ('Victory to Lord Bhairava'); *Pretraj ki jay* ('Victory to the Lord of ghosts').

The medium's body now becomes still. Her eyes, which earlier had been closed, suddenly open. She looks slowly around the room until her gaze falls upon Cataru and his wife. The medium gestures them to approach. Cataru picks up his wife and brings her before the medium. Both of them are told by the healer to kneel down. When their heads touch the floor, the medium beats each in turn on the back. Shortly afterwards, the female patient is head-butted by the medium and her hair is also pulled in an extremely savage manner. The *bhagat* then addresses the *dut* that is believed to be possessing the medium.

BHAGAT: Release their ancestor spirit from the *sankat* and bring the *pitri* also into the court.

Following this command, the malevolent spirit, which as it transpires is supposedly controlling the *pitri devata*, receives a caution.

BHAGAT: (vehemently) *Bhut* look. If you are not obedient, you will be beaten!

Before freeing the ancestor from the clutches of the evil spirit, the *dut* brings the *bhut* into the *darbar*, and all those gathered in the *dharmshala* are told by the healer that it will now be dealt with in the court. In order to do this, the *bhut* is transferred from the patient's to the medium's body.[12]

MEDIUM: (wailing loudly) Oh! Release me. Why have you caught me?

The *bhagat* takes sacred ash (*bhabhut*) from the shrine and draws a line (*rekha*) around the medium's neck with them. According to the *bhagat*, this not only traps the spirit, but it also prevents it from escaping. It is thus said to remain in this fettered state until the *bhagat* decides to free it.

BHAGAT: Tell me what you want?
MEDIUM: Don't beat me. I will go.
BHAGAT: Where will you go?
MEDIUM: Release me. I will stay in Balaji's temple.
BHAGAT: Okay. Now, promise that you will stay there.
MEDIUM: I promise.
BHAGAT: Say it again. I promise ...
MEDIUM: I promise ...
BHAGAT: to stay in the temple of Balaji.
MEDIUM: to stay in the temple of Balaji.
BHAGAT: Say, victory to Balaji.
MEDIUM: Victory to Balaji.
BHAGAT: Victory to Bhairava.
MEDIUM: Victory to Bhairava.
BHAGAT: Victory to Pretraj.
MEDIUM: Victory to Pretraj.[13]
BHAGAT: Speak the truth: victory to the court.
MEDIUM: Victory to the court.

The *bhagat* next instructs the medium's *dut* to bring the *pitri devata* into the court. This also enters the body of the medium. Before communicating with it, the *bhagat* turns to the husband of the sick woman and enquires about the patient's name. He is told that she is called Gomati.

BHAGAT: (addressing the ancestor spirit) This is Cataru and this is Gomati.

The *bhagat* motions them to bow their heads at the feet of the medium. Both prostrate themselves.

BHAGAT: You are their *pitri*. Say, Cataru is my son.
MEDIUM: Cataru is my son.
BHAGAT: Gomati is my daughter.
MEDIUM: Gomati is my daughter.
BHAGAT: I promise ...
MEDIUM: I promise ...
BHAGAT: that I will protect my children.
MEDIUM: that I will protect my children.

After the *pitri devata* is liberated (the *bhagat*, in fact, informs the audience that this has taken place and that the spirit which caused it to act malevolently has gone to dwell in Balaji's temple), and it agrees to stop troubling the patient and her husband, those who are present in the *dharmshala* begin singing another *bhajan*. While they are singing, a 21 year old woman starts running from one side of the room to the other. This behaviour continues for a number of minutes until she becomes breathless. The young exhausted woman then falls at the feet of the *bhagat*.

WOMAN: Baba, I will go. Release me, Baba. I will go back.
BHAGAT: Okay! (in a commanding tone) You will leave this girl. But why did you enter her body? She did not call you. (Pause) Who are you? Where are you from? Who sent you? Tell me everything.
WOMAN: I will tell you everything, Baba. I will tell all. Release me, Baba.
BHAGAT: I will let you go. But first tell everyone present who you are, who sent you, and from where you have come.
WOMAN: My caste (*jati*) is Pathan.[14] I am a Pathan. My *mazar* (Muslim tomb) is in Mahun. That is the place where I have come from, Baba. My master (*malik*) has sent me. All this is his work. He is very powerful (*shaktishali*), and he knows everything about magic and the occult (*tantra-mantra*). Baba, I will go. I wish to return to Mahun.
BHAGAT: Are you telling the truth? Do you really want to go?
WOMAN: Yes, Baba. (Defiantly) I will go tomorrow. I have lived with this girl for six months. But I will go tomorrow.
BHAGAT: (firmly) Speak the truth. Will you really leave, or will you stay for another six months? Why will you not go now?
WOMAN: I don't want to stay any longer with this girl, but I will go tomorrow.

The dialogue stops for a short while. The young woman remains at the feet of the *bhagat* and starts to breathe heavily. Her rate of respiration steadily increases. This is sustained for one or two minutes. She then suddenly begins to laugh loudly and also to mutter to herself. Moments later she reiterates her promise to leave.

WOMAN: I have told you. I will go tomorrow. So release me now.
BHAGAT: (after a short pause) If you are sincere and want to leave, say, victory to the true court.
WOMAN: Victory to the true court
BHAGAT: Victory to Lord Balaji.
WOMAN: Victory to Lord Balaji.
BHAGAT: I ...
WOMAN: I ...
BHAGAT: promise by the *Qur'an* ...
WOMAN: promise by the *Qur'an* ...
BHAGAT: that ...
WOMAN: that ...
BHAGAT: I will go tomorrow.
WOMAN: I will go tomorrow.
BHAGAT: I swear by the *Gita* ...
WOMAN: I swear by the *Gita* ...
BHAGAT: that ...
WOMAN: that ...
BHAGAT: I will go.
WOMAN: I will go.
BHAGAT: If I break my promise ...
WOMAN: If I break my promise ...
BHAGAT: I will eat dog shit ...
WOMAN: I will eat dog shit ...
BHAGAT: I will eat pig shit.
WOMAN: I will eat pig shit.
BHAGAT: Okay!

While kneeling at the feet of the *bhagat*, the woman lowers her head to the floor. She raises it a few minutes later, appearing composed. Shortly after she goes to sit amongst the other members of the congregation and joins with them in singing a *bhajan* in praise of the goddess Kali.

When the last verse of the hymn is completed, the *bhagat* turns the cassette recorder on. Loud, pious music fills the room. Those who are seated on the floor continue clapping. Three women are standing, all of whom are shaking and rolling their heads from side to side. One of these is Gomati, the woman from Jhansi. Although the *bhut* that caused her *pitri devata* to act malevolently is said to have been expelled, her behaviour is still unchanged. After the cassette recording has been playing for a short while, Gomati begins to walk around the room, continuing to shake and to roll her head.

GOMATI: (irreverently) Speak the truth: victory to the court.

The *bhagat* switches off the cassette recorder and tells Gomati to bow her head. Then, addressing the possessing spirit,[15] he commands the *bhut* to leave and promise never to return. The woman, however, raises her head high.

GOMATI: (with a distinct air of defiance): You speak too much! (Fearfully) You can destroy me.
BHAGAT: Yes! If you will speak, then think carefully first. Remember.
GOMATI: I will say whatever is in my mind.
BHAGAT: What is in your mind?
GOMATI: There is evil (*pap*) in it.
BHAGAT: Yes. It hasn't gone yet.
GOMATI: (changing the belligerent tone to a repentant one) Lord, forgive me. Show me the true way. Please make me a servant (*sevak*) of yours.

Gomati prostrates herself before the *bhagat* and wraps her arms around his feet.

GOMATI: You provide a place (*sthan*) for me. I want to stay in your court.
BHAGAT: Say, Mother Vaishnavi.
GOMATI: Mother Vaishnavi.
BHAGAT: I promise ...

Suddenly there is a brief pause. Then the woman moves away from the *bhagat* and rushes to the medium, placing her head at the feet of the latter.

GOMATI: (with a pitiful cry) Mother Vaishnavi. Mother Vaishnavi.

The *bhagat*'s face now becomes stern.

BHAGAT: (unyieldingly) I promise . . .
GOMATI: I promise . . .
BHAGAT: that I will stay in the court.
GOMATI: May I go to the court?
BHAGAT: Don't say, 'May I'. You are going!
GOMATI: I will stay in the court.
BHAGAT: Say, Mother Vaishnavi . . .
GOMATI: Mother Vaishnavi . . .
BHAGAT: I have given my promise.
GOMATI: I have given my promise.
BHAGAT: I will not hurt Gomati any more.
GOMATI: I will not hurt Gomati any more.
BHAGAT: I will free her.
GOMATI: I will free her.
BHAGAT: I will consider her now as my own child.
GOMATI: I will consider her now as my own child.
BHAGAT: I will never enter into this child's body again.
GOMATI: I will never enter into this child's body again.
BHAGAT: Victory to Mother Vaishnavi.
GOMATI: Victory to Mother Vaishnavi.

The *bhagat* leads the congregation in singing one more *bhajan*, and the *darbar* ends.

It is immediately evident from the above séance that the practices of the *bhagat* are strikingly different from those of Ramjilal and other *pujari* in Mehndipur. Although the *bhagat* and Ramjilal both utilise their occult powers in the sphere of diagnostics, only the former has the ability (or inclination) to expel malevolent spirits from the body. It is also clear that he differs markedly from the priest in terms of the actual way that he conducts himself during interaction with patients. While the priest is sober and often routine in approach, the *bhagat*, by contrast, is exuberant, passionate and theatrical. Moreover, the latter is never rigid or regimental in dealing with those who are possessed but constantly changes strategy to cater for the particular requirements of the individual. Ramjilal, on the other hand, not only refrains from attempting to cure the sick, but the instructions that he provides regarding ritual practice tend to be merely technical or formulaic in character.

However, while differences such as these are, perhaps, to be expected, these religious specialists are complementary figures.

In Mehndipur I found no conflict between Ramjilal and the *bhagat*; neither did I find any tension or rivalry between other priests and healers. It is true that some temple functionaries at the pilgrimage centre do not actively encourage the sick to approach healers. But I was told by priests that this is because those who are afflicted occasionally claim to have been financially exploited by magico-religious specialists in their home towns and villages; consequently, some pilgrims were said to be suspicious of healers and would perhaps be offended if advised to seek one out. In spite of this, however, priests at the pilgrimage centre view curers positively, as do many pilgrims. This is because they are held to play a significant role in enabling patients to recover from demonic illness. Healers are not only said to be particularly adept at negotiating with malevolent supernaturals but also at persuading them to cease troubling those upon whom they have preyed, a talent possessed by healers which priests themselves greatly applaud. Ramjilal and a number of other senior Brahmans, in fact, often speak highly of certain practitioners operating in Mehndipur.

Just as priests positively appraise healers in the village, so too curers greatly respect the work of temple functionaries and emphasise the importance and value of temple rituals. This itself is apparent from the fact that exorcism in *dharmshala*s usually commences when the major ceremonies at Balaji *mandir* have terminated. Healers hold *darbar*s in the morning, in the afternoon and in the evening; but they often told me that séances should not begin until the major rituals at the temple are completed. Curers themselves also exhort patients to participate in ceremonies conducted by priests and frequently stress that this is crucial for gaining recovery from ill-health and disease. Furthermore, there are times when temple *pujari* are actually called upon by healers to perform a special *havan* (fire ritual). This is usually held in a *dharmshala* in order to purify (*shuddh karna*) a patient, which, in some cases, is thought to help the sick person become free from *sankat*. The priest is summoned because *havan* is often conducted in Sanskrit and requires specialist knowledge and technical expertise. However, although a priest is sometimes required by a healer in order to carry out a ritual on behalf of a patient, the converse does not apply: in the rituals performed at the temple the priest has no need of assistance from the healer. There is thus asymmetry here; and this itself is indicative of the hierarchical or ultimate superiority of the priest and the pre-eminence of priestly ritual practice. Indeed, the asymmetry is clearly understood and often explicitly acknowledged in Mehndipur by priests and by healers alike, as both kinds of specialist not only give priority to rituals held at the Balaji shrine but also assert that it would be inappropriate for patients to take part in a healer's séance before first participating in temple ceremonies. Yet it is also important to emphasise the point that within the inferior domain of the healer into which the priest occasionally enters, the latter never makes any attempt to expel malevolent spirits from the sufferer. Indeed, as I have already pointed out, this is a task carried out only by the curer. Thus, in order to exorcise *bhuts* and *prets*, the specialist skills with which the healer is endowed are needed, particularly his ability to negotiate with spirits, an ability the priest does not possess but one that is of vital import in the treatment of *sankat* or spirit malaise. Here, then, the priest must defer to the healer. To be sure, in this particular setting, the mutual interdependence of the priest and the healer is clearly visible. In this context, it is clear that each of them requires or is dependent upon the expertise of the other.

Conclusion

This chapter has examined the different (though overlapping) roles that priests and healers play in Mehndipur; and it has drawn attention to the importance of the work carried out by each of these specialists. I have shown that, while the former practitioners are pre-eminent, the hierarchical relationship between priests and healers is based upon interdependence and complementarity: not only is it clear that there are occasions when the two varieties of religious specialist are critically dependent upon each other (and this itself is acknowledged by priests and by healers); but both of them provide services that are often said by pilgrims to be crucial for sufferers. Indeed, I have demonstrated that, although the priest ensures communion between pilgrim and deity – it is by means of the priest that the pilgrim is able to bring a petition for help or aid to the attention of the deity – it is the *bhagat* or healer who brings divinity directly into relation with the sufferer, the divinity typically manifesting itself through him (or through a spirit medium who may be called upon to assist the healer). By performing these different religious functions, each of these practitioners in Mehndipur complements the other.

CONCLUSION

In India, as in many other societies, supernatural affliction as well as its avoidance, treatment and cure are fundamental religious concerns, concerns that are ignored in much of the literature on Hinduism. Hinduism, in fact, is frequently delineated in terms of profound metaphysical tenets emanating from Vedic scholarship and the interpretation of the Upanishads, which present a picture of a religious system that is highly abstract, philosophical and speculative. With respect to devotional activities, one also finds that scholars often place emphasis upon adherence to the cults of major Sanskritic deities, such as Vishnu and Shiva, or focus on the worship of these deities during festivals as well as at shrines and temples. Important rites of passage tend to be mentioned or discussed in the literature on Hinduism too, including ceremonies concerned with the bestowing of a ritual name upon an infant child or when it undergoes tonsure; ceremonies concerned with the receiving of the sacred thread by a young adult Brahman male; and ceremonies concerned with marriage as well as with death.

However, while all these aspects of religious belief and performance cannot (and should not) be ignored, this book has shown that less well known features of popular Hinduism, characterised by ideas or practices relating, not only to affliction by malevolent supernaturals, but also their expulsion or management during rites of exorcism, equally play a prominent role in the everyday life of Hindus. Indeed, it is these features which Morris Opler persuasively argued over forty years ago are the 'most (prevalent in) the religious activity of the ordinary Hindu' (1958: 553) – an argument that still appears to carry the same force today. The research I carried out in the north Indian pilgrimage village of Mehndipur clearly reveals this, as does similar or related recent research (see, for example, the work of Assayag and Tarabout *et al.*

(1999), as well as the work of Fuller (1992) and the work of Parry (1994)).

It is to be hoped that this book will be seen as a welcome contribution, a phenomenologically oriented contribution that does not merely add to the understanding of key aspects of popular Hinduism, but, critically, one that augments understanding of the ways in which Hindus commonly draw upon or engage dimensions of their faith and culture as a means of making sense of suffering or adversity as well as means of managing, responding to, and even transforming it. To be sure, it is these very dimensions of religious faith and culture, or rather their broader embeddedness in Hindu society and tradition, upon which much attention in this book has focused; and, in terms of the phenomenological approach I have adopted, there are important reasons for this: whether one seeks, for example, to comprehend why certain individuals become the prey of malevolent supernaturals and/or enter into the orbit of exorcist practice, or whether one attempts to ascertain what participants may experience or how they feel during the course of an exorcism in order to assess its therapeutic potential or effectiveness – issues that have been of vital import in this book and ones that are also a major concern particularly in the field of religious anthropology as well as in the field of medical anthropology – I have stressed the centrality of common sense, taken-for-granted cultural and religious understandings, arguing for the need to view these directly in terms of their own authority. Indeed, from the phenomenological standpoint espoused in this volume, it has been argued that privileging the authority of quotidian discourse about supernatural malaise or its treatment means accepting the discourse itself as a social and cultural reality, a reality that in Mehndipur shapes and orients the way pilgrims describe and conceptualise ill-health or cure as well as the way they experience it ontologically. Moreover, I have also argued that placing the accent upon such discourse involves a major break with, or departure from, the theoretical direction taken by many anthropologists or writers who have carried out research on spirit possession and exorcistic healing practice. In much of the anthropological literature on the topic there is a tendency for supernatural affliction and cure to be debated within the confines of Western rationalist or Western psychological paradigms and theories, as this book has shown. And this is problematic or presents a major difficulty; for, although these common ways of accounting for, or speculating about, supernatural malaise may not in themselves be seen as a false or incorrect analytical route, their tendency to undervalue native discourse forces analysis of illness or cure indigenously conceived in supernatural terms into terms far removed from native conceptions and understandings. For this reason approaches that do this have been criticised in this book; and it has advanced the argument as well as attempted to demonstrate that the kind of phenomenology I have used offers an alternative to such approaches, an alternative that neither removes the authority of native discourse nor compromises or undermines the authority of the religious and cultural logic that underpins it. Like Kapferer (1979, 1991, 1997), whose writings have had an enormous influence on the theoretical orientation of this book and on the analysis of the data it presents, I hold that the method of phenomenology offers important advantages precisely because it does not assume an epistemology superior to those whose knowledge it endeavours to reveal or disclose. Indeed, it does not insist on dominating the materials to which it attends but seeks to give them voice, a voice that is subordinated to no other authority except its own. Phenomenology in the sense is clearly unlike the types of approach I have criticised and, as an alternative to them, I hope to have shown that it enables anthropological analysis and investigation of illness or cure supernaturally conceived to be placed on a wholly different footing, one that does not merely attend to indigenous discourse or the native voice but one that ensures that the value or force of that voice is given full recognition.

Appendix 1

TOWARDS DEFINING
A MANTRA

In Sanskrit, the word mantra (from the root *man*, literally, 'think') means 'instrument of thought'. But, although the etymology of the term is clear, no equivalent exists in English that can be substituted for it. As Padoux remarks, it is not only 'difficult to define properly'; it is 'impossible to translate' (1989: 300). This point has also been made by Gonda, whose article on 'The Indian Mantra' is still, perhaps, the most important on the subject (Padoux ibid.). Gonda writes:

> (O)ur modern languages do not possess a single term which might cover what the Indians understood, and often still understand by a mantra. The very diversity of translations in dictionaries and books touching upon 'the sacred word' in India shows us that the term is, in point of fact, untranslatable.
>
> (1963a: 246–47)

Nevertheless, despite the problem of translation as well as the difficulties that arise in attempting to understand its meaning, Gonda and others have provided definitions of the term. These definitions, as Alper notes (1989: 3–5), are extremely heterogeneous in character, though two poles or distinct view-points can be detected, particularly when comparing the approaches of Gonda and Bharati. The former treats definition in a rather loose fashion and tends to apply the term to whatever phenomena are covered by it in a particular sacred text or secondary, related source. Thus, he states that all the Vedic collections of metrical texts or *samhita*s are mantras because they are referred to by this term in the Brahmanas, the prose texts that provide detailed commentary on the employment and ritual use of the Vedic hymns (1963a: 256). Bharati, by contrast, provides a formal definition:

A mantra is a quasi-morpheme or a series of quasi-morphemes, or a series of mixed genuine and quasi-morphemes arranged in conventional patterns, based on codified esoteric traditions, and passed on from one preceptor to one disciple in the course of a prescribed initiation.

(1965: 111)

In terms of north Indian conceptions of a mantra, neither of these view-points could be considered erroneous or particularly inappropriate, as most of my Hindu informants hold that any sacred text is a mantra, whether it emerged in ancient times or in a more recent period; and they equally view the sacred utterance that is passed from guru to disciple during initiation (*diksha*) as a mantra. The informal and formal definitions offered respectively by Gonda and Bharati may thus be combined. Moreover, it should be noted that phonology or sound, which many scholars (e.g. Eliade 1958: 212 ff.; Esnoul 1987: 68–9; Gonda 1963a: 272 and *passim*, 1963b: 38 and *passim*; Gupta 1987: 176–77; Hoens 1979: 93 ff.; Kakar 1982: 172 ff.; Monier-Williams 1925: 128–29; Padoux 1989: 301; Staal 1975: 35–6, 1989: 61; Varenne 1973: 105) consider to be the main feature of a mantra, is also viewed by pilgrims, priests and healers in Mehndipur as being especially characteristic of it. This, then, should also be mentioned in an account of the term. Furthermore, it is necessary to emphasise that definition should include some reference to power or to supernatural efficacy, which sacred utterance is believed to possess. All my informants mentioned this. In fact, in the scholarly literature almost everyone who has commented on mantras has drawn attention to the Indian belief in the power of sacred words, whether they have focused on their use in the past or in the present.

Having identified some of the major facets of a mantra, then, it is possible to give a general or preliminary definition of the term. In accordance with the way it is widely employed or understood in north India today, I use the word to refer to a magical formula, a sacred verse or mystical sound, a hymn or *bhajan*, whether originating in Vedic or post-Vedic times, an incantation, a charm or a spell. This definition, it may be noted, is similar to the one found in contemporary Hindi dictionaries. However, it is important to add that a mantra is an essential component of most rituals too, and in some ceremonies, such as some types of healing rite, it may be the main device or instrument employed. But whether words alone are used or are combined with particular forms of action or display, recitation itself is a ritual performance. Indeed, as Humphrey and Laidlaw have stressed, '(r)eciting a text is a distinct ... ritual act' (1994: 194), a point which other anthropologists (e.g. Leach 1966: 407; Tambiah 1970: 195, 1985: 17–18) have also emphasised regarding the use of magical words.

Appendix 2

MANTRAS USED BY PILGRIMS IN MEHNDIPUR TO GAIN RELIEF FROM SUFFERING AND AFFLICTION

The three Hindi mantras below are dedicated respectively to Hanuman, Bhairava and Pretraj. They are employed by pilgrims for invoking the help of the gods. Priests as well as healers at the pilgrimage centre often instruct patients and/or their carers to recite them. The mantras are believed to provide relief from suffering and to cure every type of illness and disease. The particular text from which I have taken them is known as the *Sri Balaji Path* ('The Sacred Recitals of Lord Balaji') (1990: 7–10), compiled by S. Agrawal *et al*, a text that is widely available in the village. The mantras are given, firstly, in transliteration and, secondly, in translation.

Āratī Śrī Sankaṭ Mocan Kī

1 Oṁ jay Hanumat vīrā, svāmī jay Hanumat vīrā.
2 Sankaṭ mocan svāmī, tum ho raṇdhīrā. Oṁ.
3 Pavan-putra Añjanī-sut, mahimā ati-bhārī.
4 Duḥkha dāridra miṭāo, sankaṭ sab hārī. Oṁ.
5 Bāl samay meṁ tumne ravi ko bhakṣ liyo
6 Devan stuti kīnhīṁ, tab hī chor diyo. Oṁ.
7 Kapi Sugrīva Rāmā sang maitrī karvāī.
8 Bālī Bālī marāy Sugrīva gaddī dilvāī. Oṁ.
9 Jāri Lanka ko, le Siya kī sudhi, vānar harṣaye.
10 Kāraj kaṭhin sudhāre, Raghuvar man bhāye. Oṁ.
11 Śakti lagī Lakṣmana ke bhārī soc bhayo.
12 Lāy sanjīvan būṭī duḥkha sab dūr kiyo. Oṁ.
13 Le pātāl Ahirāvaṇa, jab hi paiṭhi gayo.
14 Tāhi māri prabhu lāye, jay jay kār bhayo. Oṁ.

15 Ghāṭe Mehndipur meṁ śobhit, darśan ati-bhārī.
16 Mangal aur śaniścar melā haiṁ jārī. Oṁ.
17 Śrī Bālājī kī āratī, jo koī nara gāve,
18 Kahat Indra harṣit man vāṁchit phal pāve. Oṁ.

Worship (of Lord Hanuman) for Deliverance from Affliction

1 Victory to brave Hanuman; victory to Lord Hanuman, the brave.
2 Lord, you (give) deliverance from affliction (and) are resolute in battle.
3 You are the son of Pavan (and) Anjani; great is your glory.
4 Please end suffering and poverty, conquer all troubles.
5 In your childhood you devoured the sun
6 (And) then released it when the gods beseeched you.[1]
7 You caused Sugriva (and) Rama to become friends.
8 Bali was killed; Sugriva gained his throne.
9 Lanka was burnt; (and) the monkey (Hanuman) rejoiced (with) news of Siya (Sita).
10 You Hanuman corrected the problem (and) pleased the heart of Raghuvar (Rama's grandfather).
11 Laksmana was very anxious (and) frightened.
12 (But) you brought the Sanjivan herb (a herb containing life-restoring properties); (and) his suffering was removed.
13 When Ahiravana (the ten-headed demon in the form of the snake) took (Rama) to the underworld, you entered (it).
14 You killed him and saved the Lord; victory, victory, you are awesome.
15 In Ghate Mehndipur (there) is radiance; darshan is very great.
16 Fairs are held on Tuesdays and Saturdays.
17 At Balaji's arati, anyone who sings (praises),
18 Indra says obtains happiness and the fruits of (his) action.

Āratī Śrī Bhairavajī Mahārāj Kī

1 Suno jī Bhairava lāṛile kar bintī karūṁ.
2 Kṛpā tumhārī cāhie maiṁ dhyān tumhārā hī dharūṁ.
3 Maiṁ caraṇ chūtā āpke arjī merā sun lījie.

---

1 This and other episodes in the life of Hanuman, which are referred to in the mantra, are said to be recorded in Valmiki's epic, the *Ramayana*.

4 Maiṁ hūṁ matī kā mand merī kuch madad to kījie.
5 Mahimā tumhārī bahut kuch thoṛī sī maiṁ varaṇan karūṁ.
6 　　　　　　　　　　　　　Suno jī Bhairava.
7 Karte savārī svān kī cāroṁ diśā meṁ rajy haiṁ.
8 Jitne bhūt aur pret sabke āp hī sirtāj haim.
9 Hathiyār haiṁ jo āpke, unkā kyā maiṁ varaṇan karūṁ?
10 　　　　　　　　　　　　　Suno jī Bhairava.
11 Bahut sī mahimā tumhārī Mehndipur sarnām hai.
12 Āte jagat ke yātrī, Bajarang kā sthān hai.
13 Śrī Pretrāj Sarkār ke maiṁ śīs caraṇoṁ meṁ dharūṁ.
14 　　　　　　　　　　　　　Suno jī Bhairava.
15 Niśdin tumhāre khel se Mātājī khuś hotī raheṁ.
16 Sir par tumhāre hāth rakh kar āśīrvād raheṁ.
17 Kar joṛ kar bintī karūṁ aru śīs caraṇoṁ meṁ dharūṁ.
18 　　　　　　　　　　　　　Suno jī Bhairava.

The Worship of Lord Bhairava

1 Please listen, Lord Bhairava; (with) affection (and) joined hands I beg you.
2 I need your grace (as) I meditate upon you.
3 I touch your feet; please listen to my request.
4 I am of weak intellect, so please help me a little.
5 Your glory is great; I am able to tell (only) a little of it.
6 　　　　　　　　　　　　Please listen, Lord Bhairava.
7 You ride the dog (and your) kingdom (extends) in the four directions,
8 Having conquered all spirits and ghosts.
9 Those weapons which are yours – of them could I give an account?
10 　　　　　　　　　　　　Please listen, Lord Bhairava.
11 Great is your glory; Mehndipur is celebrated (for it).
12 Pilgrims of the world come (here); it is the place of Bajarang (Hanuman).
13 I bow my head to the feet of Lord Pretraj
14 　　　　　　　　　　　　Please listen, Lord Bhairava.
15 (May) Mataji (the goddess Kali) continually be happy with your sport, (both) night (and) day.
16 Put your hand on (my) head (and may) your blessing ever remain.
17 (With) joined hands, I request you again, (as) I bow to your feet.
18 　　　　　　　　　　　　Please listen, Lord Bhairava.

Āratī Śrī Pretrāj Sarkār Kī

1 Jay Pretrāj kṛpālu merī arj sun lījiye.
2 Maiṁ śaran tumhāre a gayā hūṁ nāth darśan dījiye.
3 Maiṁ karūṁ bintī āpse ab tum dayāmay citt dharo.
4 Caraṇoṁ kā le liyā āsarā prabhu veg se merā dukh haro.
5 Sir par mukuṭ, kar meṁ dhuṣ, gal bīc motiyan māl hai.
6 Jo kare darśan prem se sab kaṭat kinke jāl hai.
7 Jab pahan bastar le khaāg bāī bagal meṁ áhāl hai,
8 Aisā bhayankar rūp jinkā dekh áarpat kāl hai.
9 Ati-prabal sena vikaṭ, yoddhā sang meṁ vikrāl hai.
10 Sab bhūt-pret piśāc bandhe kaid karte hāl haiṁ.
11 Tab rūp dharte vīr kā karte taiyārī calan kī.
12 Sang meṁ laṛāke jvān jinkī thāh nahīṁ balan kī.
13 Tum sab tarah sāmarth ho prabhu sakal sukh ke dhām ho.
14 Duṣṭoṁ ke māran hār ho, bhaktoṁ ke pūraṇ kām ho.
15 Maiṁ hūṁ matī kā mand merī buddhi ko nirmal karo.
16 Ajñān kā andherā ur meṁ jñān kā dīpak dharo.
17 Sab manorath siddh karte jo koī sevā kare.
18 Tandul burā ghṛt, mevā bheṁṭ le āge dhare.
19 Suyaś sun kar āp kā dukhiyā to āye dūr ke.
20 Sab strī aur puruṣ ākar paṛe haiṁ caraṇ hujūr ke.
21 Līlā hai adbhut āpkī, mahimā to aparampār hai.
22 Darbār meṁ āo abhī sarkār meṁ hājir khaṛā.
23 Insāf merā ab karo caraṇoṁ maiṁ ākar gir paṛā.
24 Arjī bamujib de cukā, ab aur is par kījiye.
25 Tatkāl is par hukm likh do faislā kar dījiye.

The Worship of Lord Pretraj

1 Victory to compassionate Pretraj; please listen now to my request.
2 I have sought refuge with you; Lord please give darshan.
3 I entreat you; now out of your compassion pay attention (to it).
4 I take shelter at your feet; swiftly relieve my suffering, Lord.
5 On your head is a crown, in your hand a bow, (and) around your neck a pearl necklace.
6 (For that person) who takes darshan (and) because of your love, you destroy all snares.
7 When you put on armour (and) wear a sword at your left side,
8 (It) is the Jinn's time to fear, (as it) sees such a terrible form.
9 Your very strong warrior army in accompaniment is formidable.

10 You capture (and) imprison all spirits, ghosts (and) pishacas (demons).
11 Then, in customary preparation, you put on the form of a warrior.
12 (And with) the warlike youths in (your) company, the Jinn's strength fails.
13 Lord you are almighty, you are the place of entire happiness.
14 You destroy the wicked (and) fulfil the desires of your devotees.
15 I am of weak intellect; purify my understanding.
16 In the dark heart of ignorance, place the lamp of knowledge.
17 You fulfil all the wishes of anyone who worships you.
18 You take the offering of rice, sugar, ghee and dried fruit.
19 Having heard of your renown, the afflicted come from afar.
20 All women and men, having come, fall at (your) feet, Lord.
21 Your play is wonderful; your glory infinite.
22 Come into the audience chamber; I am present now, standing in your court.
23 Render justice (to) me now; having come (to you), I fall at your feet.
24 Please grant the request and act on the matter now.
25 Please write a proclamation and make the decision immediately.

Appendix 3

MANTRA AND YANTRA

Below are (i) an example of a popular *bija* (seed) mantra and (ii) a *yantra* or magical diagram, which I acquired from a *tantrik* healer who made occasional journeys to Mehndipur from his home in Ajmer city. I was informed by the *tantrik* practitioner that both of these are employed for gaining success in litigation. However, whereas the former is uttered, I was told that the latter is usually written on paper or, preferably, on *bhoj patra* (the bark of the birch tree) and placed inside an amulet (*tabiz*).

Mantra: ॐ ऐ चचे डी ही ।

ॐ वी ये से कलि ।

(Oṁ ai cace ḍī.)

(Oṁ vī ye se kli.)

Yantra:

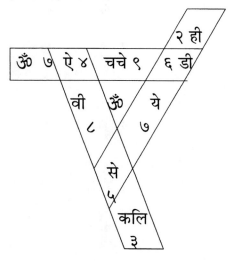

151

Appendix 4

INVENTORY OF SYMPTOMS
AND AILMENTS RECORDED
IN MEHNDIPUR

The indigenous terms below are Hindi, the lingua franca, used by patients, priests and healers at the pilgrimage centre. Symptoms and ailments are listed in terms of three levels of frequency, the frequency of their alleged occurrence. Thus, of those who agreed to be interviewed, more patients claimed (or were said by their accompanying carers) to be suffering from lethargy and weakness, for example, than withdrawn behaviour or infertility, the latter two being the types of complaint that were, respectively, less or the least commonly reported.

Indigenous Terms	*English Terms*
(Most Frequent)	
bhārīpan/sustī aur kamzorī	lethargy and weakness
bhūkh na lagnā	loss of appetite
cakkar	dizziness
circirāpan	irritability
pāgalpan	mental illness/madness
śarīr dard	aches and pains (throughout or in parts of the body)
sir dard	headache
viṣād	melancholy/depression
(Less Frequent)	
akelāpan	withdrawn behaviour
anidrā	insomnia
bukhār	pyrexia
cintā	anxiety
mūrcchā	fainting

smṛti lop	amnesia
tanāv	tension

(Least Frequent)

anupjāūpan/bāṁjhpan	infertility
apilepsi*/mirgī	epilepsy
ati-sakriyatā	hyperactivity
carm kā rog	skin disease
dāabiṭīz*/madhumeh	diabetes
duḥsvapna	nightmares
ekāgrata kī kamī	lack of concentration
galan	muscle wasting disease
garbhāt	miscarriage
gurde kī bīmārī	renal (kidney) disease
hṛday kā rog	heart disease/condition
joṛ-dard/joṛoṁ kā dard	arthritis
kabhī-kabhī andhāpan	intermittent blindness
kensar[1]	cancer
khūn kī kamī	anaemia
khūn kī ulṭī	haematemesis (vomiting blood)
khūn meṁ cīnī kī kamī	hypoglycaemia (low blood sugar)
lakvā	paralysis
madirāpān/madirā pareśānī	drinking/alcohol problem
māhavārī kī bīmārī/rajodharm pareśānī	menstrual disorder/problem
matibhram	hallucinations (auditory and/or visual)
nayan durbaltā	visual impairment
nīnd meṁ calnā	somnambulism
peśāb kī śikāyat	urinary disorder
peṭūpan	excessive eating (gluttony)
pīliyā	jaundice
raktcāp kī bīmārī	blood pressure abnormalities
śravaṇ durbaltā	auditory impairment
svās kā rog	respiratory disease
tapedik/tī bī*	tuberculosis
vazan kam honā	weight loss

---

* These are loan terms from English, which are commonly used in north India due to the impact of Western medicine. A number of other terms listed, while not being loan words, nonetheless appear to have been influenced by Western medicine, e.g. the terms for hypoglycaemia, anaemia and blood pressure abnormalities.

Appendix 5

GENEALOGIES OF PRIESTLY FAMILIES

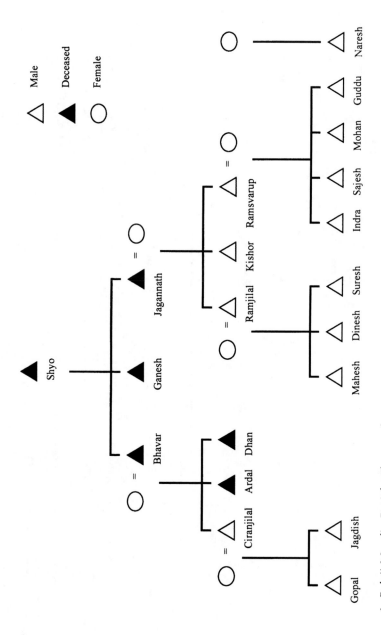

Figure 1. Balaji Mandir: Puri family genealogy

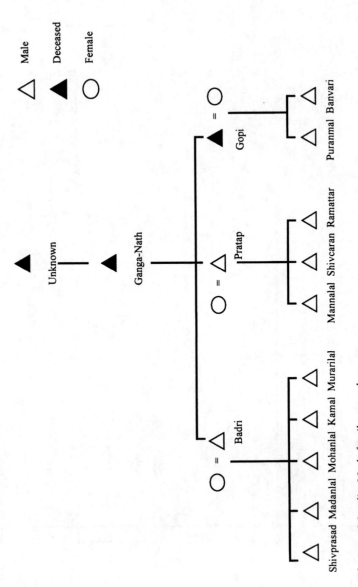

Figure 2. Bhairava Mandir: Nath family genealogy

Appendix 6

TABLES

Table 1. Categories of affliction, gender and marital status

	Male				Female				Grand Total
	Married %	Single %	Widowed/ Divorced* %	Total %	Married %	Single %	Widowed/ Divorced* %	Total %	
Possession by capricious spirits	60 (26.31)	34 (25.95)	1 (33.33)	95 (26.24)	103 (34.21)	24 (40.67)	3 (25)	130 (34.94)	225 (30.65)
Afflicted by sorcery	122 (53.50)	59 (45.03)	1 (33.33)	182 (50.27)	151 (50.16)	27 (45.76)	5 (41.66)	183 (49.19)	365 (49.72)
Possession by pitri devatas	16 (7.01)	8 (6.10)	–	24 (6.62)	21 (6.97)	3 (5.08)	2 (16.66)	26 (6.98)	50 (6.81)
Afflicted by deities	–	1 (0.76)	1 (33.33)	2 (0.55)	–	1 (1.69)	–	1 (0.26)	3 (0.40)
Uncertain of nature of supernatural affliction	1 (0.43)	–	–	1 (0.27)	3 (0.99)	–	1 (8.33)	4 (1.07)	5 (0.68)
Uncertain if affliction has supernatural cause	19 (8.33)	19 (14.50)	–	38 (10.49)	23 (7.64)	4 (6.77)	1 (8.33)	28 (7.52)	66 (8.99)
Affliction without supernatural cause	10 (4.38)	10 (7.63)	–	20 (5.52)	–	–	–	–	20 (2.72)
Total	228 (100)	131 (100)	3 (100)	362 (49.31)	301 (100)	59 (100)	12 (100)	372 (50.68)	734 (100)

*Only two divorced persons were interviewed (one male individual who claimed to be afflicted by a deity and one female individual who stated that she had been harmed by a pitri devata).

Table 2. Education and gender of the 734 patients in Mehndipur*

Age at which Education Terminated/ Level of Academic Achievement	Male	Female	Total
No education/illiterate	12	112	124
4–8 years	12	14	26
9–10 years	29	48	77
11–12 years	10	14	24
13–14 years	61	51	112
15–16 years	92	72	164
17–18 years	50	10	60
19–22 years	4	1	5
Diplomats	1	1	2
Graduates	72	32	104
Post-Graduates	19	11	30
Not Known	0	6	6
Total	362	372	734

*All those who studied from the age of seventeen onwards received (or were still receiving) college education (i.e. 146 [40 per cent] males and 55 [15 per cent] females).

Table 3. Persons invoking sorcery as agency or cause of affliction*

	Married %	Single %	Widowed %	Total %
Attacked directly by known enemy	186 (68.13)	24 (27.90)	5 (83.33)	215 (58.90)
Attacked indirectly or inadvertently	12 (4.39)	43 (50)	1 (16.66)	56 (15.34)
Attacked by unknown (or undisclosed) person	75 (27.47)	19 (22.09)	–	94 (25.75)
Total	273 (100)	86 (100)	6 (100)	365 (100)

*Because there is no difference in the number of men and women claiming to be afflicted by sorcery (182[50 per cent] of the men and 183[49.19 per cent] of the women in the sample invoked this), the figures have not been broken down in terms of gender.

Table 4. States where the 734 patients in Mehndipur were domiciled

State	Town/City	Village	Total
Assam	1	–	1
Bengal	1	–	1
Bihar	3	2	5
Delhi	142	–	142
Haryana	72	46	118
Jammu/Kashmir	2	–	2
Karnataka	2	–	2
Madhya Pradesh	43	32	75
Maharashtra	10	–	10
Orissa	3	–	3
Punjab	29	4	33
Rajasthan	70	38	108
Uttar Pradesh	161	70	231
Miscellaneous			
(Afghanistan)	1	–	1
(Nepal)	–	2	2
Total	542	192	734

GLOSSARY

agarbattī Incense stick; used in worship and for producing a pleasing aroma.

akāl-mr̥tyu Untimely death.

amāvas Last day of the dark half of the lunar month; day set apart for worship of the ancestors.

āratī Clockwise circling of a ritual object (e.g. lamp, incense stick, conch shell) before the image of a deity as an act of worship; performed twice daily: at sunrise and at sunset; also performed at Balaji temple to cure the sick and to expel malevolent spirits from the bodies of the possessed.

Arjī Healing ritual at Balaji temple in which a patient gives a large food offering to the gods; legal term, meaning petition, request or application.

aśuddh Impure, state of impurity.

āyurveda Traditional Hindu medicine/medical practice.

Bābā Term of respect in Hindi, though it also means grandfather (one's father's father); used in Mehndipur synonymously with the word *devatā* (god).

bayān Statement; a legal term; used in the context of exorcism to refer to the confession a spirit is compelled to give.

bhabhūt Sacred ash consumed by, or placed upon the head of, pilgrims; produced from spent incense sticks or burnt food offerings.

bhagat One who is devoted to a god or a goddess (cf. *bhakta*); person possessing healing power bestowed upon him or her by a deity.

Bhagvān God; Divinity in its highest and most supreme, transcendental form.

bhajan Hymn.

bhakta Devotee (of any deity).

bhog Food or incense offered to a deity.

bhoj patra Thin strips of birch bark on which *yantra*s are sometimes drawn.

bhūt-pret Generic term for ghosts or spirits.

bhūtnī Female ghost.

bhūt-pret utārnā Spirit exorcism.

bīja Seed; seed mantra, sacred utterance which is typically untranslatable and which is often both monosyllabic and nasalised (e.g. *Oṁ*).

bīmārī Disease, illness, malady (cf. *rog*).

caukī Sorcery; form of black magic causing illness or disease that progressively worsens until the victim dies.

caurāhā Cross-roads, junction where two or more roads meet; inauspicious place where demons and ghosts often congregate and/or reside.

dān Gift, donation, offering.

darbār Court, assembly; séance.

ḍākaṇ Witch.

ḍākī Wizard (cf. *nāzarū*)

darśan Viewing; both viewing a god or a goddess (resulting in blessings, etc.) and, in turn, being viewed by a deity through the medium of an idol or sacred image.

devatā-devī God-goddess.

Darkhāst Healing ritual at Balaji temple in which a patient offers a small food oblation to the gods; legal term, meaning request or application.

dūt Divine messenger or servant; helpful spirit.

ghoṭā Club; weapon used by Hanuman, the monkey god.

havan Sacred fire; used for offering oblations to deities.

jādū-ṭonā Sorcery; black magic.

jādū-ṭonā karne vālā Sorcerer; black magician.

jal Holy water; used for bestowing a blessing; sometimes consumed by those who are sick.

japa Any sacred verse uttered repetitively.

jāṛī-būṭī Roots and herbs; used for medicinal and/or magical purposes.

jhāṛ-phūṁk Sweeping and blowing; used in exorcism and for removing or counteracting mystical harm.

kaccā-kalavā Spirit of a dead baby or miscarried foetus.

kājal Soot, lamp black; placed around the eyes of babies and children to protect them from harmful, supernatural forces, particularly the evil eye.

kīrtan Devotional utterance; sacred utterance usually consisting of divine names (e.g. Sita Ram).

mālā Garland; string chain containing 108 beads; used to aid mantric recitation or meditation.

mandir Temple, shrine, place of worship.

mantra Magical formula, spell, hymn, any sacred verse or scripture.

mantrik Person who has knowledge (often secret or occult) and expert skill in the ritual use of mantras.

masān Cremation ground, graveyard.

Masān Spirit (usually malevolent) controlled by a person possessing supernatural powers.

morchal/morpankhī Large fan of peacock feathers; widely used by diagnosticians or healers in north India (though less frequently in Mehndipur) for undoing harmful magic, for removing spirits from the body, and for curing the sick.

mokṣa Emancipation; liberation or release from the cycle of rebirth and redeath.

mukti Release; a variant of *mokṣa*.

mūrti Image; image of a deity in iconic or aniconic form.

mūṭh Sorcery; form of black magic causing instant death.

nazar Evil eye, the malign gaze.

nāzarū Wizard (term rarely used).

pāp Sin, transgression.

pāṭh Sacred verse or scripture.

peśī Hearing (of a law suit); trance.

pīr (*Bābā*) Muslim holy man and occult specialist.

pitṛ Ancestor spirit.

pitṛ-loka Realm or world of the ancestors.

pitṛsthān Place of the ancestor; sacred stone platform dedicated to an ancestor spirit.

prasād Sacred remains of food left by a god or a goddess that is returned to the donor.

pretātmā Disembodied soul or spirit which resides in the air.

pūjā Worship.

pujārī Priest, temple functionary.

puṇya Merit accrued from righteous deeds or actions.

punarjanm Rebirth.

rog Disease, illness, malady.

rogī Patient, sick person.

sādhanā Ritual methods or practices.

sankaṭ Trouble, distress, adversity; supernatural affliction.

śakti Power, energy, the goddess as power.

śānti Peace, tranquility.

samādhi State of deep meditation; meditation until death; stone monument marking the site where a great master of meditation expired.

siddha (or *siddha puruṣa*) Person possessing magical or super-natural power.

siddhi Extraordinary, supernatural power.

sindūr Vermilion paste.

śuddh Pure, state of purity.

tābīz Charm, apotropaic object; brass, copper or iron object into which sacred verses and sometimes other items (e.g. holy ash or *bhabhūt*) are placed.

tāntra-mantra vijñān Science of the occult and the supernatural.

tāntrik Magician, person possessing magical power, which is often employed to cause harm.

theparī Cow-dung cake; used by some patients in Mehndipur as a plate on which to give burnt offerings of *potasā* (a sugar preparation).

vaidya Āyurvedic practitioner.

yantra Magical diagram; used in meditation and to provide protection against harmful forces.

yātrā Pilgrimage, any type of journey.

yātrī Pilgrim, traveller.

yunānī Traditional Muslim medicine/medical practice.

NOTES

INTRODUCTION

1 In Monier-Williams' *Sanskrit-English Dictionary*, a *bhuta* is literally a 'has been', that is to say, 'the ghost or spirit of a deceased person'. Similarly, the Sanskrit word *preta* means 'departed' or 'dead', 'the spirit of a dead person'.

2 It should be noted that women were not usually approached directly; for such behaviour is often viewed as an affront. However, a woman rarely arrives at the shrine without a male chaperon, especially if she has come to receive treatment or cure from supernatural affliction. Whenever I interviewed a man who was accompanying a sick woman, a great deal of the information about her was supplied by the man. But in these cases, whenever possible my research assistant and I directed the most important questions to the woman herself, questions on matters pertaining to the nature of her malaise and the supernatural agent (when mentioned by the informant) responsible for it, for example. This task was sometimes difficult, though many men did not seem to object and allowed their womenfolk to respond freely to the questions asked.

3 This Hindi word, which means 'trouble', 'distress' or 'adversity', is widely used to denote any type of affliction, though in Mehndipur it is almost invariably used to designate supernatural malaise. However, although one frequently hears the word, those who come to Balaji temple for the first time are not always familiar with the particular way in which certain terms like *sankat* are employed here. In interviews, then, this word was used only if the interviewee used it.

1 MEHNDIPUR: THE FIELDWORK SETTING

1 This is around 4.5 pence. During my period of residence in the field the standard rate of exchange for £1 Sterling was 45 rupees.

2 Today Ganga-Nath's two sons, Badri and Pratap, are the chief priests (*pujaris*), though only one of them is head *pujari* at any one time. The office is usually occupied by each in turn for a period of twelve months. When fieldwork was conducted in Mehndipur, the latter was the

incumbent. See the Genealogies of the Puri and Nath priestly families in Appendix 5.

3 For an account and general definition of the term mantra, see Appendix 1.

4 When fieldwork was carried out, Kishor was the head priest. Kishor informed me that he received *diksha* (initiation) from his paternal uncle (Ganesh Puri), becoming *mahant* at the shrine in April 1965 (*Citra* 2022 VE).

5 This is another name by which Ganesh Puri is respectfully known.

6 According to Monier-Williams' *Sanskrit-English Dictionary*, Mahavira is another name for Hanuman.

7 The eight forms are variously listed in Dange (1986: 123) and in Dowson (1992: 45).

8 Similar accounts have been recorded by Parry (1982: 82) and by Das (1976: 225). Harlan also refers to this in the context of *sati* ceremonialism (1992: 130). For an account of heat (*tapas*) produced by austerities, see O'Flaherty 1973.

9 In Mehndipur, there are over two hundred temples dedicated to pan-Hindu deities.

10 The first of these is sometimes referred to as *bari* (big) Arji. A variant of the second term, which one occasionally hears, is Darkhvast.

11 *Tamas* (darkness, inertia) is one of the three *gunas* or 'strands', the other two being *sattva* (light, goodness, truthfulness) and *rajas* (activity, passion, energy). In the Hindu Samkhya doctrine and very widely in contemporary folk belief, *sattva*, *rajas* and *tamas* are the fundamental constituents of nature (*prakriti*) (cf. Brockington 1991: 101; Monier-Williams 1925: 194–5).

12 Some pilgrims informed me that Sanskrit mantras are more effective than those written in the vernacular. The former, however, are seldom used at the pilgrimage centre. Three Hindi mantras dedicated to Hanuman, Bhairava and Pretraj, which pilgrims are often instructed to recite, are found in the *Sri Balaji Path* ('The Sacred Recitals of Lord Balaji'), a text that is widely available in Mehndipur. Both transliteration and translation of them are given in Appendix 2.

13 It is worth noting here that, while the words of a mantra may be uttered or written, the mantra itself may equally be set out in the form of a magical diagram called a *yantra*. An example of this is given in Appendix 3.

2 SUPERNATURAL MALAISE AND KEY PATTERNS OF AFFLICTION: CAUSATION, ATTRIBUTION AND VULNERABILITY

1 For the quantitative data on spirit possession and other major forms of affliction which I analyse, see Tables 1 and 3 in Appendix 6.

2 Other terms commonly employed in Mehndipur to denote sorcery are *cauki* and *muth*. *Cauki* and *jadu-tona* are terms that are often used interchangeably, though on some occasions they clearly designate different types of sorcery. *Muth* is a form of black magic that is generally held to cause instant death. (For in-depth discussion of sorcery terms, see chapter 3.)

3 On medical knowledge and popular therapeutic practice in Rajasthan, see Lambert 1988, 1992, 1996.

4 Babb (1975: 200) and Fuchs (1964: 124), exploring popular Hinduism in Madhya Pradesh, have also drawn attention to this. They point out that long term illnesses that are resistant to other modes of treatment are often assigned to this category.

5 This is a pseudonym. Pseudonyms have been used for all named patients or their carers mentioned in this chapter, as in other parts of the book.

6 *Jind* is a variant of *jinn* (cf. Jha 1969: 367; Taymeeyah 1995) from the Arabic term *djinn*, denoting a Muslim spirit or demon. In Mehndipur, the terms *jinat*, *jinayat* and *jindani* are also used interchangebly to refer to the female counterpart of the *djinn*.

7 A *tantrik* is widely believed to be capable, not only of removing mystical harm, but also of inflicting it. He is thought to have both the power to bless and to curse.

8 For a discussion of *mukti* and *moksha* in the context of pilgrimage, see Gold 1988a: 3–5 and *passim*.

9 Rebirth (*punarjanm*) may be viewed as a form of release (*mukti*), not only in terms of being freed from the realm of the ancestors (*pitri-loka*), but also in the sense of moving one step closer towards ultimate liberation (*moksha*) from *samsara*, the wheel of rebirth and redeath.

10 According to many of the pilgrims whom I interviewed in Mehndipur, ancestor spirits cannot directly call upon the high deities whose assistance and help they often need to gain rebirth. This is why a human intermediary is said to be required.

11 See Table 4. For other relevant data given in this chapter, see Tables 1 to 3 in Appendix 6.

12 According to the recent *Census of India*, only 26 per cent of the population is urban. See 'Final Population Totals' in *Census of India*, 1991. Series 1, Paper 2. Table 1.1, p. 82.

13 As I pointed out in the introductory chapter, in the case of the woman's socio-economic status, depending upon whether she was single or married, this was determined by her father's or husband's occupation respectively.

14 In India as a whole 64 per cent of males and 39 per cent of females are literate. The percentages for northern India from where the vast majority of my respondents came, however, are lower for females. When the literacy rates for Bihar, Delhi, Haryana, Madhya Pradesh, Punjab, Rajasthan and Uttar Pradesh are averaged, the percentages are 63 per cent for males as opposed to only 29 per cent for females. (See 'Final Population Totals', in *Census of India* , 1991. Series 1, Paper 2. Table 6 pp. 210–17.)

15 See Appendix 4 for the full inventory of symptoms and ailments recorded in Mehndipur.

16 To test this finding for statistical significance the Chi Square Test was used. Statistical significance is determined by the probability or p. value being *less* than 0.05. In respect of the difference between the number of men and women allegedly afflicted by capricious spirits, the p. value is less than 0.02. This finding is thus statistically significant.

17 This finding is highly statistically significant, having a p. value of less than 0.001. (Tests of association involving these person categories were also carried out for affliction by capricious spirits and the ancestors. However, the difference between the number of married and single persons who claimed to be afflicted by these supernatural agents is not statistically significant. Here the p. value is greater than 0.05.)

18 Because only three of the interviewed informants claimed to have been harmed by Hindu deities, no clear or precise statement about the patterning of affliction by them can be given here.

19 Interestingly, it may be noted that the average age of education of those who rejected supernatural causation was not different to that of other male interviewees who invoked it. In each case, the average age was 14 years. In fact, for all the categories of affliction mentioned above (and listed in Table 1, Appendix 6), the average age of education of male and female respondents (14 years and 13 years respectively) was the same.

20 For a recent, lucid account of, as well as a comprehensive guide to, phenomenology, see Moran (2000).

21 Other writers (e.g. Carstairs 1957: 73 and Daniel 1987: 172) have also noted that South Asian women are generally held to have greater sexual desire (*kama*) or needs than men.

22 There are ten kin terms in Hindi for 'aunts' and 'uncles' related to a person by blood or by affinity. These are *mama* (MB), *mami* (MBW), *mausi* (MZ), and *mausa* (MZH), on the maternal side, and *tau* (F[elder]B), *tai* (F[elder]BW), *caca* (F[younger]B), *caci* (F[younger]BW), *phuphi* (FZ), and *phupha* (FZH) on the paternal side.

3 SORCERY, WITCHCRAFT AND THE EVIL EYE

1 I agree with Crick that extreme care must be taken when terms like 'sorcery' and 'witchcraft' are employed by the anthropologist. Crick, who builds on the semantic approach of Ardener (1971), rightly emphasises the point because generalised use of such terms can lead to misunderstanding or obscure important differences between societies. However, as recently noted by Kapferer (1997: 11), while such terms do have deficiencies, they place ethnographic observations into a comparative context when (importantly) comparison 'recognises difference but *not* uniqueness' (my italics). A major difficulty with Crick's argument against generalised use of terms like sorcery and witchcraft is that his concerns about recognising difference tend to be combined with an emphasis on uniqueness. As Kapferer indicates with reference to the argument advanced by Crick, 'there is a tendency here to return to the closure of anthropological relativism' (ibid.: 18).

2 Jonathan Parry in his book, *Death in Banaras*, states that the higher castes in the Hindu sacred city of Kashi frequently disparage belief in spirit possession, etc., which they see as being nothing more than 'superstition' (*andhvisvas*) (1994: 228). He writes:

> I believe that the notion of 'superstition' – both in its older sense of something which is opposed to religion by its excess

and lack of authoritative textual sanction, ... and in its modern sense of something which has no reality – does convey the attitude which the Brahmans widely purport to hold towards spirit possession ... (T)he superior cult (of the Brahman) repudiates the beliefs and practices of the inferior (cult) as mere 'superstition' ... (Such) misgivings (are not just) confined to the matter of whether this or that victim is really possessed or is merely shamming, for some informants rate all exorcists as charlatans, claim that ghosts do not really possess the living and dismiss the whole phenomenon as *dhong* ('deceit' or 'trickery') ... Such scepticism is most commonly and stridently expressed by the men of the higher castes.

(ibid.: 228–30)

It may be noted that well-educated, middle class urbanites sometimes see spirit possession or sorcery as a 'superstition' too (though it must be emphasised that Brahman priests I interviewed in Mehndipur did not express the same sentiment). Mr Gupta's negative comment on it, therefore, is perhaps understandable. Moreover, it should also be noted that there is no anomaly in seeking a supernatural cure for illness considered to have a non-supernatural cause, which is the reason Mr Gupta first brought his son to Mehndipur. In the Indian context, this is not seen as constituting some kind of contradiction, just as in the West an ailing person may, for example, seek divine healing at Lourdes in France for a naturally occurring disease.

3 In societies where witchcraft, for example, is often said to be the cause of adversity, writers in the functionalist tradition of sociological theory have tended to see accusations as providing an index of current social tensions within these societies. Thus, commenting on the Navaho Indians of North America (cf. Kluckhohn 1944) and the Azande of the Sudan in north-east Africa (cf. Evans-Pritchard 1937), Kennedy (1967) argues that there are 'correspondences (between) outbreaks in (alleged) witchcraft activity (and) ... periods of stress ... (and) social disorganisation' in the two communities (ibid.: 221). A similar argument predicated on the social strain-gauge hypothesis (cf. Marwick 1964) has also been put forward by Macfarlane (1999) and by Thomas (1991) to explain the rise and fall of witchcraft accusations in late medieval England.

4 For the other dialogues in the series from which this is taken, see chapter 5.

5 Maharaj (literally, 'great king') is used in Rajasthan as a term of respect.

6 This is an essentially *tantrik* ceremony, which, as Parry observes, is sometimes known as *shava-sadhana* (1982: 88). For in-depth analysis of tantrism and *tantrik* rituals, see Bharati 1965; Crooke 1911; Eliade 1958; Gupta *et al.* 1979; Kakar 1982; Shrimali 1988; Woodroffe 1959 (1918); and Zimmer 1956. A more general but relevant discussion of tantrism is also found in the writings of Biardeau 1989; Crooke 1907, 1908; Monier-Williams 1925 (1919) and Sen 1961.

7 In India, infants who die before the age of eighteen months are usually buried rather than cremated (cf. Stevenson 1971: 219). Furthermore, Muslims rarely cremate their dead. Some of my respondents in Mehndipur maintained that this explains why spirits which sorcerers send to attack their victims are typically ghosts of infants or Mohammedans.

8 For descriptions and analyses of *shraddha* rituals, see Gold 1988a: 90 ff.; Nicholas 1981: 367–79; O'Flaherty 1980; Parry 1982: 84–85; and Stevenson 1971: 156–92.

9 In some cases, poisonous substances may actually be dispensed by occult practitioners. Although I have no direct evidence of this taking place, some healers in Mehndipur claiming to possess supernatural power do use medicines. I know of clients who have actually received them from these curers. Admittedly, in these instances, they were given for beneficial purposes. But some practitioners who are offered a large financial reward for administering poison perhaps yield to the temptation on some occasions. If this is true, the Indian situation could well resemble the Sri Lankan one, as reported by Obeyesekere (1975: 22 n. 2).

10 It must be pointed out that Muslims are seldom seen in Mehndipur; and those who do make the journey to the village typically come to the temple of Balaji in the hope of receiving a cure from the deity. This phenomenon in itself is a testimony to the great appeal that Balaji temple in Mehndipur has, not only for Hindus, but for some non-Hindus. In addition, it is equally noteworthy, perhaps, because it can be seen as a manifestation of religious eclecticism in the region (cf. Mayaram 1999).

11 A *nakshatra* is essentially a 'lunar house', though the term is sometimes translated as 'star' (cf. Fuller 1992: 265). As a unit of time, it is a period that lasts for approximately twenty-four hours. There are twenty-seven *nakshatra*s in total and all of them are identified by particular star constellations from which the names of the *nakshatra*s are derived (Fuller: ibid.).

12 According to Ann Gold (1988a: 181), who has carried out fieldwork in Ajmer, this term is often used interchangeably with the word *meli*. Although I did not encounter the second of these, Gold states that it usually denotes a deceased witch; whereas the first refers to one who is alive. (Also see Gold 1988b: 47 n. 15.) The word *meli* is discussed by Lambert (1988: 198) who uses the term synonymously with *dakan* as well.

13 For examples see the volumes edited by Douglas (1970) and Marwick (1982).

4 HEALING AND THE TRANSFORMATION OF SELF IN EXORCISM

1 Lévi-Strauss' classic essay 'The Effectiveness of Symbols' (1979) which not only analyses the ritual used by the Central American Cuna shaman to assist in cases of difficult childbirth, but also compares the Cuna shaman's role with the role of the Western psychoanalyst, has

been sternly criticised by Taussig (1992) and by Sherzer (1989). The principal objections of these writers must, I believe, be taken on board; however, as the work of Laderman (1987) shows, the analogical model Lévi-Strauss develops in his famous essay is still both apposite and useful. To be sure, the value of the model has more recently been confirmed by Desjarlais (1992: 207 ff.), despite the fact that Desjarlais himself has also drawn attention to its limitations.

2 Desjarlais (1992) has also emphasised the importance of emotion, as well as its psychological and, crucially, its physiological or visceral concomitants, in exorcism and in healing rituals. His phenomenological examination of exorcism and healing among the Yolmo Sherpa people of north-central Nepal complements the analysis Kapferer has advanced as well as complements the analysis I provide in this chapter.

3 On renunciation Dumont writes:

> a man can become dead to the social world, escape the network of strict interdependence, ... and become to himself his own end as in the social theory of the West, except that he is cut off from the social life proper ... (T)he renouncer ... leaves his social role in order to adopt a role that ... is both universal and personal.
>
> (1980: 184–85)

4 A number of other writers have also argued that the sense of 'I' or self-consciousness is universal (e.g. Heelas and Locke 1981; Hallowell 1971 [1955]; Humphrey and Laidlaw 1994: 248; Morris 1994).

5 Monier-Williams' *Sanskrit-English Dictionary* gives a long list of meanings for the term *rasa*, which include the following: 'juice', 'nectar', 'taste', 'flavour', 'aesthetic and religious sentiment'. (On the use of the term *rasa*, as well as its translation and meanings, see de Bary 1964: 258–59 and *passim*; Hardy 1987: 389; Hiltebeitel 1987: 356; Lynch 1988: 177 ff., 1990a: 17; Masson and Patwardhan 1970: 23 ff.) It should also be noted that the theory of emotion in conjunction with *rasa* theory was essentially laid out in the *Natyasastra* ('Treatise on Dramaturgy' – *circa* 200 BCE to 200 CE), a work which is attributed to the sage Bharata. According to Bharata, in drama there are eight aesthetic sentiments or *rasas* (erotic love, humour, pathos, fury, heroism, fear, loathsomeness and wonder), which emerge from the eight primary or enduring emotions (love, mirth, sorrow, anger, energy, terror, disgust and astonishment); and attendant upon these are the thirty-three secondary or transitory emotions (envy, anxiety, joy, etc.) (*Natyasastra* 6. 15–21).

6 It may also be noted that this notion of the self as lacking control means that Western individuals do not always view themselves as being fully autonomous. Heelas says:

> Individual autonomy and freedom demand that control comes from within and that the agent is able to 'make up his own mind', ... make his own choices and implement them by means of his will ... We also (however) speak of 'being

NOTES

consumed by a sense of dread', 'thoughts striking out of the blue', 'being possessed by an evil intention', (and we equally say such things as) 'I knew it was not my lucky day' and 'it was my destiny'.

(1981: 40–41)

Thus, while Mauss and Dumont characterise the Western self as if it were conceived of as being completely autonomous and free, it is more accurate to say that it is viewed as being relatively autonomous vis-à-vis Indian conceptions.

7 It may be noted here that devotion or *bhakti*, in fact, also has a great deal in common with possession, as Dumont (1970: 57) and others (e.g. Tanaka 1991: 78 ff.) have pointed out. Both devotion to, and possession by, a deity are similar, not only in terms of the direct experience of divinity, for instance, which the former is thought to produce and the latter to presuppose, but also particularly in terms of emotional or psychological experience held to be concomitant with them. Thus, Dumont says,

it remains that both possession, a functional feature of folk religion, and *bhakti*, a characteristic of many sects rest upon a common psychological condition.

(1970: 57)

8 Marglin (1990: 220–21 and *passim*) denotes the inseparable link between the emotions, the body and the mind by using the compound expression 'body-emotions-thoughts'.
9 Like the word Maharaj (literally, 'great king'), Baba ('exalted one') is an honorific term, denoting respect. In Mehndipur, the term Baba is also used synonymously with *devata* (god).
10 Skultans (1987a: 664) also discovered this at the Mahanubhav temple in Maharashtra.
11 The former spring festival takes place during the month of March (Phalguna), while the latter is held in October (Ashvina). Dashahara celebrates Rama's victory over Ravana, the fierce ten-headed demon who ruled over Lanka. According to the temple priests in Mehndipur as well as many visitors at the pilgrimage centre whom I interviewed, more than 5000 pilgrims come to Mehndipur on each of these occasions. It is said that on these special festive days, the possessed are immediately healed; whereas, at other times, cure may take longer.
12 This is a food offering that weighs 50 kilos. After it has been brought before the healing deities, it is usually distributed amongst the poor. A donor gives *savamani*, not only after recovering from illness, but also when his or her prayers have been answered, as, for example, when a woman gives birth to a male child. The votive offering may be made to Balaji, to Bhairava or to Pretraj. With respect to the former deity, four types of *savamani* are offered. *Laddu* and *puri* (fried bread) is the most expensive, costing 1100 rupees. *Halva* (prepared from wheat flour, mung beans, coconut, cardamom, syrup, and ghee) and *puri* costs 900 rupees. The other varieties of *savamani* offered to Balaji also cost 900

172

rupees. They are *khir* (rice pudding) and *puri*, and a dish containing three separate items in addition to *puri*, namely, *dal* (gram), *bati* (prepared from wheat flour, ghee and sugar), and *curma* (made from wheat flour, ghee, sugar, coconut, cardamom and cashew nuts). The *savamani* offered to Bhairava is *gulgule*, made with wheat flour, ghee and molasses. It costs 400 rupees. Pretraj's *savamani* consists of *caval* (rice), and *bura* (unrefined sugar). This is the least expensive of all, costing 350 rupees. Every day at the temple between five and ten *savamani*s are offered, though during a *mela* it is said that as many as one hundred may be given on each day of the festival.

13 On the comparable role of family proxies in Sri Lankan sorcery practices, see Bastin 1996.

5 HINDU PRIESTS AND HEALERS

1 The *tabiz* is a small brass, copper or iron object into which sacred verses are placed (also see Babb 1975: 75 and Carstairs 1983: 56). In Mehndipur, these are sometimes written on paper or on *bhoj patra*, the bark of the birch tree. Alternatively, magical words are simply recited by a priest (or by a healer) and then 'blown' into the receptacle. In addition, black paper may be included. This, according to some of my informants at the pilgrimage centre, is a symbol of Bhairava or of his vehicle (*vahana*), the black dog. Black, however, is generally thought to be extremely effective in warding off malevolent forces. This is why lamp black (*kajal*) is applied around the eyes of the child or in spots on other parts of its body. A small quantity of *sindur*, a vermilion paste, and a little of the gold and silver paper that is regularly removed from the idols in the main healing temple is also often put into the amulet. Finally, the last item that is commonly placed inside it is holy ash (*bhabhut*). All these contents are held to provide a potent, protective force against harmful influences. The *tabiz* is usually worn around the upper portion of the arm or around the neck as a locket. Men tend to prefer wearing it the first way, women the second.

2 It should be noted the dialogue that ensues between the father of this female sufferer and the priest Ramjilal is also reported where I discuss sorcery suspicions and accusations (see chapter 3).

3 In Rajasthan, as elsewhere in India, this type of gesture is recognised to be a way of showing or signifying respect.

4 Touching the feet of a person is a mark of profound respect for that individual as well as a way of demonstrating one's humility. In Rajasthan, it is not only common to see someone touch the feet of a spiritual superior, such as a priest, a healer or a religious teacher (guru), but also of a parent or senior relative. Wives often do this to their husbands.

5 Patients in Mehndipur who are said to be suffering from mental illness or madness (*pagalpan*) are often shackled in this way.

6 These and other comments may suggest that the patient was obese. However, he was, in fact, quite lean. Although Ramjilal never stated during the consultation that the patient had been afflicted by a spirit, in

Mehndipur it is thought that a possessed person often eats copious quantities of food and that, instead of getting fat, the exact opposite occurs: the victim becomes extremely thin or skeletal; for it is frequently said that the spirit or spirits possessing an individual absorb all the nourishment from the food which he or she consumes.

7 This is a female spirit which is held to appear sometimes as a beautiful nymph. In this guise she is believed to entice men to lie with her. But those who succumb to the temptation invariably meet their demise. Men may be alerted to her true identity, however; for it is said that her feet point backwards and never quite rest on the ground, as do those of ordinary mortals (cf. Crooke 1906: 131 and Pocock 1973: 34).

8 This is an ancient syllable or sound which is well known, not only in India, but also beyond its borders. For discussion and analysis of its alleged sacredness and power, see Brockington 1991: 51 and *passim*; Esnoul 1987: 68–69; Gonda 1963a; Gupta 1987: 177; and Hoens 1979: 93 and *passim*.

9 It may be noted that illness not only frequently precedes entry into the healing profession in India; but this is common in other parts of the world too. Taussig (1987), for example, has demonstrated that curers in central and south America 'embark on their careers as a way of healing themselves' (ibid.: 447). Thus, '(t)he resolution of their illness', he writes, 'is to become a healer ... It is as if serious illness were a sign of powers awakening and unfolding a new path for them to follow' (ibid.). Eliade (1964) has also shown the same to be the case in central Asia. In this region he says that

> the primitive magician, the medicine man, or the shaman is not only a sick man; he is, above all, a sick man who has been cured, who has succeeded in curing himself. Often when the shaman's or medicine man's vocation is revealed through an illness or epileptoid attack, the initiation of the candidate is equivalent to a cure.
>
> (ibid.: 27)

10 The laughter provoked by what Gomati says probably arises because Cataru, her spouse, is not afflicted. Moreover, it is likely that her demands (or the demands of the malevolent being thought to be possessing her) are seen as being completely ridiculous because it is said that only malevolent supernaturals are 'tried' in the court or *darbar*.

11 The healer laughs because this is probably seen as a futile threat. The *bhagat* told me on a number of occasions that he is impregnable to any type of spirit attack. His laughter could also be viewed as being a demonstration of his superior power, which in the exorcist milieu may have a profound, positive effect. For, by asserting or showing this, patients perhaps become cognisant or are reminded of the dominion that he is said to have over wayward spirits.

12 Although I was initially unsure about what was taking place at this point during the séance, the *bhagat* and his medium assured me after it had ended that this is actually what occurred.

13 It should be noted that the particular ordering of the victory slogans, as it were ('Victory to Balaji', 'Victory to Bhairava', 'Victory to Pretraj'), which are frequently chanted in Mehndipur, clearly illustrates the way in which these deities are viewed as being hierarchically ranked at the pilgrimage centre, a point which was stressed in chapter 1.
14 This is a 'tribal' group found mainly in Kashmir, Pakistan and Afghanistan.
15 The healer not only later assured me that this spirit was quite distinct from the one that allegedly caused the patient's *pitri devata* to act malevolently; he also claimed that it is common for patients to be afflicted by a large number of spirits simultaneously, and that each of them often has to be tackled individually. However, he stressed that, on some occasions, it is possible to expel many spirits at the same time, since less powerful *bhut*s may follow upon the heels of a powerful one, especially if the former have been operating under the governership of the latter.

BIBLIOGRAPHY

Agni Purana Part 1. 1984. Translated by N. Gangadharan. Delhi: Motilal Banarsidass.

Agrawal S., Y. Agrawal and H. Saraph. 1990. *Sri Balaji Path*. Delhi: Vikas.

Allen, N.J. 1976a. 'Shamanism among the Thulung Rai', pp. 124–40 in J.T. Hitchcock and R. Jones (eds) *Spirit Possession in the Nepal Himalayas*. Warminster: Aris & Philips.

—— 1976b. 'Approaches to Illness in the Nepalese Hills', pp. 500–52 in J.B. Loudon (ed.) *Social Anthropology and Medicine* (A.S.A. 13). London: Academic Press.

Alper, H.P. 1989. Introduction, pp. 1–14 in H.P. Alper (ed.) *Mantra*. New York: State University of New York.

Anonymous. 1990. *Bara Hanuman Upasana*. Ghata Mehndipur: Bhagvan Book Dipi.

Ardener, E. W. 1971. 'The New Anthropology and its Critics'. *Man* 6: 449–67.

Assayag, J and G. Tarabout (eds). 1999. *La Possession en Asie du Sud: Parole, Corps, Territoire. Purusartha* 21. Paris: École des Hautes Études en Sciences Sociales.

Babb, L.A. 1975. *The Divine Hierarchy: Popular Hinduism in Central India*. New York, London: Columbia University Press.

Banerji, D. 1981. 'The Place of Indigenous and Western Systems of Medicine in the Health Services of India'. *Social Science and Medicine* 15 A (2): 109–14.

Barnett, S. 1976. 'Coconuts and Gold: Relational Identity in a South Indian Caste'. *Contributions to Indian Sociology* 10: 133–56.

Bastin, R. 1996. 'The Regenerative Power of Kali Worship in Contemporary Sinhala Buddhism'. *Social Analysis* 40: 59–93.

Beals, A.R. 1976. 'Strategies of Resort to Curers in South Asia', pp. 184–200 in C. Leslie (ed.) *Asian Medical Systems: A Comparative Study*. Berkeley: University of California Press.

Beidelman, T.O. 1971. 'Nuer Priests and Prophets', pp. 375–415 in T.O. Beidelman (ed.) *The Translation of Culture: Essays to E. Evans-Pritchard*. London: Tavistock.

Berger, P. and T. Luckmann. 1967. *The Social Construction of Reality*. Harmondsworth: Penguin.

Berreman, G.D. 1963. *Hindus of the Himalayas*. Oxford: Oxford University Press.

—— 1964. 'Brahmans and Shamans in Pahari Religion'. *Journal of Asian Studies* 23: 53–69.

Bharati, A. 1965. *The Tantric Tradition*. London: Rider.

Biardeau, M. 1989. *Hinduism: The Anthropology of a Civilization*, trans. R. Nice. Delhi: Oxford University Press.

Bloch, S. and M. Aveline. 2000. Group psychotherapy, pp. 84–116 in S. Bloch (ed.) *An introduction to the psychotherapies*. Oxford: Oxford University Press.

Boddy, J. 1989. *Wombs and Alien Spirits: Women, Men, and the Zar Cult in Northern Sudan*. Wisconsin: University of Wisconsin Press.

Bourdieu, P. 1992. *The Logic of Practice*, trans. R. Nice. Cambridge: Polity.

Bourguignon, E. 1965. 'The Self, the Behavioural Environment, and the Theory of Spirit Possession', pp. 39–60 in M.E. Spiro (ed.) *Context and Meaning in Cultural Anthropology*. New York: Free Press.

Brockington, J.L. 1991. *The Sacred Thread: Hinduism in its Continuity and Diversity*. Edinburgh: University of Edinburgh Press.

Brown, J.A.C. 1976. *Freud and the Post-Freudians*. Harmondsworth: Penguin.

Carrithers, M., S. Collins and S. Lukes (eds). 1985. *The Category of the Person: Anthropology, Philosophy, History*. Cambridge: Cambridge University Press.

Carstairs, G.M. 1955. 'Medicine and Faith in Rural Rajasthan', pp. 107–34 in B.D. Paul (ed.) *Health, Culture and Community: Case Studies of Public Reactions to Health Programs*. New York: Russell Sage Foundation.

—— 1957. *The Twice-Born: A Study of a Community of High-Caste Hindus*. London: Hogarth Press.

—— 1961. 'Patterns of Religious Observance in Three Villages of Rajasthan', pp. 59–113 in L.P. Vidyarthi (ed.) *Aspects of Religion in Indian Society*. Meerut: Kedar Nath Ram Nath.

—— 1983. *Death of a Witch: A Village in Northern India 1950–1981*. London: Hutchinson.

Carstairs, G.M. and R.L. Kapur. 1976. *The Great Universe of Kota: Stress, Change and Mental Disorder in an Indian Village*. London: Hogarth Press.

Census of India. 1981. Sawai Madhopur. *District Census Handbook*. Series 18. Delhi: Government of India.

—— 1991. *Final Population Totals*. Series 1, Paper 2. Delhi: Government of India.

Claus, P. J. 1979. 'Spirit Possession and Spirit Mediumship from the Perspective of Tulu Oral Traditions'. *Culture, Medicine and Psychiatry* 3: 29–52.

Cohen, A. P. 1994. *Self-Consciousness: An Alternative Anthropology of Identity*. London and New York: Routledge.

Crapanzano, V. 1977. Introduction, pp. 1–40 in V. Crapanzano and V. Garrison (eds) *Case Studies in Spirit Possession*. New York, London, Sydney, Toronto: Wiley.

Crick, M. 1976. *Explorations in Language and Meaning: Towards a Semantic Anthropology*. London: Malaby.

Crooke, W. 1906. *Things Indian: Discursive Notes on Various Subjects Connected with India*. London: John Murray.

—— 1907. *Natives of Northern India*. London: Constable.

—— 1908. 'Aghori', pp. 210–13 in J. Hastings (ed.) *Encyclopaedia of Religion and Ethics*. New York: Scribner.

—— 1911. Possession, pp. 601–8 in J. Hastings (ed.) *Encyclopaedia of Religion and Ethics*. New York: Scribner.

Csordas, T.J. 1997. *The Sacred Self: A Cultural Phenomenology of Charismatic Healing*. Berkeley, Los Angeles, London: University of California Press.

Dange, S.A. 1986–90. *Encyclopaedia of Puranic Beliefs and Practices*. 5 vols. New Delhi: Navrang.

Daniel, E.V. 1987. *Fluid Signs: Being a Person the Tamil Way*. Berkeley, Los Angeles, California: University of California Press.

Das, V. 1976. 'The Uses of Liminality: Society and Cosmos in Hinduism'. *Contributions to Indian Sociology* 10 (2): 245- 63.

Daya, D.R. 1990 (1849). *Demonology and Popular Superstitions of Gujarat* , trans. A.K. Forbes. Bombay: Vintage Books.

De Bary, W.T. 1964. *Sources of Indian Tradition*. New York, London: Columbia University Press.

De Heusch, L. 1981. *Why Marry Her? Society and Symbolic Structures*, trans. J. Lloyd. Cambridge: Cambridge University Press.

Desjarlais, R.R. 1992. *Body and Emotion: The Aesthetics of Illness and Healing in the Nepal Himalayas*. Philadelphia: Philadelphia University Press.

Douglas, M. 1970. *Witchcraft Confessions and Accusations*. (A.S.A. 9). London: Tavistock.

Dow, J. 1986. Universal Aspects of Symbolic Healing: A Theoretical Synthesis. *American Anthropologist* 88: 56–69.

Dowson, J. 1992 (1879). *A Classical Dictionary of Hindu Mythology and Religion, Geography, History and Literature*. New Delhi: Heritage.

Dumont, L. 1970. *Religion, Politics and History in India: Collected Papers in Indian Sociology*. Paris, Hague: Mouton.

—— 1980 (1970). *Homo Hierarchicus: The Caste System and its Implications*. Chicago, London: University of Chicago Press.

—— 1992 (1986). *Essays on Individualism: Modern Ideology in Anthropological Perspective*. Chicago, London: University of Chicago Press.

Dumont, L. and D.F. Pocock. 1957. 'For a Sociology of India/Village Studies'. *Contributions to Indian Sociology* 1: 7–41.

—— 1959. 'On the Different Aspects or Levels in Hinduism/Possession and Priesthood'. *Contributions to Indian Sociology* 3: 40–74.

Dundes, A. 1981. 'Wet and Dry, the Evil Eye: An Essay in Indo-European and Semitic Worldview', pp. 257–312 in A. Dundes (ed.) *The Evil Eye. A Folklore Casebook*. New York: Garland.

Durkheim, E. 1926 (1915). *The Elementary Forms of the Religious Life: A Study in Religious Sociology*, trans. J.W.Swain. London: Allen & Unwin.

Dwyer, G. 1996. *Supernatural Affliction and its Treatment: Aspects of Popular Religion in Rural and Urban Rajasthan*. D Phil Thesis, Oxford.

—— 1998. 'The Phenomenology of Supernatural Malaise: Attribution, Vulnerability and the Patterns of Affliction at a Hindu Pilgrimage Centre in Rajasthan'. *Social Analysis* 42 (2): 3–23.

—— 1999. 'Healing and the Transformation of Self in Exorcism at a Hindu Shrine in Rajasthan'. *Social Analysis* 43 (2): 108–37.

Eliade, M. 1958. *Yoga, Immortality and Freedom*, trans. W.K. Trask. London: Routledge & Kegan Paul.

—— 1964. *Shamanism: Archaic Techniques of Ecstasy*, trans. W.R. Trask. London: Routledge & Kegan Paul.

Elworthy, F.T. 1895. *The Evil Eye: An Account of this Ancient and Widespread Superstition*. London: John Murray.

Epstein, S. 1967. 'A Sociological Analysis of Witch Beliefs in a Mysore Village', pp. 135–54 in J. Middleton (ed.) *Magic, Witchcraft and Curing*. New York: National History Press.

Esnoul, A.M. 1987. 'Om', pp. 68–70 in M. Eliade (ed.) *The Encyclopedia of Religion* 11. New York, London: Macmillan.

Evans-Pritchard, E.E. 1950 (1937). *Witchcraft, Oracles and Magic Among the Azande*. Oxford: Clarendon Press.

—— 1970 (1956). *Nuer Religion*. Oxford: Clarendon Press.

—— 1984. *Theories of Primitive Religion*. Oxford: Clarendon Press.

Favret-Saada, J. 1980. *Deadly Words: Witchcraft in the Bocage*. Cambridge: Cambridge University Press.

Foucault, M. 1994. *The Order of Things: An Archaeology of the Human Sciences*. London: Routledge.

Frank, J. 2000. 'What is psychotherapy?,' pp. 1–21 in S. Bloch (ed.) *An Introduction to the Psychotherapies*. Oxford: Oxford University Press.

Freed, S.A. and R.S. Freed. 1964. 'Spirit Possession as Illness in a North Indian Village'. *Ethnology* 3: 152–71.

Freeman, R. 1999. 'Dynamics of the Person in the Worship and Sorcery of Malabar', pp. 149–81 in J. Assayag and G. Tarabout (eds) *La Possession en Asie du Sud: Parole, Corps, Territoire. Purusartha* 21. Paris: École des Hautes Études en Sciences Sociales.

Freud, S. 1991 (1909). *Two Short Accounts of Psychoanalysis*, trans. J. Strachey. London: Penguin.

—— 1949 (1940). *An Outline of Psychoanalysis*, trans. J. Strachey. London: Hogarth.

Freud, S. and J. Breuer. 1956 (1895). *Studies on Hysteria*, trans. J. and A. Strachey. London: Hogarth.

Fuchs, S. 1964. 'Magic Healing Techniques Among the Balahis in Central India', pp. 121–38 in A. Kiev (ed.) *Magic, Faith, and Healing*. New York, London: Free Press.

Fuller, C.J. 1992. *The Camphor Flame: Popular Hinduism and Society in India*. New Jersey: Princeton University Press.

Gell, A. 1980. 'The Gods at Play: Vertigo and Possession in Muria'. *Man* 15: 219–48.

Gellner, D.N. 1992. *Monk, Householder, and Tantric Priest: Newar Buddhism and its Hierarchy of Ritual*. Cambridge: Cambridge University Press.

—— 1994. 'Priests, Healers, Mediums, and Witches: The Context of Possession in the Kathmandu Valley', Nepal. *Man* 29: 27–48.

Gold, A.G. 1988a. *Fruitful Journeys: The Ways of Rajasthani Pilgrims*. Berkeley, Los Angeles, London: University of California Press.

—— 1988b. 'Spirit Possession Perceived and Performed in Rural Rajasthan'. *Contributions to Indian Sociology* 22 (1): 35–63.

Gonda, J. 1963a. 'The Indian Mantra'. *Oriens* 16: 244–97.

—— 1963b. *The Vision of the Vedic Poets*. The Hague: Mouton

Good, B.J. 1996. *Medicine, Rationality, and Experience*. Cambridge: Cambridge University Press.

Gough, E.K. 1958. 'Cults of the Dead Among the Nayars'. *Journal of American Folklore* 71 (281): 446–478.

Guirand, F. 1959. 'Greek Mythology', pp. 87–212 in R. Aldington and D. Ames (ed.) *Larousse Encyclopedia of Mythology*. London: Batchworth.

Gupta, S., D.J. Hoens and T. Goudriaan. 1979. *Hindu Tantrism*. Leiden/Koln: Brill.

Gupta, S. 1987. Mantra, pp. 176–77 in M. Eliade (ed.) *The Encyclopedia of Religion* 9. New York, London: Macmillan.

Hallowell, A. 1971 (1955). *Culture and Experience*. Philadelphia: University of Pennsylvania Press.

Hardy, F.E. 1987. 'Krsnaism', pp. 387–92 in M. Eliade (ed.) *The Encyclopedia of Religion* 8. New York, London: Macmillan.

Harlan, L. 1992. *Religion and Rajput Women: The Ethic of Protection in Contemporary Narratives*. Berkeley, Los Angeles, Oxford: University of California Press.

Harper, E.B. 1963. 'Spirit Possession and Social Structure', pp. 165–77 in B. Ratnam (ed.) *Anthropology on the March*. Madras: Book Centre.

Heelas, P. 1981. 'Introduction: Indigenous Psychologies', pp. 3–18 in P. Heelas and A. Locke (eds) *Indigenous Psychologies*. London: Academic Press.

—— The Model Applied: Anthropology and Indigenous Psychologies, pp. 39–63 in P. Heelas and A. Locke (eds) *Indigenous Psychologies*. London: Academic Press.

Heelas, P. and A. Loche (eds). 1981. *Indigenous Psychologies*. London: Academic Press.

Henry, E. O. 1977 'A North Indian Healer and the Sources of His Power,' *Social Science and Medicine* 11(5): 309–17.

Hiltebeitel, A. 1987. 'Hinduism', pp. 336–60 in M. Eliade (ed.) *The Encyclopedia of Religion 6*. New York, London: Macmillan.

—— 1989. *Criminal Gods and Demon Devotees: Essays on the Guardians of Popular Hinduism*. New York: State University of New York Press.

Hobbs, N. 2000. 'Group-Centred Therapy', pp. 278–319 in C.R. Rogers (ed.) *Client-Centred Therapy*. London: Constable.

Hoens, D.J. 1979. Mantra and other Constituents of Tantric Practice, pp. 90–117 in S. Gupta, D.J. Hoens and T. Goudriaan (eds) *Hindu Tantrism*. Leiden/Koln: Brill.

Humphrey, C. and J. Laidlaw. 1994. *The Archetypal Actions of Ritual: A Theory of Ritual Illustrated by the Jain Rite of Worship*. Oxford: Clarendon Press.

Husserl, E. 1964. *The Idea of Phenomenology*, trans. W.P. Alston and G. Nakhnikian. The Hague: Martinus Nijhoff.

Inglis, S. 1985. 'Possession and Pottery: Serving the Divine in a South Indian Community', pp. 89–102 in J.P. Waghorne and N. Cutler (eds). *Gods of Flesh, Gods of Stone: the Embodiment of Divinity in India*. Chambersburg, Pennsylvania: Anima.

Jha, M. 1969. 'Spirit Possession among the Maithil Brahmins'. *The Eastern Anthropologist* 22 (3): 361–68.

Jones, R.L. 1976. 'Spirit possession and Society in Nepal', pp. 1–20 in J.T. Hitchcock and R.L. Jones (ed.) *Spirit Possession in the Nepal Himalayas*. Warminster: Aris & Phillips.

Kakar, D.N. 1972. 'The Health Centre Doctor and Spirit Medium in a North Indian Village'. *The Eastern Anthropologist* 25 (3): 249–58.

Kakar, S. 1981. *The Inner World: A Psycho-analytic Study of Childhood and Society in India*. Delhi: Oxford University Press.

—— 1982. *Shamans, Mystics and Doctors*. London: Unwin.

Kapferer, B. 1979. 'Emotion and Feeling in Sinhalese Healing Rites'. *Social Analysis* 1: 153–76.

—— 1991 (1983). *A Celebration of Demons: Exorcism and the Aesthetics of Healing in Sri Lanka*. Washington: Berg Smithsonian Institution Press.

—— 1997. *The Feast of the Sorcerer: Practices of Consciousness and Power*. Chicago and London: University of Chicago Press.

Kennedy, J.G. 1967. 'Psychological and Social Explanations of Witchcraft'. *Man* 2: 216–25.

Kluckhohn, C. 1944. *Navaho Witchcraft*. Boston: Beacon Press.

Kultgen, J. 1975. 'Phenomenology and Structuralism'. *Annual Review of Anthropology* 4: 371–387.

Kurma Purana. Part 2. 1972. Trans. S. Mukherji, V.K. Varma and G.S. Rai. A.S. Gupta (ed.) Varanasi: All-India Kashi Raj Trust.

Laderman, C. 1987. 'The Ambiguity of Symbols in the Structure of Healing'. *Social Science and Medicine* 24 (4): 293–301.

Lambek, M.L. 1981. *Human Spirits: A Cultural Account of Trance in Mayotte*. Cambridge: Cambridge University Press.

Lambert, H.S. 1988. *Medical Knowledge in Rural Rajasthan: Popular Constructions of Illness and Therapeutic Practice*. D Phil Thesis, Oxford.

—— 1992. 'The Cultural Logic of Indian Medicine: Prognosis and Etiology in Rajasthani Popular Therapeutics'. *Social Science and Medicine* 34 (10): 1069–76.

—— 1996. 'Popular Therapeutics and Medical Preferences in Rural North India'. *The Lancet* 348: 1706–09.

Leach, E.R. 1966. 'Ritualisation in Man in Relation to Conceptual and Social Development', pp. 247–526 in J. Huxley (ed.) *Ritualisation of Behaviour in Man and Animals*. London: Philosophical Transactions of the Royal Society.

Leslie, C. 1976. 'The Ambiguities of Medical Revivalism in Modern India', pp. 356–67 in C. Leslie (ed.) *Asian Medical Systems: A Comparative Study*. Berkeley: University of California Press.

Lessa, W.A. and E.Z. Vogt. 1958. Introduction to Shamans and Priests, pp. 410–11 in W.A. Lessa and E.Z. Vogt (ed.) *Reader in Comparative Religion: An Anthropological Approach*. Illinois: Row & Peterson.

Lévi-Strauss, C. 1979 (1963). The Effectiveness of Symbols in C. Lévi-Strauss, pp. 186–205 in *Structural Anthropology* 1, trans. C. Jacobson and B. G. Schoeph, Harmondsworth: Penguin, pp. 186–205.

Lewis, I.M. 1966. 'Spirit Possession and Deprivation' Cults. *Man* 1 (3): 307–29.

—— 1978. *Ecstatic Religion: An Anthropological Study of Spirit Possession and Shamanism*. London: Penguin.

—— 1986. *Religion in Context: Cults and Charisma*. Cambridge: Cambridge University Press.

Locke A. 1981. Universals in Human Conception, pp. 19–36 in P. Heelas and A. Locke (eds) *Indigenous Psychologies*. London: Academic Press.

Lynch, O.M. 1988. Pilgrimage with Krishna, Sovereign of the Emotions. *Contributions to Indian Sociology* 22 (2): 171–94.

—— 1990a. The Social Construction of Emotion in India, pp. 3–34 in O.M. Lynch (ed.) *Divine Passions: The Social Construction of Emotion*. California: University of California Press.

—— 1990b. The Mastram: Emotion and Person Among Mathura's Chaubes, pp. 91–115 in O.M. Lynch (ed.) *Divine Passions: The Social Construction of Emotion*. California: University of California Press.

Macfarlane, A. 1999 (1970). *Witchcraft in Tudor and Stuart England: A Regional and Comparative Study*. London: Routledge & Kegan Paul.

Maitra, A. 1986. *Religious Life of the Brahman*. Inter-India Publications.

Majumdar, D.N. 1958. *Caste and Communication in an Indian Village*. London: Asia.

Mandelbaum, D.G. 1966. 'Transcendental and Pragmatic Aspects of Religion'. *American Anthropologist* 68 (5): 1174–91.

Marglin, F.A. 1985. 'Types of Oppositions in Hindu Culture', pp. 65–83 in J.B. Carman and F.A. Marglin (eds) *Purity and Auspiciousness in Hindu Society*. Leiden: E.J. Brill.

—— 1990. 'Refining the Body: Transformative Emotion in Ritual Dance', pp. 212–36 in O.M. Lynch (ed.) *Divine Passions: The Social Construction of Emotion in India*. Berkeley, Los Angeles, Oxford: University of California Press.

Marriott, McK. 1955a. 'Western Medicine in a Village of Northern India', pp. 239–68 in B.D. Paul (ed.) *Health, Culture and Community: Case Studies of Public Reactions to Health Programs*. New York: Russell Sage Foundation.

—— 1955b. 'Little Communities in an Indigenous Civilization', pp. 171–222 in McK. Marriott (ed.) *Village India: Studies in the Little Community*. Chicago: University of Chicago Press.

—— 1976. 'Hindu Transactions: Diversity without Dualism', pp. 109–42 in B. Kapferer (ed.) *Transaction and Meaning: Directions in the Anthropology of Exchange and Symbolic Behaviour*. Philadelphia: Institute for the Human Sciences.

—— 1989. Constructing an Indian Ethnosociology. *Contributions to Indian Sociology* 23 (1): 1–39.

Marriott, McK. and R.B. Inden. 1977. Toward an Ethnosociology of South Asian Caste Systems, pp. 227–38 in K. David (ed.) *The New Wind: Changing Identities in South Asia*. Hague: Mouton.

Marwick, M.G. 1964. 'Witchcraft as a Social Strain-Gauge'. *Australian Journal of Science* 26: 263–68.

—— 1982. *Witchcraft and Sorcery: Selected Readings*. London: Penguin.

Masson, J.L. and M.V. Patwardhan. 1970. *Aesthetic Rapture: The Rasadhyaya of the Natyasastra*. 2 vols. Poona: Deccan College.

Mauss, M. 1985 (1938). 'A category of the human mind: the notion of the person; the notion of the self, pp. 1–25 in M. Carrithers, S. Collins and S. Lukes (eds) *The Category of the Person: Anthroplogy, Philosophy, History*. Cambridge: Cambridge University Press.

Mayaram, S. 1999. 'Spirit Possession: Reframing Discourses of the Self and Other, pp. 103–31 in J. Assayag and G. Tarabout (eds) *La Possession en Asie du Sud: Parole, Corps, Territoire. Purusartha* 21. Paris: École des Hautes Études en Sciences Sociales.

McCreery, J.L. 1995. 'Negotiating with Demons: the uses of Magical Language'. *American Ethnologist* 22 (1): 144–64.

Mines, M. 1988. 'Conceptualizing the Person: Hierarchical Society and Individual Autonomy in India'. *American Anthropologist* 90: 568–79.

Monier-Williams, M. 1925 (1919). *Hinduism*. London: Macmillan.

—— 1993 (1899). *A Sanskrit-English Dictionary*. Delhi: Motilal Banarsidass.

Montgomery, E. 1976. 'Systems and the Medical Practitioners of a Tamil Town', pp. 272–284 in C. Leslie (ed.) *Asian Medical Systems: A Comparative Study*. Berkeley: University of California Press.

Moran, D. 2000. *Introduction to Phenomenology*. London and New York: Routledge.

Morris, B. 1994. *Anthropology of the Self*. London, Colorado: Pluto.

Natanson, M. 1967. Introduction, pp. xxv–xlvii in A. Schutz *Collected Papers* 1. The Hague: Martinus Nijhoff.

Natyasastra. 1950. Translated by M. Ghosh. Calcutta: Royal Asiatic Society.

Nicholas, R.W. 1981. 'Sraddha, impurity, and relations between the living and the dead', pp. 367–79 in T.N. Madan (ed.). *Way of Life: King, Householder, Renouncer: Essays in Honour of Louis Dumont*. Delhi: Vikas.

Nichter, M. 1980. 'The Lay Person's Perception of Medicine as Perspective into the Utilization of Multiple Therapy Systems in the Indian Context'. *Social Science and Medicine* 14 B (4): 225–33.

Nuckolls, C.W. 1991. 'Becoming a Possession-Medium in South India: A Psychocultural Account'. *Medical Quarterly* 5 (1): 63–67.

Obeyesekere, G. 1970. 'The Idiom of Demonic Possession: A Case Study'. *Social Science and Medicine* 4 (1): 97–111.

—— 1975. 'Sorcery, Premeditated Murder, and the Canalization of Aggression in Sri Lanka'. *Ethnology* 14: 1–23.

—— 1977. 'Psychological Exegesis of a Case of Spirit Possession in Sri Lanka', pp. 235–94 in V. Crapanzano and V. Garrison (eds) *Case Studies in Spirit Possession*. New York, London, Sydney and Toronto: Wiley.

—— 1984. *Medusa's Hair: An Essay on Personal Symbols and Religious Experience*. Chicago, London: University of Chicago Press.

O'Flaherty, W.D. 1973. *Asceticism and eroticism in the mythology of Siva*. Oxford: Oxford University Press.

—— 1980. 'Karma and Rebirth in the Vedas and Puranas', pp. 3–37 in W.D. O'Flaherty (ed.) *In Karma and Rebirth in Classical Indian Traditions*. Berkeley and Los Angeles: University of California Press.

O'Malley, L.S.S. 1935. *Popular Hinduism*. Cambridge: Cambridge University Press.

Opler, M.E. 1958. 'Spirit Possession in a Rural Area of Northern India', pp. 553–556 in W.A. Lessa and E.Z. Vogt (eds) *Reader in Comparative Religion: An Anthropological Approach*. Illinois: Row & Peterson.

Padoux, A. 1989. 'Mantras – What Are They?', pp. 295–318 in H.P. Alper (ed.). *Mantra*. New York: State University of New York.

Pakaslahti, A. 1996. *Temples and Healers: Traditional Treatment of Psychiatric Patients in India*. (Video Presented at X World Congress of Psychiatry, Madrid).

—— 1998. 'Family Centred Treatment of Mental Health Problems at the Balaji Temple in Rajasthan, pp. 129–66 in A. Parpola and S. Tenhunen (eds). *Changing Patterns of Family and Kinship in South Asia*. Helsinki: Studia Orientalia.

Parry, J. 1980. 'Ghosts, Greed and Sin: The Occupational Identity of the Benares Funeral Priests'. *Man* 15: 88–111.

—— 1982. 'Sacrificial death and the necrophagous ascetic', pp. 74–110 in M. Bloch and J. Parry (eds). *Death and the regeneration of life*. Cambridge: Cambridge University Press.

—— 1994. *Death in Banaras*. Cambridge: Cambridge University Press.

Pocock, D.F. 1973. *Mind, Body and Wealth*. Oxford: Blackwell.

Rogers, C.R. 2000. *Client-Centred Therapy*. London: Constable.

Satija, D. C., D. Singh, S.S. Nathawat and V. Sharma. 1981. A Psychiatric Study of Patients Attending Mehandipur Balaji Temple. *Indian Journal of Psychiatry* 23 (3): 247–50.

Scheff, T.J. 1977. The Distancing of Emotion in Ritual. *Current Anthropology* 18 (3): 483–90.

Schutz, A. 1967. *Collected Papers* 1. Edited by M. Natanson. The Hague: Martinus Nijhoff.

—— 1970. *On Phenomenology and Social Relations*. Edited by H.R. Wagner. University of Chicago Press.

Seeberg, J. 1992. *Sankatfolk*. Moesgaard: Aarhus University.

Sen, K.M. 1961. *Hinduism*. London: Penguin.

Shaara, L. and A. Strathern. 1992. A Preliminary Analysis of the Relationship between Altered States of Consciousness, Healing, and Social Structure. *American Anthropologist* 94: 145–60.

Sherzer, J. 1989. *Namakke, Sunmakke, Kormakke*: Three Types of Cuna Speech Event, pp. 263–82 in R. Bauman and J. Sherzer (eds) *Explorations in the Ethnography of Speaking*. Cambridge, New York, New Rochelle, Melbourne, Sydney: Cambridge University Press.

Shrimali, N. 1988. *The Power of Tantra*. Delhi: Hind.

Singh, S. 1961. Religious Beliefs and Practices of The Sansis of Punjab, pp. 220–40 in L.P. Vidyarthi (ed.). *Aspects of Religion in Indian Society*. Kedar Nath: Ram Nath.

Siva Purana. Part 3. 1970. Translated by a board of scholars. Edited by A. Kunst and J.L. Shastri. Delhi: Motilal Banarsidass.

Skultans, V. 1987a. 'The Management of Mental Illness among Maharashtrian Families: A Case Study of a Mahanubhav Healing Temple'. *Man* 22 (4): 661–79.

—— 1987b. 'Trance and the Management of Mental Illness among Maharashtrian Families'. *Anthropology Today* 3 (1): 2–4.

Spiro, M.E. 1978. *Burmese Supernaturalism*. Philadelphia: Institute for the Study of Human Issues.

Srinivas, M.N. 1965 (1952). *Religion and Society among the Coorgs of South India*. London: Asia.

Staal, F. 1975. *Exploring Mysticism*. Harmondsworth: Penguin.

—— 1989. Vedic Mantras, pp. 48–95 in H.P. Alper (ed.). *Mantra*. New York: State University of New York.

Stevenson, S. 1971. *The Rites of the Twice-Born*. New Delhi: Oriental Books Reprint Corporation.

Survey of India. 1973. Delhi: Government of India.

Tabor, D.C. 1981. Ripe and Unripe: Concepts of Health and Sickness in Ayurvedic Medicine. *Social Science and Medicine* 15 B: 439–55.

Tambiah, S.J. 1970. *Buddhism and the Spirit Cults in North-East Thailand*. Cambridge: Cambridge University Press.

—— 1985. *Culture, Thought and Social Action: An Anthropological Perspective*. Cambridge, Massachusetts, London: Harvard University Press.

Tanaka, M. 1991. *Patrons, Devotees and Goddesses: Ritual and Power among the Tamil Fishermen of Sri Lanka*. Kyoto: Kyoto University Press.

Taussig, M. 1987. *Shamanism, Colonialism, and the Wild Man: A Study in Terror and Healing*. Chicago: University of Chicago Press.

—— 1992. *The Nervous System*. New York, London: Routledge.

Taymeeyah, I. 1995. *Essay on the Jinn (Demons)*, trans. A.A.B. Philips. Saudia Arabia: International Islamic Publishing House.

Thomas, K. 1991 (1971). *Religion and the Decline of Magic: Studies in Popular Beliefs in Sixteenth and Seventeenth Century England*. Harmondsworth: Penguin.

Tulsidas, G. 1991. *Sri Ramcaritmanas*. Delhi: Gita.

—— 1993. *Sri Hanuman Calisa*. Delhi: Gita.

Varenne, J. 1973. *Yoga and the Hindu Tradition*, trans. D. Coltman. Chicago, London: University of Chicago Press.

Vitebsky, P. 1993. *Dialogues with the Dead: The discussion of mortality among the Sora of eastern India*. Cambridge: Cambridge University Press.

Waghorne, J.P. and N. Cutler. 1985. *Gods of Flesh, Gods of Stone: the Embodiment of Divinity in India*. Chambersburg, Pennsylvania: Anima.

Weber, M. 1968. *On Charisma and Institution Building: Selected Papers.* Edited by S.N. Eisenstadt. Chicago: University of Chicago Press.

—— 1969 (1947). *The Theory of Social and Economic Organization,* trans. A.M. Henderson and T. Parsons. New York, London: Free Press.

Woodroffe, J. 1959 (1918). *Sakti and Sakta: Essays and Addresses on the Sakta Tantrasastra.* Madras: Ganesh.

Yalman, N. 1963. 'On the Purity of Women in the Castes of Ceylon and Malabar'. *Man* 93 (1): 25–58.

Zatzick, D.F. and F.A. Johnson. 1997. 'Alternative Psychotherapeutic Practice among Middle Class Americans: II Some Conceptual and Practical Comparisons'. *Culture, Medicine and Psychiatry* 21 (2): 213–246.

Zimmer, H. 1956. *Philosophies of India.* New York: Meridian.

Zimmerman, F. 1978. From Classical Texts to Learned Practice: Methodological Remarks on the Study of Indian Medicine. *Social Science and Medicine* 12 B: 97–103.

—— 1980. 'Rtu-satmya: The Seasonal Cycle and the Principal of Appropriateness'. *Social Science and Medicine* 14 B: 99–106.

INDEX